COLUMBO
EXPLAINS THE SEVENTIES
A TV COP'S POP CULTURE JOURNEY

By Glenn Stewart

To Ma and Dad
for their love and support

Columbo Explains the Seventies: A TV Cop's Pop Culture Journey

Published by
BONAVENTURE PRESS
Aliso Viejo, CA
USA
www.bonaventurepress.com

All rights reserved. No part of this book may be reproduced or transmitted in any form or by any means, electronic or mechanical, including scanning, photocopying, recording or by any information storage and retrieval system without written permission from the author, except for the inclusion of brief quotations in a review.

Cover art by Stefan Prodanovic

Copyright 2025 by Glenn Stewart

Publisher's Cataloging in Publication Data
Stewart, Glenn, 1957-
    Columbo Explains the Seventies: A TV Cop's Pop Culture Journey
        p. cm.
    Includes annotated references and index.

    1. Columbo (Television Program)   [1. Columbo (Television Program)
    2. Mystery and detective television programs.   3. Television programs] 1. Title.
    791.4572

ISBN 978-1-937878-28-3 (Paperback)
ISBN 978-1-937878-29-0 (Hardcover)
ISBN 978-1-937878-30-6 (Kindle ebook)

Contents

Acknowledgments   5

Preface   8

I. Introduction   11
Crime Solving in the Columboverse
Columbo Redux

II. Columbo's Cultural Footprint   22
Watching the Detective
Playing Columbo
Lasagna for Sinatra
Trivia Wars and Name Games
Columbo Bites Crime
The Columbo Rebellion
Columbo Around the World

III. Columbo and Social Culture   42
The "Me" Decade

1. Class Conflicts and Power Plays   46
2. Liberation and Lady Killers   59
3. Coping with Future Shock   74
4. Race and Representation   87
5. Murder for the Whole Family   98
6. Deconstructing Murder and Media   111
7. Just One More Think: The Psychology of *Columbo*   124

8. The Politics of Murder	141
9. Columbo in the Nineties: A Man Out of Time	147
IV. Columbo and Popular Culture *Crossing the Cultural Streams*	162
10. The Legacy of the Thinking Detective	164
11. A Hitch in Crime	177
12. Columbo Gets His Wings	188
13. The Curious Case of *Columbo Takes the Rap*	194
14. The Debacle of *Mrs. Columbo*	201
15. Explaining Patrick McGoohan	213
V. Watching and Rewatching *Columbo*	227
Footnotes and Sources	229
Index	237

Acknowledgments

First, thank you to the guy with the flashlight.

Seventies *Columbo* watchers know exactly who I mean. He would appear at the beginning of every installment of the NBC Mystery Movie, a shadowy figure in the distance against a flat horizon and an ominous sky, walking toward the viewer with an illuminated flashlight, occasionally arcing it and approaching us in mysterious darkness while we were reminded who were the crimesolvers to be chosen from that particular evening. Henry Mancini's stirring, memorable theme was my teenage Sunday night siren song. If my family's *TV Guide* wasn't handy, I would have to wait in anticipation of the announcement at the end of these introductory credits to learn who would be gracing our 25-inch TV screen that evening. It was with excited delight that I would hear, "Tonight, starring Peter Falk as *Columbo*." It was with deflated disappointment that I would hear, "Tonight, starring Rock Hudson and Susan St. James as *McMillan & Wife*." I was ambivalent about *McCloud*.

But it was that guy with the flashlight who introduced the possibility of a new *Columbo* episode on, first Wednesday, then Sunday nights from 1971-1978. I'm sure countless others join me in thanking him for his service to mystery lovers everywhere.

There are others to thank, of course. They may not have carried flashlights, but their thoughts and contributions were nonetheless enlightening. Most significantly, this book would not exist without the Columbophile Blog and its fearless leader, Columbophile (CP). I randomly stumbled across the Blog several years after its 2015 creation and quickly realized that it was way more than mere gushing fan devotion to Peter Falk, crumpled raincoats, and "Just one more thing." It had a readership with intelligence and the honesty to call out episodes like *Last Salute to the Commodore* as pieces of junk.

When I saw the assortment of articles posted by Columbophile and some rare guest contributors, I thought that I might try my hand at writing for the Blog as well. I submitted my first piece to CP on spec—speculative, without any guarantee that it would be printed—in the summer of 2020. Nerd alert: It was about the use of phone records in classic *Columbo* episodes. About six months later, CP published it, and over the following months he graciously printed several other articles. A small handful of these have been repackaged and reappear in this book. Without the positive reinforcement and generosity of Columbophile in letting me use his Blog space, I simply would not have continued writing. CP is as close to that guy waving the flashlight as it gets, so thank you.

One of those Columbophile Blog guest writers was Richard Weill. I read his piece, "The Five Key Steps to Crafting a *Columbo* Mystery" and figured that this guy knew what he was talking about. In subsequent years, we'd exchange *Columbo* thoughts through the Blog and emails, and his sharp observations have elevated my own. Although we are generally like-minded, we do disagree vehemently about Columbo's name, and in the limited paragraphs where I discuss the controversy, know that I had Rich in mind. He made other insightful contributions over the years that helped my thinking in the chapters "Crime Solving in the Columboverse," "Just One More Think," "A Hitch in Crime," "Explaining Patrick McGoohan," and likely others that have slipped my mind.

Because *Columbo* didn't explicitly deal with political sides, my book hadn't planned on touching that third rail. A fellow *Columbo* fan from my days in radio, Craig Mustard, convinced me otherwise. His thoughts provided me with some jumping-off points for that chapter and others.

Dene Kernohan was a valuable resource for script points. Comparing what was on the printed page with what made it to the screen is always interesting and often useful, and I was only able to do that through Dene's efforts.

I spoke with several people who kindly gave me their time and allowed me to complete my own research. These included Sherry Nemmers, Norm Boucher, Ron OJ Parson, Bill Paxton, and especially Elizabeth Cava. It was through her, and her usage permissions, that I had access to the documents of the chapter "Explaining Patrick McGoohan."

There are not many, but this is far from the first book about *Columbo*. I am grateful for the observations provided in their works by Amelie Hastie, Lilian Mathieu, David Martin-Jones, Christyne Berzsenyi, CP, and of course the grandfather of *Columbo* writers, Mark Dawidziak. David Koenig's book, *Shooting Columbo*, came with the facts, and David also provided support and shape for this book's final look.

As an early-Seventies teen at Brooks School in North Andover, Massachusetts, I have to note the critical contribution of the late Paul Keaney. Paul taught History at Brooks for many years and his demanding standards in both research and writing raised my own game, although I may not have realized it at the time. I like to think that PJK would enjoy this book.

There are others who provided readership of drafts, encouragement, advice or all of the above, including Andrew Jenkins, Eric Schultz, my son David, and most especially my wife Cyndi. She indulged me my many hours in the Columboverse while I scribbled notes, captured dialogue, and beat Columbo to his best Gotcha lines. My favorite is from *An Exercise in Fatality*: "You tried to contrive a perfect alibi, sir, and it's your perfect alibi that's going to hang you."

My alibi for all things is simple. I was watching *Columbo* at the time.

Preface

Columbo's popularity has been consistent from its 1968 *Prescription: Murder* debut and is persistent through whatever moment in time you happen to be sampling this book. The character's mass appeal, worldwide recognition, and our continuing interest in his investigations confirms that *Columbo* has a unique position in television and entertainment history.

With the official beginning of the series in 1971, Peter Falk and the role he so expertly and effortlessly embodied became cultural touchstones. This was a person that the middle-class masses could identify with, having ordinary character traits not often found in a television authority figure. He was unassuming, mild-mannered, rather sloppy, forgetful, maybe even a bit absent-minded, humble, kind, and polite. Unconcerned with appearance, his look was unique to television detectives. He stood out among the conventional coat-and-tie types or the impeccably dressed Kojaks patrolling the American streets. He was us.

Many TV critics of the era used the word "bumbling" to describe him. In an interview with Johnny Carson on *The Tonight Show* in 1973, Falk made it clear that he had no time for that characterization. "I don't think he's dumb, and I don't think he plays it being dumb. There's a difference between being dumb and being distracted. There's a difference between being foolish and being perplexed. There's a difference between being stupid and being preoccupied. If you play it being a chump or an oaf, there's no dignity there. People wouldn't like a character that doesn't have dignity."[1]

In the 1970s, *Columbo* owned a significant swath of the popular culture landscape, at a time when there was no internet, social media, or widespread cable offerings to dilute interest. Its prominent status and repute as quality, prestige television lends itself to an intriguing thought experiment: If a Classic

Columbo box set (VHS, DVD, Blu-ray, take your pick) were unearthed 100 years from now as a time capsule, what would it tell us about the decade of the Seventies? The first views would be of the crisply manicured lawns of the sumptuous mansions of Los Angeles, populated by handsome men wearing turtlenecks, cravats and expensive wide-lapel suits, side-by-side with gorgeous women sporting chic furs, fashion turbans, and colorful split-leg pantsuits.

But beneath the very stylish veneer of Seventies haute couture, 100-years-hence pop culture archaeologists might be able to get clues to the weightier elements that stitch together a society's culture. What could the original 45 episodes of *Columbo* explain about class conflict, power struggles, feminism, race relations, sex, technology, media, psychology, politics and violence? What values did Columbo share with his viewing audience? How does *Columbo* intersect with other cultural icons and platforms?

While the term "popular culture" has potentially several different meanings, for our purposes, we'll define it as the cultural products consumed by much of a society's population. This would include film, music, art, literature, dance, television, radio, magazines, social media, and other forms of expression and communication with mass accessibility and appeal.

Pop culture is one niche of a population's overall culture. In the broader sense, culture is "all the ways of life including arts, beliefs and institutions of a populace that are passed down from generation to generation. Culture has been called 'the way of life for an entire society.' As such, it includes codes of manners, dress, language, religion, rituals, art, norms of behavior, such as law and morality, and systems of belief."[2]

To this could be added a population's own social culture, encompassing sociocultural factors such as race, ethnicity, ethnic identity, sex and sexual identity, value systems, and attitudes. Our goal is to glean some insight into how one particular popular television detective transected and reflected these cultures.

Columbo's position in the Seventies mass-appeal mainstream deserves some attention, for popular and social culture interconnect, and popular culture is not just mindless entertainment separated from the world around it. As writer Hua Hsu explains, "In a free society, culture... embodies an unconscious sense of the values we share, of what it means to be right or wrong."[3] If so, one of the defining TV shows of the Seventies could tell us something about the values we shared in that decade.

This is not likely to be expected of *Starsky & Hutch, Barnaby Jones*, or even any of the other shows sharing NBC's weekly Mystery Movie wheels with the LAPD Lieutenant. Maybe *Kojak* can tell us about gritty urban morality or lollipops as cigar substitutes. Perhaps *Ironside* can teach us about the struggles of the disabled, or *Cannon* about the persistence of societal fat-shaming.

Those conversations might be worth having, but they would probably be as brief as the TV careers of *Bronk, Toma, Griff* and plenty of Columbo's other fellow Seventies crime busters. What is it about *Columbo* that made the character a product of the times, and how did this detective connect with the changing attitudes and values of the Seventies television consumer?

The answers to these questions can point to why this particular TV cop is a unique cultural artifact who can help our understanding of a key American decade. Popular culture is, after all, a form of history, a piece of the historical puzzle fitting together with contemporaneous news accounts, journals, video chronicles and the like. The history of social movements can be reflected and studied in a wide variety of these pop culture forms, and the 45 episodes of a scruffy L.A. detective are a more than suitable place to focus our attention.

At its best, the primary feature of *Columbo* is its intelligence. It is, of course, a smart show in its plotting and the unravelling of the crime. But beyond that, the very premise of a cop without a gun, without an office, and without a car (well, a speedy one) means that the cop must have something else going for him if he wants to catch the killer every week. That's intelligence. And *Columbo* is an intelligent program, designed for intelligent viewers, and worthy of intelligent discourse.

That's what this book humbly tries to accomplish.

I.
Introduction

Crime Solving in the Columboverse

As TV viewers, we like to imagine that our popular shows could somehow align with our own reality, as if our favorite fictional characters co-exist right here with us in our own universe on planet Earth. This probably applies even more so to our favorite lieutenant. In our world, a lone dedicated detective named Columbo can right the wrongs committed by the rich and privileged, providing us with otherwise unattainable moral victories against the forces of power. It's a comfort to think that Columbo could be flesh-and-blood, on our side and fighting for us.

So when we see something in *Columbo* that doesn't fit into our reality, like perhaps a closing Gotcha clue that would never survive actual trial scrutiny, we notice.

Too bad for us, Columbo is a fictional character. Co-creators Richard Levinson and William Link never aimed to put him into a universe that was meant to be totally genuine, at least by our standards of realism. "We had no intention of dealing with the realities of actual police procedures. Instead, we wanted to pay our respects to the classic mystery fiction of our youth. In the interest of flavorful characterization, we deliberately chose not to be realistic. Our show would be a fantasy, and as such it would avoid the harsher aspects of a true policeman's life: the drug busts, the street murders, the prostitutes, and the back-alley shootouts."[1] The show was never meant to be a documentary, but Classic *Columbo* did strive to make the show *plausibly* realistic, which would help immerse us in the storylines and strengthen our connection with the character. In many ways, it had to conform to the world around it.

Seventies *Columbos* weren't pure realism, but they made the effort to be faithful to their own reality. Looking at the series in this way, we can concede that *Columbo* episodes were not perfect fits into our real, non-fictional world. However, the show generally did play fair by its *own* rules in its *own* universe that had its *own* conventions and assumptions. Which leads to wondering—what exactly was Columbo's reality?

Fans of the Marvel Cinematic Universe have experienced the Multiverse, where parallel universes exist and collide, providing us with a variety of villains and an array of realities. This is by no means a new concept in fiction: H.G. Wells' 1903 *Modern Utopia*, television's *The Twilight Zone*, *Star Trek's* Mirror Universe, *Fringe*, *Dr. Who*, among many others. In 2019's *Yesterday*, the film's protagonist finds himself in an alternate reality where The Beatles didn't exist.

Since Columbo himself does not exist in our real world, let's playfully suggest that Columbo might solve his murders in a very close facsimile to our own Earth, a parallel universe where our hero matches wits with California's killer elite. Professor David Martin-Jones uses the term "Columboverse" in his book *Columbo: Paying Attention 24/7*, and while his use of the expression has a different thrust than it does in this book, I'll appropriate it here with proper credit paid.[2] What does this Columboverse accept as possible, and how does it differ from our own humdrum actual experience?

Columbo's version of reality is immediately apparent whenever he steps into a crime scene, as actual LAPD detective norms would never allow for a scruffy, rumpled raincoat to be worn on the job as standard attire by any investigator. And while Columbo usually does coat-and-tie it underneath, he is nonetheless described as "shabby" as early as the second pilot *Ransom for a Dead Man*, and an "unmade bed" in episode 3, *Dead Weight*. The coat and tie wardrobe becomes a low bar with passing episodes, so by the time we get to *Double Shock*, his shirt is barely buttoned. For the plainclothes officers you and I might meet, the business casual look is preferred to reinforce the aura of professionalism when dealing with the public.

But of course, that's precisely the impression that Columbo does not want to give to the killers, whom he hopes will underestimate him (as Dr. Ray Flemming correctly surmises in *Prescription: Murder*). In each of his cases, Columbo uses his sloppy physical appearance to diminish himself and appear ineffectual. The goal is to lull the villain into a false sense of superiority in order to secure the killer's "help" in solving the crime and provide key clues to their guilt. The coat and unkempt look further that goal, although Columbo will tell you that in any other attire, like even a new raincoat in *Now You See Him*, he simply can't think properly.

Speaking of style etiquette, no officer in our reality, plainclothes or otherwise, would fail to carry a gun as part of their gear. But of course, Columbo also hasn't passed the every-six-months LAPD gun test in almost 10 years (*Forgotten Lady*). In Columbo's universe, that puts him at high risk in a job where a city homicide detective has not only divined who committed the murder, but follows him/her around with antagonizing questions, veiled accusations, and several possibilities of becoming a homicide victim himself. This alternate-reality LAPD apparently has no problem with turning a blind eye (or Peter Falk's glass eye) to a pesky officer gun requirement.

Appearance is not merely clothes and weaponry. Pulling up to a crime scene in a clunky 1959 Peugeot convertible Model 403 is not going to inspire public confidence, and would hardly make the LAPD proud. But in the Columboverse, it's another way to downgrade the Lieutenant's competence to the unsuspecting killers. And even in this pseudo-reality, the durability of this particular Peugeot is remarkable. It first rolled into view in *Murder by the Book*, by 1973's *Any Old Port in a Storm* had clocked over 100,000 miles, and was still chugging down L.A. freeways through 2003.

Some fans get frustrated with the complete lack of awareness that sharp, wealthy and connected L.A. killers have about the detective who's put away so many other sharp, wealthy and connected L.A. killers. The cosmetics queen, the art critic, the chess master, the orchestra conductor, the TV detective, the exercise guru—the litany of the famous and infamous collared by Columbo grows with each passing year, yet it would appear that he languishes in semi-anonymity outside of his own police force.

Instead, it's an obscure Mexican comandante in *A Matter of Honor* who seems to know more about Columbo than anyone stateside. But in the Columboverse, that's precisely the point. If the killers are going to let their guards down, the belief that Columbo is a nobody-working-class stiff plays to the Lieutenant's advantage. The more famous and notorious Columbo becomes, the more the villains would become wary of him, and the tricks that Columbo uses to get them talking would be ineffective. For Columbo, fame is certainly not the name of the game, so in the fictional *Columbo* world, that inevitability is simply ignored.

Might better writing have accounted for this, and balanced at least some recognition for Columbo with clever killers who still thought they could best him? Perhaps, but that would only make more obvious another convention of alternate-reality Columbo, the almost total lack of lawyers to advise their killer clients. Rare are the moments when we see the murderers have any legal counsel to advise them to simply shut the fudge up. Of course, even if they appear, their clients, like Riley Greenleaf (Jack Cassidy) in *Publish or Perish*, conveniently ignore or castigate them. But the more famous Columbo gets, the harder it would be for the guilty to avoid this common-sense legal strategy that is common in our real world. Over time, a more celebrated Columbo becomes a less effective Columbo. So in parallel-universe *Columbo*, the solution is to keep him practically a detective nobody.

Of course, this also means that he never gets promoted. This, despite Sergeant Wilson (Bob Dishy) in *The Greenhouse Jungle* noting that Columbo is "fast becoming a legend in the department." One suspects that keeping that Lieutenant's badge is exactly what our Columboverse cop wants, as moving up to the Captain's chair would take him off the street doing what he loves. And multiverse Columbo also has plenty of time to hound suspected killers around town and follow up leads that real-world lieutenants would never have a chance to do. The administrative, community and desk duties that are part of the job description of actual LAPD lieutenants leave practically no time to bunk at military academies, attend magic shows, play chopsticks at the Hollywood Bowl, and other such crime-solving diversions.

For younger consumers of television raised in the cable and streaming era, it's easy to scoff at the quick and bloodless nature of the murderous acts depicted in Seventies TV. But during *Columbo's* original run, there was a seemingly endless national debate, complete with congressional hearings, over television violence. No Seventies show was ever going to show the real bloody aftermath of vicious acts. That was left to the movies, where you had to actually pay to see blood on the screen. And that's exactly why the sanitized murders of *Columbo* weren't ever mocked or questioned in their day. That's how these killings were expected to be seen. This also provided an advantage to the writers who never had to worry about blood-soaked evidence or villains taking too long to clean up their murderous messes.

This doesn't mean that our Columboverse killings were all ho-hum homicides. The Columbophile Blog chronicles the most shocking and unsettling ones, and it's really not until the Nineties revival that the violence gets ratcheted up a notch or two.[3] But even when brutal and upsetting, the blood flow in the Classic Era murders was negligible.

Clean Columboverse kills were convenient for everyone, and not just the episode writers. This is a world where the most inexperienced gunslingers can get their missions accomplished with just a single shot, slaying the victim with brutal efficiency and no bloodletting. That's quite a feat in the real world, but

"YOU HAVE TO FORGIVE ME..." it's not me, it's my mind; it's very slow, and I have to pin everything down." (from *By Dawn's Early Light*)

commonplace in Columbo-place. For the up-close killers like Leslie Williams (*Ransom for a Dead Man*) and Hayden Danziger (*Troubled Waters*), this may have been easier than for distance-shooters like Ruth Lytton (*Old Fashioned Murder*) and Nelson Hayward (*Candidate for Crime*). But the results were the same. Anyone could pick up a gun, anyone could pull the trigger, anyone could handle the backfire, and anyone could hit the precise spot guaranteeing instantaneous and blood-free death.

Of course, this rarely enters into Columbo's reasoning. But when it does, it creates pesky inconsistencies in the Columboverse, and it fails to be faithful to its own reality. Unsurprisingly, it's an inexperienced *Columbo* writer who opens up this Columboverse can of worms. In *Fade In to Murder*, scribe Peter Feibleman has Columbo get the evidence of Ward Fowler's (William Shatner) Army marksmanship skills that would come in handy for the fatal shot to Claire Daley. And yet Feibleman, writing the very next episode *Old Fashioned Murder*, doesn't have Columbo questioning the considerably more expert firing skills required by Ruth Lytton (Joyce Van Patten) to knock off *both* thief Milton and brother Edward. (Perhaps there are some WAC records buried in paperwork somewhere with Ruth's shooting scores). In the Columboverse, you shouldn't ever question the killer's aim.

But nothing jolts *Columbo* viewers into reality like a Gotcha built on flimsy legal evidence. This is completely understandable. We like to think of our hero catching the killers of our universe, dispensing justice to the villain with long and well-deserved jail time. The reality is, the baddies will lawyer up and introduce reasonable doubt into their defense, and that can be a bit deflating. We look at each Gotcha and apply logic to it, and logic tells us that many of these cases would have trouble standing up in court.

But in the Columboverse, that hardly matters. As author Dana Schwartz explains, "I'm fantasizing about *Columbo* villains, and the way they react when Columbo bests them. When the murderers are outsmarted, they politely turn themselves in...." In the real world, we sense that there are many criminals who will avoid their justice with extravagant lies and legal slow-playing. The Columboverse presents an alternative. "At this point [the Gotcha], the exquisite character-actor playing the murderer will sigh, or smile, or sometimes even laugh. He will all but shake hands and congratulate the Lieutenant whom he had so underestimated. Columbo had outsmarted him, fair and square. 'Well done, detective, you may take me to jail now.'"[4] When the Gotcha happens, we see the reaction of the killer, and in that precise moment, we know that Columbo has won their mental competition. It may or may not be an iron-clad legal victory, but it is the emotional victory in the Columboverse that counts.

Let's take *The Most Crucial Game*. Watching this as a 1972 teen, I was completely blown away by the conclusion—it wasn't what Columbo heard on the tape, it's what he *didn't* hear! Sealing the deal was the gobsmacked reaction of Paul Hanlon (Robert Culp) when he realized that Columbo had just clocked him. That's all I needed. In adult retrospect, Hanlon would surely hire a battery of high-priced legal talent to provide about 37 different reasons why you don't hear a clock chime on the incriminating recording. But so what? This isn't *Law and Order*. We're not going to see Part 2 with the prosecuting team in court. That's not the point in the Columboverse. Having a legally solid Gotcha is obviously desirable, and certainly contributes to our overall enjoyment of the episode. But the killer's acknowledgement of defeat, however momentary, is what drives the sense of justice that satisfies the viewer.

Occasionally, the killer initially resists giving us this gratification. In those cases, it falls to someone close to the murderer to provide the viewer with emotional closure. When killers like Alex Benedict, Harold Van Wick, and Grace Wheeler fail to cop to their crimes, it's the reactions of Janice Benedict (*Etude in Black*), Elizabeth Van Wick (*Playback*) and Ned Diamond (*Forgotten*

Lady) that tell us that Columbo has won. With those rare exceptions, the Gotchas of alternate-universe *Columbo* only need to convince three people—Columbo, the murderer, and the viewer. The additional 12 in the jury box don't matter.

Much of television has historically been used as escapist fantasy, an idealized fiction of American life. The Columboverse is not designed to reflect the actual practices of the Los Angeles Police Department, courtroom evidence, slam-dunk convictions, bloody crime scenes, or amateur marksmanship. For entertainment purposes, we should understand that there is an element of un-reality to every *Columbo* episode.

But it would be a mistake to think that because of this, those hundred-years-hence discoverers of our *Columbo* time capsule wouldn't learn anything about the Seventies. Much of what we see on TV should ideally also act as a mirror for different elements of our society. If it's not accurate, if it strikes a wrong note, we notice. So, there are no limousines in the *Brady Bunch* neighborhood, no farmers in overalls at the *Cheers* bar, no high rises on the horizon in Andy Griffith's Mayberry. The goal is to depict a convincing, or at least plausible, reality. Popular culture echoes the world around it. Even on a 23rd century starship surrounded by fantastic contraptions and exotic aliens, there is at least an accurate reflection of human emotions.

It's a credit to creators Levinson and Link, the writing staff, and most especially to Peter Falk that the Columbo character is so well-developed that we like to imagine him as a part of our own world. That doesn't mean we're delusional—we all know that he's a fictional creation, right? But most Seventies fictional TV sleuths don't inspire us to think about much beyond largely superficial traits: Kojak's lollipop, Ironside's wheelchair, Cannon's weight, McCloud's cowboy hat, Charlie's Angels', uh, assets.

The (slight) downside to this is that we sometimes expect Columbo to follow all the rules and conventions of our own universe. He doesn't. He was never meant to. And that's OK. If he's faithful to his own reality in the Columboverse, that's more than enough.

Columbo Redux

Before we lean more into *Columbo* of the Seventies, we'll take a brief detour to *Columbo* of the Nineties. Surely, if we can draw intelligent conclusions about the cultural impact of 45 episodes of the Classic *Columbo* era, we can do the same for the 24 episodes between 1989-2003, right? After all, it's the same show with the same lieutenant played by the same actor with the same lovable character traits. Seems simple enough.

And as a huge *Columbo* fan, I would more than welcome the opportunity to expand the scope of this book or provide a breathless tease for *Part II: New Columbo Explains the Nineties*. Alas, that will have to come from someone else. Post-1989 *Columbo* is—I take no joy in saying this—just not a strong or enduring enough program to be worthy of the same intelligent discourse.

There were some notable moments dotted throughout the revival. In particular, Peter Falk excelled when he had compelling actors to verbally spar with. His interactions with Faye Dunaway in *It's All in the Game*, William Shatner in *Butterfly in Shades of Grey*, and Rod Steiger in *Strange Bedfellows* all matched the interplays with many of the previous era's film stars that filled out the guest lists of killers and supporting performers. Unfortunately, there was just not enough star-power chemistry to fuel the newer episodes.

In 1975's *Playback*, Columbo looks to solve the crime by minutely examining still shots of two almost identical video recordings, side-by-side. One playback machine shows the shooting of Margaret Meadis, and the other is of the immediate aftermath, as a security guard enters the murder room. Columbo is looking for anything that would point to a difference in the two settings, a difference that could reveal the murderer's identity. He finally sees it—a spot that is lighter in one scene than the other. Zooming in, Columbo finds the clue that cracks the case.

Our task is similar, as we put the two incarnations of *Columbo* side-by-side and examine them closely. On a surface level, the shows appear to be somewhat the same. But we have to zoom in to find those tell-tale spots that mark the differences in quality. To fans whose entry point into the series was 1989 or beyond, their perceptions of these differences are very likely to be different than those of someone first exposed to Classic *Columbo*, perhaps as they were growing up. Because *Columbo 2.0* still retained the charm and likeability of Peter Falk's character, it's understandable that more recent viewers were drawn into the series on the strength of that performance and the entire Columbo persona. And sure, you could stick around for the murders, too. If you enjoyed New *Columbo* thanks to Peter Falk and the character, that's very reasonable, and I sincerely intend no disrespect.

Those who first discovered *Columbo* in its original Seventies form had more than an idiosyncratic detective to enjoy. In today's parlance, we would call it Prestige TV. Each episode was produced as if it were a theater feature, with lavish sets, movie guest stars and supporting cast, thoughtful scripts, convincing clues, elegant costuming, and striking, chilling music to accompany the stylishly executed murders. Peter Falk and the Columbo character of course held it all together, and without him at the show's core, it may not have thrived.

But the show wasn't just beholden to Peter. There was so much quality and care displayed in every *Columbo* that even when there was an inevitable clunker, for whatever reason, the episode was usually strong enough to at least mildly appreciate, and even warrant repeat viewings.

As the years progressed, the Columbo character veered more and more into self-parody. To be fair, this pre-dated the revival. In her book *Columbo: Make Me a Perfect Murder*, Amelie Hastie speculates that it began creeping into his performances upon Falk's portrayal of parodic detectives in 1976's *Murder by Death* and 1978's *The Cheap Detective*.[5] The broad interpretations probably weren't helped by the advice of Falk's close friend Patrick McGoohan. David Koenig's *Shooting Columbo* reveals that McGoohan "had long encouraged Falk to think beyond the format, to realize that the most enduring component of *Columbo* was Columbo himself, Columbo the character."[6]

The revived *Columbo* exacerbated this problem. Yes, the character was a strength of the show. But it could also be an Achilles heel. As the Classic Era concluded in 1978, the lasting memory for many people was the Columbo schtick, made famous by repeated ham-handed impersonations and a farcical image of the Lieutenant that lingered in those 11 years between series. Instead of being a serious character with a comedic edge, New *Columbo* seemed to flip the dynamic to service that caricature and play up the sillier elements.

This is nowhere more evident than in the increased placement of what seemed to be Designated Comedy Scenes in the later years. In the Classic Era, Columbo's appearance and quirks produced reactions from those around him, and the observational humor came from how those in Columbo's orbit responded to his presence. The gold standard for this is the soup kitchen scene from *Negative Reaction*.

Columbo is on the search for a witness to the murder of Alvin Deschler, who Paul Galesko (Dick Van Dyke) has set up as the fall guy in Paul's murder of wife Frances (Antoinette Bower). Thomas Dolan (Vito Scotti) is a wino who was at the scene of Deschler's demise, and Columbo has traced him to St. Matthew Mission in downtown Los Angeles. Columbo enters the mission, and the Sister of Mercy (Joyce Van Patten) immediately, and understandably, pegs him as a homeless man in need of a meal and a place to stay.

Columbo himself does not do anything remarkably funny here. It's the reactions of the Sister, in a terrifically oversolicitous but not overplayed performance from Van Patten, that generate the laughs. The humor comes from the context, as she makes her assumptions about Columbo from his appearance. He eventually realizes this ("Uh... I think there's a misunderstanding"), but the Sister is quick to try to put him at ease. "Oh no, brother, no false pride between friends. A man's worth is not judged by the size of his purse." If you look closely, it's clear that Peter Falk is holding back laughter and breaking character, relying on the presumption that Columbo himself might find this amusing. Vito Scotti contributes a funny portrayal moments later. The scene has no music, relying instead on the actors involved for its humor.

Contrast this with a typical "humorous" scene from 1991's *Caution: Murder Can Be Hazardous to Your Health*. Columbo, in his battered wreck, keeps cutting off Wade Anders (George Hamilton) trying to park his sporty Mercedes-Benz in the parking lot of Anders' office. It's a low-brow vaudeville comedy clinic, with repetition, yelling, hand gestures, Peugeot backfires, bumper-falling sound effects, tire screeches, and exasperated expressions, all put to a silly soundtrack. That cop with dignity that Falk so eloquently described to Johnny Carson in 1973 was losing his own.

The difference is that the best Seventies humor came from the amusing reactions to Columbo. Maybe it's lawyer Cunnell's expressions to Columbo's curiosity about his shoes (*The Most Crucial Game*). Or perhaps Vito Scotti's character fitting Columbo for a suit in *Candidate for Crime*. The jokey Nineties scenes, unfortunately, invite us to laugh *at* him.

Without the high-value elements that elevated every Seventies episode, Columbo was often stranded in what resembled an ordinary television police procedural. It is, to be sure, a subjective task in differentiating the quality of Old versus New *Columbo*. I also appreciate that this might spark honest disagreement. For the record, though, I would argue that the music, guest stars, scripts, Gotcha clues, direction, acting and balance of humor to serious crime solving were all vastly inferior in the later years.

There were also distressingly sloppy characterizations and inconsistencies in bringing Columbo into a new era. For example, it was a well-known and reliable trait of Columbo that he hated heights, established with both villains and secondary characters. So when Columbo hops into a helicopter without a care in 1990's *Columbo Cries Wolf* and climbs ladders set against rooftop chimneys, one has to wonder: Peter Falk essentially ran the show in the Nineties, and if he and the producers didn't care about getting the character details right, why should *we* bother caring?

The *Columbo* revival's reflection of the decade was usually in the most superficial ways. There were technology updates like the pager of *Columbo Cries Wolf*, and the fax machine of *Agenda for Murder*. There were tawdry pseudo-R-rated villains like sex therapist Dr. Joan Allenby (Lindsay Crouse, *Sex and the Married Detective*) and openly womanizing artist Max Barsini (Patrick Bauchau, *Murder: A Self Portrait*). But as we will observe in a later chapter, the Nineties simply may not have been the best decade to launch a second life for *Columbo*. Even if the show had maintained something near the high-quality standards of the Classic episodes, it may have been doomed to indifference.

Should the failings of *Columbo 2.0* be held against the overall *Columbo* legacy? Fortunately, no. *Columbo's* comeback seemed less organic and more economic, as ABC was looking to revive the Mystery Movie format, but only if *Columbo* and its co-creator William Link was involved (Richard Levinson had passed away). This errant phase of *Columbo* can be dismissed as easily as Michael Jordan fans can dismiss his declining Washington Wizards comeback years. We can acknowledge that it has a place in his history, but it doesn't need to be defining, or even well-remembered. It is likely that if this particular updated production of *Columbo* had made its debut in 1989, without the legacy of 45 previous episodes behind it, it would probably have never made it past a handful of murders, grinding to a halt on the ABC Mystery wheel just as surely as *Gideon Oliver* and *Christine Cromwell*.

II.
Columbo's Cultural Footprint

The massive popularity and cultural impact of the Columbo character has been worldwide since his introduction in 1968. *Columbo* movie pilots and episodes have been repackaged as films for theaters across the Atlantic. Striking, colorful foreign posters for *Ransom for a Dead Man* (*Riscatto Per un Uomo Morto*), *Etude in Black* (*Concerto con Delitto*), *Dagger of the Mind* (*Scacco Matto a Scotland Yard*), and *A Friend in Deed* (*Un Amico da Salvare*) might still be had on eBay.

Columbo's mainstream sway extended well beyond a simple "Just one more thing" catchphrase. Fans who discovered *Columbo* through the re-introduction of the character in 1989 or in the 2020 pandemic lockdown may not have a frame of reference for understanding just how large a cultural footprint *Columbo* had in the Seventies. It's worth racking up a few more miles on the Peugeot odometer to journey through the era and examine just how popular this guy in the wrinkled raincoat was.

Watching the Detective

Pre-internet, pre-Instagram, and pre-iPhone, the surest way to gauge a celebrity's popularity was through magazine covers and coverage. For kids, the plastering of teenage idols' pictures on the fronts of *Tiger Beat*, *16*, and *Teen Beat* told young people who the hottest faces in youth pop culture were.

For adults, other magazines spread the word. And in the Sixties and Seventies, the magazine with the largest overall circulation in America

A RARITY: Columbo depicted without his cigar!

was *TV Guide*. Viewers and families planning their evenings depended on having a *TV Guide* atop the coffee table next to the television. With the 24/7 programming details of the three commercial networks and Public Broadcasting, it was indispensable. It also carried brief articles about the shows and their stars, helping to fill the star-gazing void between the decline of lurid Hollywood mags like *Confidential* and the rise of *People* and *Entertainment Tonight*. In 1972, *TV Guide* circulation was 16 million, behind only *Reader's Digest* and doubling its closest competition. Mid-'70s readership later reached 19 million.[1] Beginning with its debut issue cover of April 3, 1953 featuring "Desiderio Alberto Arnaz IV" (Lucille Ball's baby), the cover of *TV Guide* has been a reliable pop culture barometer, tracking the meteoric rise of household television watching.

Peter Falk appeared on the cover of *TV Guide* four times in the Seventies, either as himself or as his Lieutenant alter ego. On March 25, 1972, after the first season concluded, the magazine announced, "America Discovers Columbo." Subsequent covers included one on Aug. 14, 1976, from famed caricaturist Al Hirschfeld, noted for hiding the name of his daughter Nina in his portraits. For his Columbo, "Nina" was worked into the Lieutenant's coat folds.

In 1975, Falk hit the cover of *Rolling Stone* in a slovenly pose to promote not *Columbo*, but his movie *A Woman Under the Influence*. The headline: "The Bars Stay Open at Night for Columbo." In 1976, he was on the cover of *People*, topping fellow issue subjects Paul Newman and Aerosmith. Beyond the entertainment publications, however, the major exposure was in 1973, when the November 26 issue of *Time* magazine declared the new season to be "TV's Year of the Cop," with a rather unconvincing likeness of Columbo pointing at... well, we don't know, but Columbo was generally too polite to point.

The article inside referenced the slew of new cop, detective and lawyer/crime shows cramming the airwaves, but gave particular focus to Columbo, clumsily describing him as looking like "an ambulatory cypress stump in baggy brown pants."[2] In the serious magazine niche, *Time's* circulation of 4.25 million broadened *Columbo's* scope and made the newsmagazine's exposure significant.[3] So, amidst the cigarette ads for Vantage, Lucky Ten, Belair and Doral, and the articles about energy conservation and President Nixon's vow to put Watergate to rest, we learn that Columbo takes on the wealthy "to play off a well-heeled villain against the down-at-the-heel Columbo." This is not precisely correct, as we will note in a later chapter, but as *Columbo* was expanding its reach in popular culture, a *Time* cover story certainly didn't hurt.

As a testament to popularity, comedy also plays a role, and Columbo's traits made him a ridiculously easy and ripe subject for parody, as in January of 1973, when *Mad* magazine featured a "Clodumbo" layout. Seven months later *Cracked* magazine, often described as the poor man's answer to *Mad*, featured "Columbore" on its cover.

As you might expect, the jokes practically wrote themselves. *Mad's* spoof had the Lieutenant bothering the Police Commissioner with an endless stream of inane conversation, until finally called to a murder at the home of Dr. Robert Culpable, a dead ringer for the striped-shirt, square-glassed Robert

Culp of *Death Lends a Hand*. The doctor is innocent, but is bothered so much by Clodumbo that Culpable confesses just to be rid him. The artwork from longtime *Mad* illustrator Angelo Torres was sharp and realistic, the parody gentle.

Cracked didn't vary the formula much, but it took a more mean-spirited tack: "Right off you know who the murderer is, so there's no suspense. What there is however, is the sheer boredom of watching a clumsy, sloppy detective hamming it up." *Mad* would be back in 1975 to imagine the "final" *Columbo* episode, as the previously unseen Mrs. Columbo, in curlers, shoots (!) her husband after he announces his retirement and intention to stay home with her all day. As hit-or-miss as these parodies were, *Columbo* clearly wouldn't be fodder for comedy unless it was already a popular and recognized cultural phenomenon.

TV sitcoms had their day with *Columbo* as well. NBC's *Sanford and Son* featured Redd Foxx in a wig-raincoat-cigar disguise, calling himself "The Falk-on… Peter Falk-on," while competing network ABC used the disguise bit on *The Odd Couple*. But the most fascinating reference comes from CBS' off-center and underrated comedy *Green Acres*. In a Season 3 episode, future *Columbo* villain Eddie Albert (as Oliver Wendall Douglas) and wife Lisa (Eva Gabor) learn about a new play being put on by the locals of Hooterville. It's a murder mystery, with the investigator being played by a police dog—who goes by the name of Columbo. In true *Green Acres* fashion, nobody considers this bizarre except for Oliver. What's remarkable is that this episode aired in April 1968, only two months after the debut of the Columbo character on *Prescription: Murder*![4]

Another *Columbo* spoof aired in 1975, as Johnny Carson popped up in file cabinets, closets, and wall safes with "one more thing." Carson's *Tonight Show* was the only real late-night entertainment option of the era, producing 17 percent of NBC's profits as the most prolific moneymaker in TV history.[5] Carson had no serious competitors in the 11:30 p.m.-1 a.m. timeslot. His popularity and domination of late-night scared off CBS and ABC, whose own talk shows from Merv Griffin and Joey Bishop were replaced in favor of grab bags of assorted specials, concerts, movies and prime time reruns.

The Tonight Show was a logical place for Falk to promote *Columbo*, which he did on several occasions early in the fall TV seasons. For the first of these, in September of 1972, he wore his raincoat to plug *Etude in Black*, which would be debuting the second season in the show's new Sunday nighttime period (the NBC Mystery Movie originally began on Wednesday nights). In later years, the character was established enough to allow Falk to forego the coat, although Carson had him try on some different slicker styles after hyping *Any Old Port in a Storm* in 1973. The following year, Falk excitedly promoted the shoe-tying Gotcha twist of *An Exercise in Fatality* without a spoiler; it was described as something everyone did every day.

The Carson appearances did more than alert viewers that summer rerun season was over. They allowed Peter Falk to shed the Columbo routine and character tics in favor of simply being natural, casual, warm, funny and human. Falk's effortless charm was a selling point for the Lieutenant, too, and the convergence of the personable Falk with Columbo helped drive the popularity of both.

Meanwhile, CBS' attempt to dent Johnny Carson's pop culture supremacy led to an unusual approach. In 1975, they began airing repeats of one of NBC's prized gems—the Sunday Mystery Movie. *Columbo* began showing up during bedtime hours, unfortunately hacked to near incomprehension by the need to squeeze more commercials into an already tight timeslot. Both *Columbo* and Carson survived the ploy.

Playing Columbo

By 1974, *Columbo* was on the air for over two seasons. It had been featured on the cover of *Time* magazine and multiple *TV Guides*, been nominated for Best Drama Emmys, and Peter Falk had already snagged his first Best Actor award. Its status in popular culture was growing. It was time for a board game. At first blush, this would seem to be a cherished milestone. The show was not just being watched, but now became an interactive activity, a part of the rich *Columbo* experience. But that would be overselling it. Board games based on television programs have a long and financially-incentivized history, with networks and studios looking to reap whatever momentary windfalls they can from a show's fleeting fame.

So, how exactly do you make a board game based on *The Waltons* interesting? *The Love Boat, Little House on the Prairie, Mork and Mindy, M*A*S*H, Laverne and Shirley, The Brady Bunch, Happy Days, The Partridge Family,* and *All in the Family* all received the table-top game treatment. *Space: 1999* was floundering and uninspired, yet inspired a board game.

On the criminal front, 1959's *Perry Mason: Case of the Missing Suspect* had players competing to see who would be first to whisk a murder suspect to the courthouse (sounds like a Paul Drake mission more than Perry's). *Peter*

THERE'S A GUN hiding behind that badge, so we know that can't possibly be Columbo! *(Photo courtesy of Jim Pulles)*

Gunn, Dragnet, Get Smart, Batman and *The Man from UNCLE* pre-dated the *Columbo* game. There was *Kojak: The Stake Out Detective Game, CHiPs, Starsky and Hutch Detective Game, Charlie's Angels,* and *Scooby Doo, Where Are You?*

Some of these diversions had enough imagination to at least attempt to emulate the spirit of the TV show that provided the game name. In *Space: 1999*, participants had to get their spaceship home to Earth first, Chinese checkers-style. *M*A*S*H* players could race a jeep or copter to the base camp and receive their transfer orders to go home. The goal of *Charlie's Angels* was to have everyone work as a team to trap a villain, using each Angel's "talent." The subtitle of the *All in the Family* game was "Is there a little bit of Archie in all of us?," and players answered questions so others could try to match the responses to things Archie or Edith Bunker might have said.

As a television program of the highest quality, with a distinctive format, becoming renowned and revered the world over, the *Columbo* game would certainly be one of the shining stars of the board game universe, would it not? It would not.

The object of this basic memory game was to roam through a mansion to collect cards that would, when put together, make up drawings of the murderer and weapon involved in the chosen crime. It was, in fact, almost a direct steal from 1958's *Alfred Hitchcock Why Mystery Game*. The setting was different in *Hitchcock* (a ghost house), but the cards were much the same, and players were looking to align them puzzle-style to create a picture. Each game allowed one to pick up clues from a Discard area. In *Columbo's* case, it was the mansion's lawn, I suppose much like the lawn where Ken Franklin dumped the body of Jim Ferris in *Murder by the Book*.

Unfortunately, there was no semblance at all to elements of the TV *Columbo*. The game goal was to discover the murderer, whom television viewers of course already knew. Most distressing, though, were the obvious licensing issues that prevented Game Columbo from even showing us his face. He's wearing a raincoat and holding a cigar, but his head is awkwardly turned away, forever shrouded in mystery. The "real" Columbo would not be rolling the dice to save this game.

Lasagna for Sinatra

In 1973, NBC's *The Dean Martin Show* added a feature designed to juice its declining ratings. It was called the "Man of the Week Celebrity Roast," with numerous Hollywood actors and comedians (the so-called roasters) ribbing a celebrity or otherwise noteworthy person, much in the style of the private and infamously bawdy dinners held at the New York Friars Club since 1950. When Dean's show was cancelled in 1974, NBC recognized the popularity and potential of the roast segment, and contracted with Martin to host a series of specials now titled *The Dean Martin Celebrity Roast*.

The guest lists of both the roasters and the roastees is a remarkable study in Seventies entertainment popular culture, with some light crossover into sports, politics and then-current affairs. Some heavyweight names transcend the decade, while others are head-scratching whodats to observers today, and only serve to highlight the cliché about fleeting fame.

Some of the roasted were Lucille Ball, Bob Hope, Bobby Riggs, Jackie Gleason, Peter Marshall, Joe Namath, Ralph Nader, Zsa Zsa Gabor, Bette Davis, Hugh Hefner, Kirk Douglas, Barry Goldwater, Wilt Chamberlain, Monty Hall, Gabe Kaplan, Redd Foxx, Sammy Davis Jr, Evel Knievel, Joe Garagiola, Truman Capote, Bette White, Mr. T, Hank Aaron, and Dan Haggerty. If you're not up on your Seventies decade, you may need to do some Googling. They even tried a roast of someone dressed up as George Washington (hopefully you won't need to Google him).

Roasters included Don Rickles, Rich Little, Neil Armstrong, Joey Bishop, Nipsey Russell, Florence Henderson, Henry Kissinger, Freddie Prinze, Dionne Warwick, Phyllis Diller, Ed Asner, Hubert Humphrey, Shelley Winters, Tony

Orlando, Ruth Buzzi, William Conrad, Henry Fonda, Rex Reed, Charo, Ernest Borgnine, Howard Cosell, Army Archerd, Vincent Price, Mark Spitz, Mel Tillis, and Telly Savalas.

These lists are by no means exhaustive, and the nuts-and-gum mix of pop culture figures is truly astounding in this era of narrow-casting and niche TV programming. Since many of these people were not exactly renowned for their comedy stylings, the specials retained many of the writers from Martin's original show to provide the jokes.

On February 7, 1978, an impressive gaggle of celebs gathered at Las Vegas' MGM Grand Hotel in the Ziegfeld Room, the roasting venue for the past four years of specials.[6] The spotlighted roastee was a true legend of Hollywood and popular culture, Frank Sinatra. The list of Hollywood heavy hitters for this event would be understandably prestigious, including Jimmy Stewart, Gene Kelly, Orson Welles, Milton Berle, and Jonathan Winters. Ronald Reagan, two years removed from California governorship and two years away from another political office, was there to tease Ol' Blue Eyes: "Frank worked for me on all my campaigns. He was with me all the way to the governor's mansion. Without his help, who knows, I might have been President."

Another roaster was so well known that he attended the event as his popular television character—Peter Falk as Columbo. Early on in the proceedings, toastmaster Dean Martin, doing his usual tipsy routine, introduced the Lieutenant with a story about how Sinatra was looking for the perfect prop to add to a photo shoot. Holding up an album cover from the movie *Pal Joey*, Martin said that Frank suddenly asked a random passerby to lend him his raincoat, which was then slung over Sinatra's arm for an iconic image of the singer under a lamppost. "This guy with the raincoat was a nice fella, and he's in the audience tonight as Frank's invited guest, Lieutenant Columbo!"

The camera cuts to the side of the stage, where Falk-as-Columbo gets up and acknowledges a rousing wave of audience applause. Ambling to the dais with a paper bag of… something, he begins his selection of jests and jokes.

Except, he's not really there to tease Frank at all. The only semblance of a joke about Sinatra comes when "Columbo" asks a question for his "family" and references Frank's 1971 retirement. "They claim that now, when you make a record, that Jerry Vale does the singing for you." But even this is as much a rib at the numerous Columbo relations that have received mentions in the series. The entire 10 minutes is pure Columbo character riffing.

He asks Dean, "Those shoes, they're not rented, are they?" He makes a self-deprecating crack about his own wardrobe. He politely calls Frank "Sir." He reaches over several guests to borrow a pen from Dom DeLuise and a napkin from Martin. He wants Sinatra to autograph it, and dithers about who to address it to, finally deciding on "To Rose" (presumably the unseen series wife, although this shouldn't be considered canon). He presents the guest of honor with the paper bag, containing a dish of lasagna cooked by Mrs. Columbo. Throughout, he and Frank work the Ziegfeld Room like a well-oiled comedy machine. And, in fact, they did work together in the 1964 movie *Robin and the Seven Hoods*.

This was not a roast of Sinatra. This was simply a concentrated, virtuoso performance of Peter Falk as Columbo. The humor didn't come from any standard setup-punchline jokes, although there are a couple of those that might qualify. The belly laughs from the Vegas audience, the TV viewers, and the assorted stars come from seeing the ordinary reactions of a relentlessly ordinary man thrust on stage with bigger-than-life celebrities and talking about his ordinary family. As he told Carson years before, Columbo was not being dumb, he was not foolish, and he was not stupid.

It is highly likely that Peter Falk, so obsessive and fiercely protective of his character, was himself responsible for most if not all of this routine. Comedian and impersonator Rich Little, a regular fixture at the Martin roasts, had perhaps the best perspective on how the specials were put together. "They wrote jokes for everybody except Don Rickles," he says. "They didn't write anything for Rickles. Now, you could use all of the material, or just some of it. But everybody was given a script with jokes."[7] It is likely that Falk did indeed get a few Sinatra jokes from the writers, and probably ditched them.

Falk-as-Columbo was such a smash that in a roast rarity, the show producers kept the entire performance in the final cut, at the expense of other guests. But, as those who had worked with Peter before would no doubt attest, he was such a perfectionist that he insisted on retakes of his routine. He did so later that evening with no Vegas audience and minus Frank and Dean. On the *Columbo* set, Falk was the boss, and that re-do would have been the final say. But this time, he wasn't on the *Columbo* set. Producers tossed the endless retakes and went with the original tape.[8]

The Dean Martin Celebrity Roast of Frank Sinatra, recorded in February 1978, was broadcast on NBC the evening of July 2, a Sunday night. By this time, *McCloud* and *McMillan* (minus "*& Wife*") were long gone, cancelled in April of 1977. New episodes of *Columbo*, though, continued in the familiar Sunday Mystery Movie slot rotating with various specials and reruns.

While the Sinatra roast was happening that evening of February 7, the *Columbo* production team was wrapping up *The Conspirators*, with the Lieutenant going after a colorful Irish poet who murdered an arms dealer.

The episode would be broadcast on May 13, ahead of the Martin-Sinatra special. At the time, Peter Falk was going through the usual yearly dance with the network of deciding what the terms would be for him to return to the show. There were always concerns that either NBC or Falk would scuttle it, but things had always worked themselves out.[9]

This year, however, NBC had hired a new president and CEO, Fred Silverman. He arrived at the network for his first official day on the job in June 1978. He was not a fan of keeping Columbo, but there would be no official announcement to the public of a cancellation. Instead, Peter Falk's contract would simply not be renewed.

In the meantime, though, *The Conspirators* aired in May. Peter Falk, NBC and the viewing public had no way of knowing that this would be the decade's last episode. So when the *Dean Martin Celebrity Roast of Frank Sinatra* was broadcast two months later in July of 1978, it could well be that only one person on the planet, Fred Silverman, knew that this would be the very last time that Peter Falk would perform as Columbo for NBC.

Trivia Wars and Name Games

By 1979, the heralded reign of Peter Falk as Columbo at NBC was done, and the brief infamy of Kate Mulgrew as Mrs. Columbo had begun (more on that piece of TV history later). But 1979 also began a chain of events that would thrust *Columbo* back into the popular culture spotlight.

"Well, my friends, I have a very sad announcement to make. At this time, this is the last *Jeopardy!* telecast on NBC."
– Art Fleming, *Jeopardy!* Host, March 2, 1979

With this declaration, America's intelligent, fact-based game show was over. Its 1979 death knell as mass appeal entertainment meant that there were few options available for anyone who had a hunger for the brainy, arcane and obscure information that *Jeopardy!* provided. But there was one outlet left.

In 1979, Fred L. Worth was an air traffic controller in Sacramento, California. As a side hustle, he had been amassing hundreds of little-known facts and small details into two books, 1974's *The Trivia Encyclopedia* and its 1977 follow-up, *The Complete Unabridged Super Trivia Encyclopedia*.

Worth explained, "Once I was established as a controller and I had time to myself, I decided to write down all the information I'd been collecting all my life." Alphabetized index cards held the thousands of factoids collected from his own memory and California libraries, as well as trips to Toys R Us and anywhere else he could scrounge information from both the real and the fictional worlds.[10]

The volumes were successful, encouraging Worth to try creating a board game based on his collection of trivia. It never got off the ground. But in 1979, two Canadian journalists, frustrated with losing their *Scrabble* game tiles, began designing their own board game. Two years of data research and development paid off in 1981 with the creation of *Trivial Pursuit*. But the game was not an immediate success... until it had the help of a Hollywood star.

The introduction of *Trivial Pursuit* in 1981 came at a particularly bad time for Fred Worth. In August, he was one of the 11,000 federally-employed air traffic controllers fired by President Ronald Reagan after their union went on an illegal strike for better pay and working conditions. As *Pursuit* slowly gained traction, Worth noticed that the game featured many facts from his Seventies trivia books that were simply re-written into the form of questions. He felt that this was blatant stealing of the fruits of his hard work and labor. But crafty Fred had earlier hatched a plan to ensure that he would not be taken advantage of.

Most accounts have Worth devising his ruse based on an old practice of cartographers inventing minor geographic elements into their maps to prove any appropriation, but that's not what Worth told the *New York Times*. "I knew that lexicographers used to make up a word and put it in the dictionary to see if it turned up in other dictionaries," Mr. Worth said, "so I decided to plant a ringer of my own to see if anyone copied it." In this case, it was not a word, but a name, which Worth did not yet disclose.[11]

In the meantime, actress Glenn Close had been living in Canada and was familiar with *Trivial Pursuit*. She was filming *The Big Chill* in 1983, and director Lawrence Kasdan had his large cast spend several weeks together for extensive rehearsals before shooting. It was here, off-set, when Close introduced her castmates (William Hurt, Jeff Goldblum, Kevin Kline, and more) to the game. It was a huge hit with everyone, and when this was reported in the Hollywood press, *Trivial Pursuit* was suddenly the newest pop culture rage.[12] By 1984, the game had generated $256 million in sales. Fred Worth now had his target in sight with a price tag, and in October of 1984, he filed a $300 million lawsuit against the makers of *Trivial Pursuit*.

Worth had his own *Columbo* Gotcha moment ready for the courtroom, a "fact" that he totally invented for his book to smoke out any copycats, the ringer he teased the *New York Times* with. It had been carefully inserted into *The Complete Unabridged Super Trivia Encyclopedia* as a declaration that Columbo's real, authentic and actual first name was Philip. When this popped up in the "Genus" edition of *Trivial Pursuit*, Worth was convinced that his copyright trap had been sprung. He sued the game for lifting his material.

Of course, Columbo's first name was not Philip. It was a well-established show legend that the Lieutenant's given name was never said, and it is likely that Worth chose this fakeout for his plan precisely because Columbo was a pop culture icon who would generate the proper amount of attention for this obvious inaccuracy.

But Worth was wrong. He had certainly demonstrated that *Trivial Pursuit* had used information from his books, but they readily admitted this, and to taking from other sources as well. Worth's problem was that facts themselves couldn't be copyrighted, only how they were presented. Fred's facts were presented in his books as direct statements alphabetized by topic. *Trivial Pursuit* used the information from these statements, but phrased as questions. The court ruled that this was not infringement. Worth's subsequent appeals to higher courts, including the U.S. Supreme Court, were rejected.

Following this trivia war, ironies abounded. There were other, unintentional factual errors that were used in *Trivial Pursuit* based on Worth's work, and his reputation suffered, so much so that he was labelled "Fred L. Worthless" in trivia circles and many trivia guides still ban using his books.[13] As for "false facts" of the type that Fred had created, in an unrelated 1992 lawsuit, the courts ruled that copyright traps were not themselves copyrightable. A federal court ruled that if that were the case, "no one could ever reproduce or copy actual facts without risk of reproducing a false fact and thereby violating a copyright... If such were the law, information could never be reproduced or widely disseminated."[14]

But Fred L. Worth had kept the trivia flame alive while *Jeopardy!* was cooling its heels, awaiting a 1984 comeback with brand new host Alex Trebek, thanks in large part to the mania generated by *Trivial Pursuit*. Unfortunately, Worth's efforts have had a lingering effect. For example, Peter Falk's pumpkin lasagna recipe in *Cooking with Columbo* makes the "Philip Columbo" error (hopefully the actual recipe ingredients suffer no such blunders).

Alas, some people are still convinced that Columbo is a Philip. This is unfortunate, because Columbo's name is not Philip—it's Frank.

The issue of Columbo's first name is a thorny one, with the most thorough debate, accounting for both Classic and New *Columbo*, coming in the

Columbophile Blog.¹⁵ It was clearly the intention of co-creators Levinson and Link to never give their detective a first name. Said Link in 2002, "He never had one and he never will, because it becomes a signature thing and people talk about it. You'll never hear a first name—ever. Peter's very adamant about that and so are we."¹⁶

Discussion of the first name has for decades always circled back around to the "Frank Columbo" prop badge flashed in a post-production insert in the third episode, *Dead Weight*. Said Link, "That was a prop man screwing up, creating a badge without even knowing the series. Peter didn't even catch that on the set. But I guess he was too involved with other things. The [prop person] who did it didn't really know the show, and didn't care, apparently."¹⁷

The decade didn't feature mass-consumer VCRs to freeze-frame scenes, and Columbo's (lack of) first name wasn't really drawing attention, so many fans easily wave it off as an Oopsie and move on. But the Frank Columbo prop badge insert also shows up four-and-a-half years later, in *A Matter of Honor*. Even more consequential, Columbo is seen holding it in his hand and showing it to Pat Morita's manservant character at Alex Benedict's mansion in *Etude in Black*. And before he displays it, Peter Falk *looks at the ID and points to it*. Hard to say Peter didn't catch that on set.

It must be noted that few in the Seventies would have anticipated the continuing interest in *Columbo* in future decades, in tandem with advanced technology's ability to allow us to repeatedly rewatch and stop the action. Those of a generous nature can allow for these errors and maintain that, as intended, the Lieutenant hadn't actually given us his first name. After all, as Link declared, it's never been said; as Columbo tells Colonel Rumford (Patrick McGoohan) in *By Dawn's Early Light*, "I do [have a first name], but my wife is about the only one who uses it."

And that's how Classic *Columbo* left the matter when it went off the air in 1978. But when New *Columbo* arrived in 1989, the intervening years had seen an explosion of precisely the technology that would allow fans to freeze any details. Retail sales of VHS machines were in the $4 billion range by 1984.¹⁸ *Columbo* VHS tapes were available by 1994. People were aware that his first name wasn't spoken, nor was it supposed to be revealed. And it certainly wasn't Philip.

Yet the revived *Columbo* continued to treat the Name Game as if it were still the Seventies, blithely giving viewers more visual evidence, either through sloppy and lazy production, or with the expectation that it could be ignored. *Grand Deceptions* shows us a production insert of an evidence bag with the name Frank Columbo. The Lieutenant holds and flashes his neatly typed

"Frank" badge twice at the Gotcha scene in *Death Hits the Jackpot*. He shows it clearly to the victim's lawyer in *A Trace of Murder*. Even after these episodes, in 2002, William Link said, "You'll never hear a first name, ever."

Technically, he was correct. Columbo's first name has never been explicitly verbalized, in the Seventies or the Nineties. If it had been said, even only once, viewers would proclaim that the puzzle of Columbo's first name was solved, ruining a perfectly fine mystery. So it seems incongruous that although the name has been seen by us on multiple occasions, the myth persists that Columbo's first name is unknown. Accepting "Frank" is up to individual tastes, but it is known.

Columbo Bites Crime

Even after the final NBC episode, Columbo was up to his old crime-fighting tricks beginning again in 1980. He wasn't quite himself, though. He had a different name and a few other detective quirks. Oh, and he changed his species, too.

McGruff the Crime Dog was the much-beloved, enormously popular animated answer to rising U.S. street crime and fears of violence that sprouted in the Sixties, soared in the Seventies, and crested in the Eighties. In a 1988 study, it was estimated that 99 percent of all children 6-12 recognized McGruff's familiar raincoated, wise and wizened appearance, making him as well-known as Ronald McDonald and bigger than Smokey the Bear.[19]

Baby Boomers have a particular fondness for McGruff, as the Crime Dog Public Service Announcements plastered the TV airwaves through the 1980s and are now forever ingrained in pop culture. And one of the inspirations for McGruff was an earlier pop culture feel-good phenomenon—Lieutenant Columbo.

Sherry Nemmers proudly and happily calls herself "McGruff's Mom." She is a Creative Director/Writer who has envisioned, conceived, written and put her personal imprint on upwards of 700 television commercials for over 40 years. The Charmin Bears are her creation. Anyone consuming television in the Eighties and beyond has witnessed her handiwork.[20]

"I'm a major Peter Falk fan," says Nemmers. Just not for the reason we might expect. "I knew who Columbo was, certainly, but I was not really watching, primarily because I didn't have the time. I loved it, but I wasn't an avid fan. Of course, he was a popular figure with everybody. But I do remember going to a movie, and I had no idea what it was going to be about, but my husband and I were on the floor." Sherry was watching Peter Falk and Alan Arkin in 1979's *The In-Laws*. "It was hilarious."

A 1975 Harris poll had 55 percent of people feeling uneasy simply walking the street; 45 percent were afraid to walk alone in a 1977 Gallup poll. To ease fears, the Department of Justice turned to the Advertising Council to create a crime prevention campaign. The Ad Council is a non-profit extension of the advertising industry, founded in 1942 to work pro bono with top ad firms to create public service campaigns. The assignment was given to Dancer Fitzgerald Sample, a top ad agency that had recently spearheaded the nationwide Keep America Beautiful campaign (Google the Crying Indian commercials). DFS strategy was to fashion a campaign that would emphasize the small steps that citizens could easily do on their own to discourage lawbreakers.

Advertising legend has it that DFS executive VP and creative director Jack Keil had a 3 a.m. brainstorm on an emergency layover at a Kansas City airport: "Take a Bite Out of Crime." Looking to emulate the success of the first public service mascot from the Ad Council in 1944, Smokey the Bear, an image was needed to carry the slogan. Nobody at DFS liked Keil's Snoopy-ish pooch with a Keystone Cops hat, so agency personnel were whipped into a competition to spark the creative juices. Losing out were a J. Edgar Hoover bulldog, a puppy called Spot the Wonder Dog, a golden retriever, and Sarge the German Shepherd. Left standing was the winner, described in Wendy Melillo's *How McGruff and the Crying Indian Changed America* as a lonely-looking hound who was "tired and had seen the world."[21]

This was 1979, and Sherry Nemmers was then a 21-year-old DFS copywriter in a stiff canine competition. She teamed with a DFS art director, Ray Krivascy, and they became co-creators of the trench coated talking dog, who at that point didn't have a name yet. Results of a cereal contest favored the moniker "Sherlock Bones," but McGruff the Crime Dog eventually won out.

As Nemmers explains, "McGruff was really an amalgam. Private detectives were huge for me. I had a lot of influences in mind. The humor probably came more from Clouseau. I loved the Pink Panther, Sam Spade, and all those great characters. Now, you could say this about Columbo and a lot of private eyes—they had a casual approach, that was very appealing to me. And what PI doesn't have a trench coat?" As for any direct character lifts in McGruff's creation, "Well, you know that in advertising, you're not going to copy anyone. You can't."

1979-1980 CONCEPTION of McGruff prior to initial campaign rollout, featuring creator Sherry Nemmers with niece and nephew. *(Photo courtesy of Sherry Nemmers)*

The McGruff look did originally feature a prominent cigar. But the image of an animated smoking character was quickly vetoed by the Ad Council. It's in Nemmers' description of McGruff's nature and disposition that the qualities of both Columbo and Peter Falk spring to mind. "He's friendly, avuncular, approachable… that's what McGruff had more than the other proposed characters. They were rescuers, all about law and order to make things right again, but they didn't have approachability. They were more about the cop than about the people. Columbo would certainly have been mentioned because we were creating a character that had that persona." The Crime Dog was less a savior, and more like a favorite uncle or helpful Dad.

McGruff was voiced by adman Keil. Nemmers disputes the rumor that DSF was looking for Falk to do it, before realizing that his folksy cadence would never work in a 30-second TV PSA. But even without that distinctive voice, Keil nailed the raspy, informal approach, and those initial spots in particular had a very Columbo-esque feel to them.

In the very first 60-second PSA, the then-nameless crime hound enters a home and says, "You know what I think? I think you forgot to lock your door." Scratching his head, he continues, "It's a funny thing. A lot of people do that, they, uh… they forget." After a few quick theft prevention tips he concludes, "Oh, you don't know me, see… It's my job to teach you to protect yourselves. Make it your job to learn."[22] It wasn't our lieutenant, but in 1980, viewers would certainly have identified the character as more Columbo than Sam Spade or Philip Marlowe.

McGruff's success continues decades later, inspiring nationwide neighborhood watch programs and allowing citizens to help take ownership in the fight against crime. "Successful advertising campaigns always have somebody's finger on the pulse of popular culture," observes Wendy Melillo. "And at the time, Peter Falk's Columbo was a very important piece of Americana."[23]

Sherry Nemmers, McGruff's Mom, has a final apt description for her team's Columbo-inspired creation. "We created a hound who was dumb like a fox."

The Columbo Rebellion

Peter Falk loved to tell stories. And one of his favorite stories was of the time that he addressed the people of Romania in 1974 to convince them not to engage in an armed uprising against Communist leader Nicolae Ceausescu. It went like this:

Romanian television was airing episodes of *Columbo* that were hugely popular across the country, so much so that when the American TV season ended and episodes stopped arriving there, the citizenry was instead convinced that the Romanian government was simply sitting on the most recent shows and refusing to broadcast them. In a panic, Romanian officials contacted the U.S. State Department to try to reach Peter Falk, with a plan to tape a message addressed directly to the Romanian people that would convince them to trust the government when they said that they were not holding back episodes. Falk was asked to tell Romanians to "put down their guns, be patient, your government is not responsible, there will be more *Columbos*."[24] The message was made, 10 million Romanians saw it, and a crisis was averted.

The core fact of this story is that *Columbo* was indeed hugely popular in Romania in 1974, another measuring stick of the show's cultural cachet not only in the United States, but around the world. Much of the rest of the tale is pure showbiz imagination.

The Romanian government came under Communist Soviet domination in 1948, and through the years, elements of Russian culture were imposed upon its people. This began to change in 1965, with the elevation of Nicolae Ceausescu to General Secretary of the Romanian Communist Party. Under Ceausescu's leadership, "de-Russification" allowed for more Western influences in Romanian popular culture. Increasingly, outside television programs were imported, like *The Saint*, from England's British Broadcasting Channel.

American President Richard Nixon, looking for an opportunity to influence Communist direction and attitudes, embarked on a policy of "differentiation," selecting potentially sympathetic Communist leaders like Ceausescu to work with more closely. This strategy included using cultural influence, the chance for the United States to introduce Western values into Romanian society.

In the early Seventies, meanwhile, Nicolae Ceausescu was getting tired of watching *Mannix* on Saturday nights. An underling sifted through some potential replacements, and found *Columbo*. With this, the General Secretary, leader of the Romanian Communist Party, became hooked, reportedly having copies of episodes made for him to watch while travelling to state events. And the Romanian love affair with *Columbo* began.

Then, the alleged *Columbo* crisis—the episodes had run out and new ones weren't available yet. Falk writes about it in his *Just One More Thing* autobiography, he tells Mark Dawidziak about it for *The Columbo Phile*, and plays it up in an interview with David Letterman on March 1, 1995. Letterman gleefully helps Falk along by punching up the dramatic points ("They were arming themselves over this? My God!").[25] The Communist government had a trust problem with the Romanian people and needed Columbo's help.

Falk's account of events might have stood were it not for Julian Assange. His WikiLeaks site had been publishing millions of leaked official state documents and emails related to human rights, surveillance, freedom of the press, government corruption, and political maneuvering. In 2007, it released a cache of diplomatic cables. Nobody expected any of them to be about Peter Falk and *Columbo*.

The request from the American embassy to the office of Secretary of State Henry Kissinger is benign. The Romanian government was asking for a short film clip of Falk thanking the Romanian people for watching *Columbo* and noting that the "series had come to an end. We hope that some day in the not-too-distant future, we may again put together a TV show that will become just as popular in Romania." (The series had not ended, only the recent season, so this looked to be a miscommunication).[26]

There was no plea for Falk to ask Romanians to trust their government. There was no fear that a gun-toting revolt was brewing. There was no diplomatic crisis that needed Columbo's assistance to quell. The message aired on June 1, after the last *Columbo* episode available to Romania, at least until the following season. The film has never been found, but diplomatic cables preserved the content.

"Excuse me. Do you have a minute? I'm Lieutenant Columbo. Sometimes I'm known as Peter Falk. When an actor portrays a role, he hopes he's creating a character that their audience can identify with, and from what we've heard here in Hollywood about Romania's acceptance of the *Columbo* show, I guess we must have been doing something right. Seriously, I can't tell you how much everyone connected with the *Columbo* show feels about receiving such heartwarming news. We would like to thank Romanian television for having put us on the air Saturday and Sunday nights. But most of all, all of us, myself and the crew and the other actors, we want to thank the Romanian people for their great response to our show. I hope someday I can come to your country and enjoy the traditional culture and hospitality of the Romanian people. In the meantime, Columbo will be seeing you again on television this fall. Until then, thanks again and my best to everybody."

Willa Paskin's "Decoder Ring" *Slate* podcasts on the topic thoroughly searched for anyone at the American embassy in Bucharest in 1974, or Romanian officials, to look for corroboration of the political details of Falk's yarn. There was only the fact that the message was recorded and aired as requested, but there was no dramatic response in Romania, no emergency. In fact, the same type of message was requested and received the following year from another actor with a hit TV show that sparked a craze for American-style coffee mugs and thin cigarettes—Telly Savalas as *Kojak*.[27]

As his interview with David Letterman wrapped, Peter Falk laughed and asked the host, "Was that a good story?" Yes, it certainly was.

Columbo Around the World

The cultural impact of *Columbo* began in the United States, and from there it has broadened throughout the world. Since 1971, Romania has been just one of over 40 countries that have aired episodes, and the original has remained consistently and enormously popular in the UK, Germany, Finland, the Netherlands, South Africa, Spain, Australia, France, Iran, Israel and many others in Europe and across the planet.

In the late Eighties, the food chain Coop Italia aired three commercials starring Peter Falk in a thinly disguised version of "Tenente Columbo." To avoid copyright conflicts, there was no raincoat and no cigar, but there was an off-screen barking dog, distracted pocket fumbling, references to his wife, a signature hand wave, and "one last question." The latter was dubbed into Italian by Giampiero Albertini, who had also handled Falk's dialogue in the *Columbo* broadcasts.[28]

In Budapest, a life-size bronze statue of Columbo with Dog stands along Falk Miksa Street, erected as part of a city renewal project in 2014. Columbo's popularity in Hungary traces back to theater showings of *Ransom for a Dead Man* in the early 1970s, and speculation was that the Hungarian roots on one side of Falk's family were linked with late 19th century politician Miksa Falk. A Budapest archivist combed through Miksa's descendants' birth certificates and found no such connection. Even the Budapest Mayor who promoted the statue idea himself admitted that this might be an urban legend. Those of a cynical bent might say that it was an urban legend to stimulate urban renewal.[29]

It may be in Japan where the *Columbo* influence is strongest. After its television introduction in 1972, it often attracted over a quarter of the available audience. Japanese-language novelizations of *Columbo* episodes followed, and through the years, Falk appeared as Columbo in Toyota Corolla ads and as a caricature in spots for Pepsi Trymax-E drink. Two Japanese TV detectives have been inspired by *Columbo*. One, *Furuhata Ninzaburo*, is an inverted mystery; the other, *Columbo of Shinano*, features a detective who purposely imitates the character. Anime writer Sean Aitchison traces Japan's love of *Columbo* to a popular Japanese mystery genre (Honkaku), the stylized physical acting traits of kabuki performance, and an established Japanese storytelling trope of the underrated protagonist.[30]

Columbo producers had long wanted to film an episode in Japan, and although it was not to be, locales of London (*Dagger of the Mind*) and Mexico (*A Matter of Honor*) served as backdrops during the show's run. It was obvious that the Columbo character travelled well across different countries and cultures. But it was in America where we can most closely examine how Columbo reflected and viewers responded to the cogent issues of the Disco Era and the Me Decade.

III.
Columbo and Social Culture

The "Me" Decade

"Hi, I'm Suzie! I've tried Esalen, Primal Scream, Pyramid Power, Synanon, a black mass in San Francisco, Open Marriage, EST, TA, TM, 'I'm OK – You're OK'… and I'm still a target."
– *The Bye-Bye Sky High IQ Murder Case* (1977)

In 1976, writer Tom Wolfe coined a term that, for many, would define the Seventies: "The Me Decade." Wolfe's cover story in *New York* magazine was a sensation, proposing that the country was being swept up in a Great Awakening that was directing Americans' focus inward, to the individual ego, and away from the anti-war, anti-racism, social justice causes that had defined the youth movement of the Sixties. This was, as Wolfe described, "The new alchemical dream—changing one's personality, remaking, remodeling, elevating, and polishing one's very self."[1]

The Me Decade was not about selfish, individual monetary greed. That would come in a later era of *Columbo*, to be discussed. Rather, to be self-directed was to be probing one's own nature, sometimes referred to as the Human Potential Movement, which grew out of the Sixties counterculture. In *Columbo*, when Suzie meets accountant George nightclubbing in *The Bye-Bye Sky High IQ Murder Case*, her lengthy chronicle of self-help attempts is a genuflect to Wolfe's belief that we were all becoming inner-directed to seek spiritual renewal.

The focus within for self-actualization ostensibly arose from events of the

Seventies. The year 1973 saw the ignominious end to U.S. involvement in the Vietnam War. The Watergate hearings were bumping soap operas and game shows off daytime TV. In October of '73, a Middle East oil embargo squeezed American oil supplies, forcing citizens to endure gasoline rationing and serpentine lines at the pumps. Coupled with peak inflation and the mounting unemployment of an economic recession, every national setback was factored into a collective feeling of American angst.

President Nixon was out, Gerald Ford was in. The latter's 1974 pardoning of his former boss for crimes yet-to-be-charged in the Watergate scandal was an act of self-immolation that put mild-mannered Jimmy Carter in the White House in 1977. *Columbo* was not around when Carter gave his infamous 1979 "crisis of confidence" address (dubbed the "malaise speech") but it was an all-too-fitting end to an uninspiring era in American life. If the nation itself had been wearing one of the decade's faddish mood rings, it would have turned gray or black.

As a tonic, it was suggested that many turned inward to self-help books, self-exploration, and self-examination. Religious and spiritual movements abounded with Eastern philosophies and values, such as Buddhism and Hinduism. In 1971, the Reverend Sun Myoung Moon moved to the United States to spread the word among his acolytes, the Moonies. Transcendental Meditation had no religious leanings, but its popularity, based on silent repetition of a mantra or sound, ascended through the decade as well.

Columbo himself was never clued into these movements, and the show sometimes used the Lieutenant to hold a skeptical mirror up to them. Even so, Columbo was actually empathetic with the TM-practicing Lisa in *Last Salute to the Commodore*. Investigating the clubbing and drowning of Commodore Otis Swanson (John Dehner), Columbo encounters her in mid-meditation on the deck of a yacht. After observing and politely asking if she was alright, he doesn't disturb her, instead choosing to sit down on the deck next to her.

Because this is such a reviled episode among *Columbo* fans for its wildly overplayed attempts at physical comedy, it's easy to forget that Lisa's silent self-improvement is not being mocked by Columbo. Yes, Columbo's attempt to put his legs into a yoga position is broadly played for yuks, but he's sincere in his attempt to, like all good investigators, get on the same wavelength with her.

Lisa was massaging her own mental health, but the decade also saw an explosion of physical health programs. Killer fitness guru Milo Janus (Robert Conrad, *An Exercise in Fatality*) was likely modelled after Joe Gold, who opened Gold's Gym in 1965 in Venice Beach, or an earlier bodybuilding entrepreneur, Vic Tanny. Commercial health facilities began to flourish.[2] Milo's health regimen, though, is too much for Columbo, who is particularly doubtful of the pills that Janus suggests ingesting with some morning carrot juice ("Yeah, I'll save these for lunch."). Columbo stood on the sidelines while the Me Decade witnessed a jogging boom, and millions of runners across the country joined Milo in pursuing better health as part of their own self-improvement.

A variety of psychoanalytic and Cognitive Behavior Therapies (CBT) were prevalent in the Seventies, and Helen Stewart (Suzanne Pleshette, *Dead Weight*) no doubt signed up for more than a few. "I'm just a mass of therapeutic studies lately," she says to Columbo in the cluttered pottery corner of her living room. "Failing art classes... I even went back to work." Stewart is unsure of her own persona, as she looks for meaning in her art. "I try to go beyond the surface, to find a deeper meaning, a truer reality..." Sheepishly, she adds, "At least, that's what I think I do."

Helen is looking to find herself in her pottery creations. "They say it's important to work with your hands" (as therapy, her disapproving mother adds). Columbo is making the effort to understand, but it's clear that he's unconvinced. To him, Helen's embrace of therapy is impacting her reliability as a murder witness. The era encouraged the journey to find the Self, but it didn't make Columbo's job any easier.

If you called Dr. Eric Mason (Nicol Williamson, *How to Dial a Murder*) a mere therapist, he would no doubt sic his killer Dobermans on you. For one of its last episodes of the Seventies, *Columbo* created a murderer modeled after one of the decade's self-improvement leaders, EST founder Werner Erhard.[3] Mason's specialty is in using specific words to control personal behaviors: "Words! Food! Money! Boss! Wife! Sex! Mommy and Daddy started setting you up right from the cradle, conditioning you. Words lock you into your locked-up little lives. We're going to teach you to smash the lock!"

Mason is presented as a behavioral psychologist genius in the field, with a doctorate in psychology, schooled in science and heavily steeped in computer technology to buttress his research. Interestingly, Werner Erhard himself came from a background as a used car salesman, deserted his wife and child, phonied up a new identity, and was later critiqued as a scam artist. In other words, he could have been a great *Columbo* villain.

In Wolfe's view, the Me Decade saw the Sixties counter-culture movement gradually pivoting away from public protest causes to private personal ones. But this was still a rebellious group. At the dawn of the Seventies, when *Columbo's* premiere season was beginning to attract viewer attention, there was a widespread catchphrase bumper sticker that crystallized in two words what Columbo himself was up to, even if we didn't yet realize it. Those words were "Question Authority."

1.
Class Conflicts and Power Plays

    The very first scene in the very first *Columbo* pilot tells us all we need to know about the 44 Classic Era killers to come. In the opening establishing shot, the camera begins at city street ground level, then slowly pans right and upward, relentlessly upward, past at least 21 stories of an expansive high-rise complex, finally stopping at the tippy-top apartment perched at the apex.

    Inside, we join an obviously exclusive and upper-crust dinner party. The medium-shot camera puts our point-of-view at the fringes of this elegant affair. The men are tuxedoed, the women showing off sparkly, glamorous evening gowns. Leather chairs, white shag rug, ornate latticework, faux support columns, multiple chandeliers, a wet bar with stools, champagne glasses, and flower arrangements all mark various points in our depth of perspective that extends ahead and out the curtained windows, to where we can make out the peak of the high-rise across the street.

    A piano tinkles lightly in the background underneath the murmur of conversation. A formally-dressed waiter enters the frame, and the camera follows him to move closer to the party's epicenter, gently swiveling to slowly zoom in and allow us to view the stylish framed artwork behind the stylishly attired and seated party guests. They are playing a sophisticated game of "Who Am I?," and the insufferable focus of this exercise is asked, "Are you a famous murderer?" We cut to our first close look at our first *Columbo* killer as he smugly replies, "Nice try… I am not Lizzie Borden."

    The high-society setting of *Prescription: Murder* would become quite familiar. There's a running theme threading through every post-2020 online pandemic appreciation of *Columbo*, and it's likewise a key element in any book, article or news story about the show—class conflict. After ticking off the Lieutenant's character foibles we can all recite, this is overwhelmingly the main subject of writings about *Columbo*, whether from veteran viewers or series newbies.

Headlines such as "Columbo: A Class of His Own" leave no doubt about the social context. "It's a piece of mainstream entertainment with an unexpected social message. The murderers firmly believe their higher class status is to be flaunted. [They] are so rich that they presume their wealth affords them intelligence.... The killer assumes the cop is a dolt. Columbo may not seem like an obvious example of culture portraying class warfare from either side of the battle, but it's a major ingredient of this procedural. And when you compare *Columbo* to other procedurals of the 1970s and 1980s, that ingredient is not only unavoidable—it's what makes this show special."[1]

From a 2020 *New York Times* piece: "Columbo is one of the very few American series fueled by class warfare. Whether they are driven by coldblooded entitlement, delusions of grandeur, or simple greed, the murderers treat the self-deprecating, ostentatiously low-grade cop with seething annoyance, willful condescension, or hypocritical benevolence."[2]

The monied murderers have everything they need to commit the crime, as well as a thinly veiled air of superiority and plenty of ego. Almost immediately after the March 1973 close of the second season with *Double Shock*, then-*New York Times* columnist Jeff Greenfield's review summed up the cultural contrast and *Columbo's* popularity. His contemporaneous analysis is worth an extended excerpt, as it tells us much about the cultural zeitgeist of the Seventies Classic *Columbo* era.

"The popularity of *Columbo* is as intense as it is puzzling. Why? Peter Falk's characterization is part of the answer of course, [but] there is something else which gives *Columbo* a special appeal—something almost never seen on commercial television. That something is a strong, healthy dose of class antagonism. The one constant in *Columbo* is that, with every episode, a working class hero brings to justice a member of America's social and economic elite.

"*Columbo's* villains… live the lives that are for most of us hopeless daydreams: houses on top of mountains, with pools, servants and sliding doors; parties with women in slinky dresses, and endless food and drink; plush, enclosed box seats at professional sports events; the envy and admiration of the Crowd. His aristocratic adversaries tolerate Columbo at first because they misjudge him. They are amused by him, scornful of his manners, certain that while he possesses the legal authority to demand their cooperation, he has neither the grace nor wit to discover their misdeeds.

"All of them are done in, in some measure, by their contempt for Columbo's background, breeding and income. Further, Columbo knows about these people what the rest of us suspect: that they are on top not because they are smarter or work harder than we do, but because they are more amoral and devious. Time after time, the motive for murder in *Columbo* stems from the shakiness of the villain's own status in high society.

"This is, perhaps, the most thoroughgoing satisfaction *Columbo* offers us: the assurance that those who dwell in marble and satin, those whose clothes, food, cars and mates are the very best, do not deserve it. They are, instead, driven by fear and compulsion to murder. And they are done in by a man of street wit, who is afraid to fly, who can't stand the sight of blood, and who never uses force to take his prey. It is delicious."[3]

Peter Falk himself would add a qualifier about Columbo's motivation. As he explained to Mark Dawidziak for *The Columbo Phile: A Casebook*: "People like to see the powerful brought down, but Columbo had no argument against the rich. He's regretful when he arrests the murderer. He thinks, 'Gee, here's this guy with a wonderful home and wonderful clothes. He talks well, he has a good education. It's a terrible thing he should have to do this.'"[4]

No, Columbo feels that the wealthy killers do not deserve to get away with it just because of their status. Their status has given them the comfort of deference by others and escape from consequences. But their breeding and upper-crust lifestyle do not, in fact, insulate them from justice in Columbo's world, and it's that sense of justice that's really driving our hero, not a blanket class condemnation.

A 2013 French academic piece titled "Columbo: Class Struggle on TV Tonight" from sociologist Lilian Mathieu briefly speculates on how this class conflict impacted a 1970s television audience and propelled *Columbo* to popularity. Mathieu premises that in the United States, the Sixties youth movement was roiling the nation, challenging free speech restrictions, gender and racial inequalities, capitalism, sexual norms, and the Vietnam War.

At the same moment that 1968's *Prescription: Murder* dinner guests were clinking their champagne glasses, this youth movement provided the social cultural environment that could seed class antagonism. To Mathieu, this "directly relates *Columbo's* success to the rebellious mood infused by the 1968 unrests. It is possible that as the time was passing, and their revolutionary dreams were fading, they found in *Columbo* some soft and subtle reminder of the class struggle they vehemently denounced a few years ago."[5]

For all the trumpeting of the class conflict elements of *Columbo*, the truth is actually simpler. It was drama, and not social division, that drove the original concept of co-creators Richard Levinson and William Link. In reality, the perceived anti-class subtext comes not from Columbo's disdain for the wealthy, but because it simply made for good television. As they explain, "When the series went on the air, many critics found it an ever-so-slightly subversive attack on the American class system in which a proletarian hero triumphed over the effete and moneyed members of the Establishment. But the reason for this was dramatic rather than political. Given the persona of Falk as an actor, it would have been foolish to play him against a similar type, a Jack Klugman, for example, or a Martin Balsam. Much more fun could be had if he were confronted by someone like Noel Coward."[6]

Levinson and Link were correct, and this contrast drove the show's best plots and favorite killers. It was a clash of styles that also happened to be a clash of classes. The upshot, likely unintentional but no less real, was the perception that *Columbo* was a class-based series that became a crowd-pleaser when the forgotten and marginalized everyman working stiff brought down the prosperous and privileged killers.

But this is not the whole explanation for *Columbo's* Seventies popularity. There's an element to the class conflict that is rarely, if ever, discussed. Greenfield obliquely hints at it at the close of his 1973 piece: "I wait only for the ultimate episode: Columbo knocks on the door of 1600 Pennsylvania Avenue one day. 'Gee, Mr. President, I really hate to bother you again, but there's just one thing....'"

Greenfield doesn't acknowledge for us the key difference between this closing example and all that he referenced before it—power. Over the years, viewers and pundits have been so focused on the affluence of the killers that their power and authority, while usually in the open, has been downplayed for the class element. Wealth often breeds power, and what Columbo frequently encounters is not the villain throwing their money in his face, but their presumed authority.

"Question Authority"—those two words of hippie counterculture lingo don't get associated with our polite, genial, respectful Lieutenant. But perhaps they should.

Sociologist Mathieu noted the confrontations initiated by youth of the Sixties, particularly in opposition to the Vietnam War. She did not detail the logical extension to events of the Seventies, as faith in government institutions slowly deteriorated under the weight of public skepticism. On the cusp of 1970, Americans learned of the My Lai massacre of upwards of 500 Vietnamese civilians at the hands of U.S. troops, and in April, President

Nixon ordered the invasion of neighboring Cambodia. Demonstrations spiked across America, with four unarmed students gunned down by National Guardsmen in a protest at Ohio's Kent State University on May 4, 1970.

In 1971, an April demonstration drew over 200,000 to the National Mall, and a simultaneous anti-war rally in San Francisco saw 156,000. The following month, Washington, D.C.'s Mayday Protests resulted in the largest mass arrests in American history, with over 12,000 detained. CIA Director Richard Helms credited Mayday with pressuring Nixon to look for a Vietnam exit ramp.[7] The tsunami of protests across the country continued.

In June of 1971, the Pentagon Papers were revealed by the *New York Times*, leaked by one of its authors, Daniel Ellsberg. It was a massive report commissioned for the Department of Defense outlining the history of U.S. involvement in the Vietnam War, and the facts, goals, and targets of American incursions were at odds with the those released for public consumption. Authorities had lied.

Almost exactly one year later, on June 17, 1972, a security guard making his nightly rounds at the Watergate Hotel in Washington, D.C. found a piece of scotch tape on an exit door lock, triggering an investigation and revealing the illegal affairs of Nixon's Committee to Re-Elect the President (CREEP). Their burglary of the Democratic National Committee headquarters and the subsequent attempts at a cover-up threw the shadow of the Watergate Scandal across the entire decade, even after the resignation of President Nixon in August of 1974. (Two months later, another prominent government authority figure would be forced to resign—the Columboverse's military symbol, Colonel Rumford).

The instinct to "Question Authority" was no longer just a sticker slapped onto the rear bumper of smoke-filled multi-colored vans blaring Grateful Dead music. It was becoming a critical sentiment of a decade in which many believed that power was corrupting, absolutely.

Mathieu elaborates on the dynamics of power and wealth. "It is more precisely domination that defines the relations between the two main characters of each episode. In *Columbo*, the murderers are always dominant."[8] Mathieu continues, "Dominants are arrogant and sure of their power, and show condescension or even contempt for the Lieutenant, who seems to be intimidated and helpless. Power and wealth have led them to lose basic respect for humanity."[9]

Mathieu further differentiates between the types of capital, or resources, that the killer has amassed to maintain this dominant position. Most commonly displayed are the economic resources that show off the murderer's lifestyle.

But Mathieu also catalogues political capital (politicians or authoritarian positions), cultural capital (institutional diplomas or high aesthetic tastes), social capital (network of relationships), and body capital (attractiveness or elegance). These resources all contribute to prestige or authority, in different shares and quantities for each villain.[10]

Before continuing, it should be noted that Columbo himself encourages these distinctions between classes of wealth and power, in order to allow himself to be underestimated by his opponent. It's part of the psychological gamesmanship employed by the shabbily-attired, distracted and firmly middle-class lieutenant when he encounters his affluent adversaries. These tactics will earn a separate chapter of discussion later on.

Demonstrations of Los Angeles wealth and economic capital are self-evident throughout Classic *Columbo*, as Greenfield reminds us. In addition, many characters possess the attractiveness and style of body capital, often remarked upon by Columbo. It might even be a feature of their profession, as with exercise guru Milo Janus (*An Exercise in Fatality*), cosmetics queen Viveca Scott (*Lovely But Lethal*), or famous actress Nora Chandler (*Requiem for a Falling Star*).

Examples of the other capitals are planted throughout the Seventies. Nelson Hayward, the *Candidate for Crime* played by Jackie Cooper, is the most obvious example of political capital, but it's also built into Colonel Rumford's (Patrick McGoohan) position as the head of Haynes Military Academy in *By Dawn's Early Light*. As Director of the Cybernetic Research Institute, Dr. Marshall Cahill (Jose Ferrer) wields clout in *Mind Over Matter*, and authoritarian businessmen like Paul Hanlon (Robert Culp) in *The Most Crucial Game* also qualify.

Social capital accrues to those who have a wide range of friends and contacts for connections and influence. Although Inspector Brimmer (Robert Culp, *Death Lends a Hand*) is a private businessman, he has considerable political influence through his extensive surveillance network, and social pull through his legitimate associates like publisher Arthur Kennicut (Ray Milland). But when one of Brimmer's intended social capital contacts, Kennicut's wife Lenore, resists a blackmail attempt, she becomes a murder victim. Louis Jourdan's culinary critic character Paul Girard has similar blackmailed social connections with powerful restaurateurs throughout Los Angeles (*Murder Under Glass*).

We see the social capital possessed by high-rise and high-society architect Elliot Markham (Patrick O'Neal, *Blueprint for Murder*), as he first meets Columbo at the public unveiling of his sparkling new Williamson City skyscraper model. And it's the social connections of murderer Joe Devlin (Clive Revill) with the O'Connell family that grease the arms-trading skids for the affable Irishman. That connection also points Columbo to where to find the guns Devlin's dealing in *The Conspirators*.

Like economic capital, the cultural capital of the *Columbo* murdering class is tangible. Note the elegance of Grace Wheeler (Janet Leigh) in *Forgotten Lady*, the showmanship of conductor maestro Alex Benedict (John Cassavettes, *Etude in Black*), and the Shakesperean flair of Nicholas Frame and Lillian Stanhope (Richard Basehart and Honor Blackman, *Dagger of the Mind*).

There are also the highly refined aesthetic tastes of killers like gastronomic expert Paul Girard in *Murder Under Glass*, renowned oenologist Adrian Carsini (Donald Pleasence, *Any Old Port in a Storm*), and horticulturalist Jarvis Goodland (Ray Milland, *The Greenhouse Jungle*).

One thing that most of these antagonists have in common is their dim view of Columbo's ability to pin the murder on them. They underestimate him and overestimate themselves. In the dominant position, they display a litany of disrespectful behaviors to the Lieutenant. These include, but are hardly limited to: snobbery, perceived intellectual superiority, belittling remarks, sarcasm, patronizing comments, ignoring, impatience, eyerolls and sometimes even outright hostility.

There's a psychology at work with these behaviors, as disrespect is a weapon in the power dynamics between individuals. Those who believe themselves to be in positions of power or authority often put down others to keep their status or control. For the killers of *Columbo*, many have already murdered to maintain their high standing or fat wallet, and they feel compelled to continue masking their crime with displays of disrespect and contempt.[11]

Our first series villain, Ken Franklin of *Murder by the Book*, provides an early example of this type of assumed authority. Of course, Jack Cassidy was the perfect actor to embody the smarmy, contemptuous and overbearing self-importance required for the role. Significantly, although we do see Franklin's pricey 1968 Mercedes convertible in the opening credits (flaunting his arrogance by driving into the parking garage under the "Exit Only" sign), Columbo himself doesn't see Franklin's displays of conspicuous wealth until 33 minutes into the episode.

Up to that point, though, there is a continual spew of disrespect and not-so-thinly veiled insults directed at Columbo. There is no wealth attached to this conceit—it's all character-driven. "If Mrs. Melville were on this case, she would be leaps and bounds ahead of you by now;" "Tell me something...how long have you been a lieutenant, Lieutenant?;" "Alright, let me see if I can explain it to you;" "Dawning on you now?"

Cassidy delivers these lines with a series of facial expressions, smirks and exasperation usually directed at small children. When not demeaning Columbo, director Steven Spielberg might choose to frame Franklin from a low angle for a classic crossed-arms power pose. Even before Columbo steps into Franklin's home stuffed with valuable paintings ("Gee, I only thought they hung this fellow in museums!"), it's established that the killer is pulling a power play. Meanwhile, Columbo acquiesces and pretends to go down the dubious rabbit holes that Franklin has set up to keep his investigator off the real scent.

Robert Culp's three Classic Era appearances provide ample opportunity to demonstrate a wide range of commanding behavior. In his first, *Death Lends a Hand*, it's not outward disrespect to Columbo, but rather the job offering for the Lieutenant to join Brimmer Investigations. Brimmer's extensive surveillance and investigative resources already infer control, and although Columbo sees through the job offer as a maneuver to get him off the case, it's no less a show of power on Brimmer's part.

In *The Most Crucial Game*, Culp, as sports maven Paul Hanlon, snarls his way through his chats with Columbo, perhaps walking ahead of him or dismissively checking his watch. Columbo gushes about how Hanlon takes charge of business after Eric Wagner's death, marveling, "You really know how to get things done!" It's hardly enough to appease Hanlon, who later pays the Lieutenant an obvious disrespect by calling him "Mr. Columbo."

As Dr. Bart Kepple in *Double Exposure*, Culp's character dings Columbo by referring to him condescendingly as "an extraordinarily amusing fellow." In the office, Kepple eschews polite norms by pouring himself a drink without offering one. And later, on the golf course, he openly ignores him as Columbo carts his way toward Kepple's foursome. Finally, Kepple earns a special place in the power hierarchy by brazenly flouting rules and convention in cheating at golf while Columbo watches. "There's my ball. I'll just toss it out a bit… and no one will ever know."

Physical humiliation is another form of disrespect. Leslie Williams (Lee Grant) is the first to employ this, in *Ransom for a Dead Man*. Flying with Columbo, it's not merely her piloting the plane through 360 degree rolls and steep banks to unsettle her passenger. She also practically orders a protesting Columbo to take the controls to fly the plane himself. In *Dead Weight*, titled authority figure General Hollister (Eddie Albert) is similarly aware of the queasy effect his yacht ride is having on Columbo, and he guns the engine to prove it. Milo Janus (Robert Conrad, *An Exercise in Fatality*) leaves Columbo behind as he tries to ask him questions along the beach, as the jogging Janus implores, "Come on, Lieutenant, get those knees up!"

Uniformed institutional authority figure Colonel Rumford (Patrick McGoohan) in *By Dawn's Early Light* doesn't need to impose his power, as it's already self-evident from the reactions of the other officers and cadets in Rumford's orbit. Observing this, Columbo is clearly intimidated by the Colonel and the unfamiliar Haynes Academy protocol, especially in the scene at the mess hall, where the Lieutenant is obliged by Rumford to finish his meal early and pocket some rolls for later.

But in a notable turnaround, marked by a superb performance from McGoohan, Rumford softens the power display later in his office, even while still surrounded by all the trappings of authority that accompany his position. Rumford kindly offers Columbo a quality cigar and affectedly searches for a bond with his opponent. "Do you have a first name?" he asks. "We have similar jobs, in a way," he reflects, trying to make a connection as reluctant warriors in the good fight for humanity. Rumford, highly emotional and contemplative, can only string together some phrases as he considers his life in the military. "It's the wars, you see, the wars… nations, when that stops… the uniform, I'll hang up my uniform. I'll go and take care of my backyard… I've got some roses, white roses… and I suppose when people stop abusing each other, you'll hang up your uniform." There's no show of wealth here, just vulnerability.

The turnaround is quite different for Beth Chadwick (Susan Clark). She begins her episode as the literal *Lady in Waiting*, attending to the needs of family members, especially her domineering mother (Jessie Royce Landis). When Columbo visits the Chadwick manse, it's Mrs. Chadwick who immediately assumes authority over him, ordering, "You there! Pay the cab and bring my luggage!" Columbo allows this case of mistaken identity to play out, an unlikely but dramatically helpful choice, for it gives everyone a chance to observe the household's power dynamics.

Beth is vindictively slapped by her mother upon arrival and verbally abused: "Always impossible, blundering, making mistakes, causing trouble wherever you were." Beth dutifully serves coffee in her subservient role, but it's here where she puts her transition from wallflower to powerbroker into motion by declaring her intention to run the company over her mother's objections.

Standing at the head of the long conference table in snappy chic fashion at her first board meeting, Beth takes control by assuming the presidency, elevating her boyfriend Peter Hamilton, announcing abrupt policy changes, refusing any advice, and threatening the job of a veteran underling. This, with accompanying facial shocks of expression from Peter and Mrs. Chadwick.

And now, her demeanor with Columbo changes, too. There's no subtlety to her demands as she stands over him, proclaiming, "Alright, Lieutenant, I think that'll be enough. I want you to listen to this very carefully—I don't ever want to see you again. You'll be refused admittance to my house and this office. I'm warning you, no more questions."

Being new to the power game, Beth does not yet have the social or political capital to threaten Columbo off the case. But Dale Kingston (Ross Martin, *Suitable for Framing*) does. Kingston has already given a verbal slap to "Mr. Columbo," and his lawyer has the proverbial "a few friends at city hall"—or so he thinks—to get a new lead detective in charge. This would appear to be the ultimate expression of authority, affecting Columbo's status as a police lieutenant and his ability to solve the crime.

In *Prescription: Murder,* we get the first glimpse of this power tactic when Dr. Ray Flemming (Gene Barry) calls on District Attorney Burt Gordon (William Windom). Gordon becomes an authority proxy for Flemming when he challenges Columbo with, "I hope he's [Flemming] not going to be annoyed by a lot of tactless remarks, especially at a time like this." When Columbo does exactly that, Gordon says he'll "pull a few strings" to ice out the Lieutenant. Flemming has taken advantage of his social standing in the form of his D.A. friend.

This being the very first *Columbo* movie, and not the series, the viewing audience has no way of fully realizing that this is an empty threat, even when the Lieutenant himself tells Flemming he's been pulled from action. In subsequent years, others would try the same show of dominance, but by that point we always knew that Columbo would find a way to dodge the figurative bullet.

In *A Friend in Deed*, no authority proxy is required when Deputy Commissioner Mark Halperin (Richard Kiley) tells Columbo to change his theory on the death of Mrs. Halperin. Technically, the Commissioner does get to fire him and exercise his political capital, but that dismissal lasts for all of two minutes and 42 seconds, until Columbo ferrets out Halperin as the killer.

In *A Case of Immunity*, the U.S. State Department tells our hero to lay off Suari Legation First Secretary Hassan Salah (Hector Elizondo), to which Columbo replies, "That's all very well and good, except for one thing—he's the murderer." Nonplussed, the protocol minion shoots back, "We don't care if Salah is guilty or innocent." Salah can bellyache to the State Department, and he can throw Columbo off the Suari embassy grounds, but the boy King of Suari has the final say-so, and with his help, Columbo gets the confession and necessary waiver of immunity to bring Salah to American justice.

Amusingly, the power figure in *A Matter of Honor* is not killer matador Luis Montoya (Ricardo Montalban), but Mexican Comandante Sanchez, who holds Columbo's impounded Peugeot hostage to make sure that the unkempt gringo detective stays on the Montoya case. That's because the legendary Montoya has enough pull to get Sanchez canned if the Comandante himself opens up the investigation that would sully the Montoya name. It's a unique twist on the dominance dynamic.

Of all the implicit power threats that Columbo has to parry, though, the most serious one comes from the head of the U.S. spy network himself in 1975's *Identity Crisis*. President Ford had pardoned Nixon almost a year prior, but this Band-Aid hardly healed a nation still skeptical of authority figureheads. In this episode, a shady ringleader is operating at the heart of our government, and Columbo has to channel his inner Woodward and Bernstein to get at the truth. The character is never identified on his card as being from the C.I.A., but as "Director Special Department Phil Corrigan Secret Agent X-9." (If this seems rather cartoonish, that's because it's an inside homage to a '30s-'40s comic strip authored by *The Maltese Falcon* writer Dashiell Hammett).

In a demonstration of his political capital, the Director is directing Columbo to forget about spymaster Nelson Brenner (Patrick McGoohan). Naturally, Columbo won't do that, but it's clear at this point that this case will never see the inside of a California courtroom. What Columbo can do is engineer what Mathieu terms the "reversal of domination."[12] Although this is a feature of all *Columbos* by the time the Gotcha rolls around, the scene inside Brenner's manor is one of the most fascinating of these power reversals in the entire Seventies catalogue, and benefits from a detailed look.

After the Director has his confab with Columbo, Brenner not-so-subtly follows the Lieutenant to a vintage Mobil (Seventies Pegasus logo!) gas station, where Brenner bestows the needy Columbo $10 and invites him back to his estate for "a cocktail or something… You rather fascinate me."

At his mansion, Brenner has pulled out all the stops in a show of domination. He has previously tried to neuter Columbo's lawman status by referring to him as "Mister," but now, the secret agent is practically preening as he walks his adversary through his expansive collection of wealth and power symbols.

He speaks an exotic language with his chef to detail the precise menu at that evening's dinner gathering and piano recital (cultural and social capital). He ignores Columbo's attempt to repay the $10 and get out from under

Brenner's debt. His living room is covered with enormous post-Renaissance paintings and dotted with ornate vases, statues and china pieces around the massive wall-length couch. Elaborate trim surrounds the doorways and large half-circle fireplace. The delicate hors d'oeuvres are set out by two servants as Columbo asks, "Do you have any wine?" "A cellar full" is Brenner's smug response. Columbo makes the plebian choice of red.

The sound system, playing a cheesy jazzified version of Elton John's "Philadelphia Freedom," is Quadrophonic. Although technologically outdated today, in 1975 the quad system was a costly four-channel audio setup emulating a 3-D sound experience. So far, Brenner has trotted out quite a bit of the economic capital at his disposal.

But it's here where Brenner's braggadocio is most flagrant, as he makes the gleeful admission that he has had Columbo's house bugged. And it is at this precise moment where Columbo begins to turn the tables on Brenner to swing the balance of dominance. Moments before, Columbo had taken a $10 bill and placed it on Brenner's thick coffee table. His debt repaid, the crafty Lieutenant is now free to look for ways to crack Brenner's façade of self-confidence. The stereo system gives him the opening to do just that.

COLUMBO: Gee, I wish my wife could hear it [*Madame Butterfly*] like this.
BRENNER: Well, it helps to calm the nerves, you know.
COLUMBO (with a shrewd, knowing expression): Are you nervous, sir?

As they move to an adjoining room for cigars, the camera slowly zooms in to Columbo's pensive face, visually telegraphing to us that he is deep in thought. After he allows Brenner to demonstrate his prowess with a cigar cutter, Columbo notices the array of diversions on Brenner's table.

COLUMBO: Do you like to play games, sir? I know this one—backgammon. And I know poker…. Do you like to gamble?
BRENNER: What else is there?

Having established the cat-and-mouse, Columbo walks about to admire the pictures, certificates and awards adorning Brenner's walls. At first, he seems to brush past the photo of Brenner standing alongside a Korean War plane, focusing his attentions elsewhere. For this mini-inspection, the seated Brenner has lost his gregarious front and is increasingly brooding and concerned. Columbo suddenly shifts back to studying the war photograph, and Brenner is all attention.

COLUMBO (moving his face close to the photo): What kind of a plane is that, sir?
BRENNER (hesitantly, drawn out): That, uh… that's the T-33… Silver Star.

Brenner's extended pause between "T-33" and "Silver Star" is only eight seconds, but it feels like an eternity, as Brenner seems to resignedly realize what Columbo's up to, namely, identifying him as the elusive Steinmetz. Columbo confidently prowls the room, and Brenner's following glare is now positively steely. The body language and verbal tones of each protagonist has shifted, and by the end of the encounter, as Columbo is pulling out of the driveway, Brenner is nervously tapping the rolled-up artist's rendition of Steinmetz against his leg. Authority has been questioned, and the reversal of domination is complete.

Needless to say, reversal of dominance is easier to pull off in 90-120 minutes than reversal of class, which is why the popular conception of *Columbo* as a series about class warfare seems a bit overstated. Each episode's solution is a change in the power dynamic, not social status. That rebellious mood of the Sixties extended into the Seventies and provided the groundwork for this pushback against authority. In *Columbo*, this pushback came often, though not always, against the rich. Serendipitously, just as Link and Levinson intended way back in the beginning, it also came against the acting world's classy Jack Cassidys or Donald Pleasences or Louis Jourdans and not the cruder Jack Klugman-types.

When *Columbo's* golden era ends, it's below decks on a lowly tugboat (*The Conspirators*), where the Coast Guard is about to seize a shipment of terrorist arms. That's a long way from the lavish dinner parties and centers of cultural and economic capital that provided the backdrop for many a suave villain. By 1978, though, a shipment of guns for the N.R.A. signals a very different kind of power and influence. While the arms are confiscated, Columbo and killer share a bottle of Full's Irish Dew, invoking the whiskey's slogan "This far and no farther." Many have interpreted that as a fitting parting line for our hero after 45 cases. It is. But for someone who's witnessed up-close the dark side of the upper crust and connected, it might also tell us something about Columbo's thoughts on the limits of wealth and power.

2.
Liberation and Lady Killers

DETECTIVE (at the dead body of Janice Caldwell): Good-looking broad, except for the marks around her neck.
COLUMBO (lifting sheet): Certainly is.
– *A Friend in Deed* (1974)

If gawking at the hotness of female corpses sounds archaic and tactless today, well, this was the state of television and our collective culture in 1974. And our hero, Lieutenant Columbo, has no objection to objectifying the body of one of the victims whose murders he will solve every third or fourth Sunday night.

It is telling that mere minutes later in this episode, he will rescue a black man from incipient racial harassment at the hands of this same fellow detective. In this awkward transition period of a society learning to come to grips with racial bias and the gender issues of women's liberation, Columbo's first instinct is to help the African-American. That act is laudable, of course, but also highlights how gender matters could be overlooked.

This is not a knock on *Columbo*. Nor is it a knock on judging the merits of attractiveness found in our culture. But perhaps we can all agree that rendering that same type of judgment to barely-cold cadavers nowadays would be a tad, uh, insensitive.

Television being what it is, turn it on at any moment in history and you'll see pretty women. *Columbo* is no exception. And while the show was also noteworthy for the roles it gave to distinguished older actresses, this was more a function of those particular stories and not a societal trend. But it is useful to examine how Seventies *Columbo* was a product of its times, gender stereotypes, viewer expectations, and how this all might play into our perceptions of *Columbo's* female killers.

Before the Seventies, the roots of the women's movement had been seeded and spread through the efforts of such Sixties activists as Betty Friedan and Gloria Steinem. As the Me Decade began, though, women had been substantially closed off from professions traditionally dominated by men, and were paid less. To remedy this, there were social movements for reforms on women's issues, including passage of the Equal Rights Amendment by Congress in 1972. The ERA proposed that gender would not determine the legal rights of men or women, effectively eliminating discrimination based on sex. Two months later, Helen Reddy would sing "I Am Woman" as an anthem of the liberation movement. The euphoria would not last.

Congress and the courts were codifying anti-discrimination in education programs, housing, obtaining credit, and jury selection. In 1973, Roe v. Wade legalized abortion. But the comprehensive principles of the Equal Rights Amendment were in trouble. To become law as a constitutional amendment, the ERA needed the ratification of three-quarters of U.S. state legislatures. It fell short, in large part because of the Stop ERA movement led by Phyllis Schlafly, a proponent of traditional female gender roles. Schlafly's group effectively scared off conservative state legislators worried that the ERA would legally mandate a nation of unisex bathrooms.

The timeline of the ERA, it's tug-of-war for progress, and its ultimate fate all embody the decade as one where women would have significant victories, yet also suffer disappointing setbacks. As *Columbo* viewers, we can recognize this in the see-sawing of approaches toward women and women's issues through the Seventies. But when the detective's decade began, how was television itself framing the women's liberation movement?

Rowan & Martin's Laugh-In was TV's top-rated show for 1968-1970, and remained in the Top 25 programs in America through 1972. At 250 jokes per 52 minutes, *Laugh-In* was a barrage of verbal and sight gags sandwiched between quick sketches spanning a comedy range of vaudeville, silly puns, slapstick and topical one-liners. It provided viewers with a popular barometer of social culture issues of the late Sixties and early Seventies, a Rorschach test of America's acceptance of fringe groups as stereotyped punchlines. That included hippies, elders, Native-Americans, gays, an occasional racial jab, and women as feminists. Or women as dumb blondes. Or women as bikinied dancers. Or women as objects of (mild) physical abuse.

It's all terribly dated but highly instructive of how television was reflecting American values as the women's lib movement developed. Judy Carne was dropped through trap doors, pelted with water, or hit with a spring-loaded boxing glove whenever she said the catchphrase "Sock It to Me." Her time on the show was over when the *Columbo* series began, but this joke comes from Season 5, in November of 1971: "The planned Women's Liberation motorcade failed to materialize today when the entire 454 ladies hopped into their cars, started their engines, and backed into each other." *Those chicks who want equality can't even drive straight! That's hilarious!* In retrospect, the sexism was astonishing, and must be a part of the Seventies context in which *Columbo* was cautiously handling women's issues.

TV disapproval of women's liberation didn't have to come from the snide jokes of a wacky comedy show. In 1971, Gloria Steinem's *Ms. Magazine* debuted, and instantly drew the cynical attention of seasoned *ABC Evening News* anchors Harry Reasoner and Howard K. Smith, who felt compelled by this affront to good taste to broadcast their innermost thoughts to the nation. Reasoner called the publication "pretty sad… in the irrelevant tradition of shock magazines" that were specializing in tabloid journalism and soft-core nude photos. Smith ignored the 1970 reality that women were making 58 percent of what men did, proclaiming, "I'm not persuaded by women's lib—indeed, there may be a case for man's lib."[1] The older white male establishment breathed a sigh of relief as these older white male establishment mouthpieces pronounced the feminist movement virtually dead in its tracks.

We know that in the course of his policework, Columbo could succumb to the male gaze. His reactions to pretty/naked/half-naked girls was sometimes used by the writers as comedy schtick for an easy chuckle, or, no doubt, a chance for male viewers to engage in covert ogling. Episodes where the appearance of lightly-clad ladies is natural to the plotting make sense, and Columbo's self-conscious reactions are appropriate. So when he turns his back to the nude model being painted by cranky artist Sam Franklin in *Suitable for Framing*, we recognize his embarrassment.

In *The Most Crucial Game*, it's clear that Eve Babcock is a high-class lady-of-the evening. Of course, this can't be said directly on 1972 television, and it takes Columbo a few moments to realize this as he visits Eve in her apartment, a crowded mishmash of elegance and kitsch (a dime-store Indian figure is prominently displayed). Eve is played by Valerie Harper, who had already been honing her comedy chops on *The Mary Tyler Moore Show*, so her interactions with Falk are wonderful as it slowly dawns on him what she does for a living. "Hi, darling… don't be embarrassed, I've been expecting you." Columbo's shyness continues; he has yet to disclose his reason for being there, and Eve lightly smooches him on the cheek. He smiles and slowly shakes his head as he seats himself in one of the bright pink wicker chairs in the room.

His shy demeanor transitions after announcing to Eve and her just-arrived dinner guest that he's with the LAPD, and Columbo now has a few questions for his hostess. In paying Eve a compliment, though, the '72 dialogue is a bit cringey today, as he says, "You'd be an ornament in any office." One imagines that Eve has heard cruder flattery in her line of work, but for the era, this is what *Columbo* considered being a gentleman.

A sexy predicament arises in *Blueprint for Murder,* as Columbo questions Goldie (Janis Paige) while she's receiving a massage in her sumptuous boudoir. Casually, repeatedly referring to Columbo as "Lover," Goldie is certain that her ex-husband's disappearance is actually murder. "Would you like to turn around, Lieutenant, I don't want to corrupt you," Goldie warns before shedding her post-rubdown towel. But even after Goldie gives the OK, Columbo plays it safe and remains with his back to her. All of these interactions are quick, humorous character-checks on Columbo as someone who is bashful, virtuous and respectful in the presence of women.

As a red-blooded male, Columbo is guilty of the occasional sideward glance to acknowledge the presence of a pretty lady. And opening a volume such as *The New History of Erotic Art* (in 1978's *The Conspirators*), Columbo has license to do some off-the-books inspecting. It might get a disapproving look from a nearby customer, but hey, it's a public bookstore.

The tome that Columbo is seen holding up like a *Playboy* centerfold is fictional.[2] But by 1978, there had already been two volumes published of *The Joy of Sex*, illustrated manuals that brought sexuality into the wide-open spaces of those public bookstores and challenged people on their comfort with sexual conversation and values. In a decade with changing attitudes toward women, there was a simultaneous shift in attitudes toward sex. *Columbo* certainly reflected the anxieties of many viewers when touching on those topics, even as we recognize scenes like that in *The Conspirators* as existing simply for an audience titter.

Viewers doing a Columbo ogle-count may note that his history of enjoying belly dancers seems a bit disconcerting. In *Try and Catch Me*, he catches up to Veronica Bryce (Mariette Hartley) at her exotic dancing lesson, which has zero significance to the plot, but does put a lot of ladies in skimpy outfits. However, belly dancing is much more socially acceptable than stripping. As Veronica's instructor implores, "Make it sensual, but dignified... It's *not* a striptease!" And appearances are deceiving in *Identity Crisis* when Columbo's attention is intently focused on a dancer at an oceanside bar. He points out to Sgt. Kramer that it was the woman's eyes that he was eyeing: "She's shy!"

CAROLINE: You know something, Lieutenant, that's the very first time that anyone ever told me that they liked me for my body instead of my mind.
– *The Bye-Bye Sky High IQ Murder Case*, 1977

Did I mention that Caroline is 14 years old, and Columbo is an older man wearing a rumpled raincoat and smoking a stinky cigar? To be fair, Columbo didn't really compliment her body, just that she was pretty. And, as blogger The Columbophile notes, "I see it as an example of Columbo telling someone something they need to hear to brighten their day rather than him being a mac-wearing old creep. We know Columbo to be pure of heart, after all."

This is a textbook case of a generational culture shift skewing perceptions. Keep in mind that this is the era where it was acceptable for executives to keep copies of men's magazines replete with centerfolds in their office waiting rooms (*Make Me a Perfect Murder*). In 1977, that exchange with young Caroline was perfectly acceptable. Certainly, the *Columbo* producers and Peter Falk himself would never knowingly corrupt the character's brand.

In the same episode, Columbo sees a male secretary in Oliver Brandt's office and wonders, "What is that, women's lib in there? They don't let ladies do that kind of work anymore?" Decades away from the woke generation, it's no surprise that for middle-aged men like Columbo, the feminist movement and the changing role of women brought some confusion.

Sometimes, the well-intentioned Lieutenant couldn't catch a break. In *Etude in Black*, he wants to question a youthful neighbor of murder victim Jennifer Welles. Looking to put Audrey at ease, he notes, "For a young girl, you're a very independent-minded person." Her response tells us how girls and women were being re-educated about men in a feminist era: "Don't bother with any male chauvinistic compliments." Genuinely perplexed, Columbo replies, "Is that what that was? I'm sorry. Forgive me." Nowadays, Audrey's response seems a tad defensive, but in the Seventies, Columbo joined everyone in learning what the new ground rules were for relating with the opposite sex.

Unfortunately, our hero wasn't immune to also yielding to the "strong woman" stereotype of the era. As *Ransom for a Dead Man* was being filmed in 1970, women managers and supervisors made up only 13 percent of the private sector workforce. This gave Columbo pause.

COLUMBO (to an associate lawyer in Leslie Williams' office): I don't know how you do it.
LAWYER: Do what?
COLUMBO: Work for a woman.

Another stereotype is the erratic female witness. A 2022 exhibit from artist Morgan Ogilvie uses the Helen Stewart character from *Dead Weight* to visualize Oglivie's concept of the woman seen by men as unreliable narrator of her experience.[3] Helen saw a shooting. And in 1971, there were surely many women who shared her point of view, not as a murder witness, but as a doubted woman. As the accusers of Bill Cosby, Harvey Weinstein, and Deshaun Watson will tell you, the credibility of women as witnesses remains a problem today. Those cases unfortunately needed the bolstering of multiple accusers. Helen was alone.

It's not a good look for Columbo when he asks Stewart if she had been drinking when she reported witnessing a murder at the hands of Major Hollister. Stewart is written as something of a flaky divorcee whose unusual, sculptured clay pieces, as we noted earlier, "try to go beyond the surface for a deeper meaning and a truer reality." Being more grounded, Columbo is skeptical of her art, and therefore of her. In the Lieutenant's defense, there's no physical evidence of murder to confirm Helen's story, so it takes awhile for him to begin to see her as credible. Questioning the specifics of her account, Columbo's just doing his job. To his credit, Columbo does eventually come around to advise Helen to believe in herself. But this happens only after she has succumbed—with a nudge from Columbo—to doubting her own story.

Perhaps a female LAPD detective could have fared better with Helen. Too bad there were almost none to be found in 1971 Los Angeles. Court-ordered mandates to actively hire and promote women in police roles didn't happen until the Eighties, and this Seventies rarity was reflected in *Columbo*, which had the very occasional attractive policewoman on hand, but never a female investigating detective, even as a background extra at a crime scene.

In her book *Columbo: A Rhetoric of Inquiry with Resistant Responders*, Associate Professor Christyne Berzsenyi devotes a full chapter to "Columbo, the Women of His Investigations, and the Equal Rights Movement." Placing Columbo's actions in the context of the times, Berzsenyi's assessment highlights the difficulty of analyzing the attitudes and motivations of a detective who isn't always presenting a 100 percent authentic self to the killer.

In the service of Seventies social equality, Berzsenyi notes that "viewers long for more diverse, accurate, and valuing portrayals of real women—strong, hardworking and courageous human beings and survivors. The wealthy, villainous women of *Columbo* are brilliant, self-serving, cunning and capable of committing mortal trouble."[4] Women's equality forges both positive and negative paths.

Berzsenyi identifies multiple interactional strategies for Columbo with such lady killers. They are not mutually exclusive, but they recognize different female-centric approaches that our sly Lieutenant might use as weapons of psychological gamesmanship against fairer-sex targets to soften them up for the inevitable Gotcha moment.

He could play what Berzsenyi labels the "sensitive, compassionate consoler and caregiver," extending condolences and asking subordinate officers to escort or otherwise take care of the supposedly vulnerable woman. He could be the picture of "gentlemanly politeness, taking care of the 'weaker sex,'" right down to offering his arm to a just-confessed Ruth Lytton in *Old Fashioned Murder*.[5]

More likely, he'll employ a variation of "flirtation, flattery or both… so the murderers relax their guard because, if the investigator is doting on them for their beauty and femininity, he appears less likely to suspect them of murder."[6] Examples include Nora Chandler (Anne Baxter) in *Requiem for a Falling Star* and Viveca Scott (Vera Miles) of *Lovely But Lethal*.

An extension of this strategy would be presenting as paternalistic and patronizing. Berzsenyi notes, "Sexism *projected* [my emphasis] by Columbo shows him to be stupefied by the departure from traditional female sex roles. He acts as if he presumes women cannot be demanding and scheming corporate executives or strategic agents of their professional lives… because they are women. He pretends to underestimate them."[7]

It's a psychological ploy. As he does with their male killer counterparts, Columbo feeds their egos to lower their defenses. So in *Ransom for a Dead Man* he'll ask Leslie Williams with amazement, "You can fly? By yourself? No kidding!" He'll gush over Kay Freestone's advanced film production knowledge in *Make Me a Perfect Murder*. He'll say to Viveca Scott (calling her "Miss Scott" and not the more professionally-respected "Ms. Scott"), "I had no idea you had such top secrets in such a nice lady's business like this." Later, he tells Scott, "It might not have been a murderer. I think the killer was a woman." The Lieutenant's language choice here is revealing of the gender distinction. The female killer is the outlier.

While some might interpret such mildly misogynistic comments as revealing of Columbo's true nature, I'd opt, as I do for much of his behaviors, for a mix of authenticity and exaggeration. We've already seen isolated examples of interactions outside of those with the killer where he expresses confusion with changing male/female roles; embellishing these attitudes serves the greater purpose of encouraging female villains to drop their guard. He does it with male murderers, why not with women?

Separating psychological gambits from genuine attempts at compliments isn't going to be conclusive. But we can state with some certainty that Columbo is not demonstrating what we would today call "toxic masculinity." He is not the aggressive, gun-wielding cop of other television artifacts that conform to a cultural stereotype. Even so, his acceptance of women's equality could stand a gentle push in that direction. Sometimes, it takes a symbolic victory to help the cause.

On September 20, 1973, a pudgy 55-year-old, long-ago Wimbledon champ named Bobby Riggs took to the court against tennis pro Billie Jean King in what was billed as "The Battle of the Sexes." Riggs proclaimed that because he was a man, he could easily whip King at the net game. Riggs was a huckster, skilled at hyping a good marketing opportunity. He had already bested the top female player, Margaret Court, in May, using enough soft drop shots and high lobs to win handily in the insensitively-dubbed "Mother's Day Massacre."

The match with King was totally inconsequential as an actual event, yet monumentally symbolic for women's fight against the pervasive social inequalities with men. The build-up was enormous, as 50 million people tuned in to either revel in men's superiority, or watch the strutting, arrogant male get knocked off his perch. By the time it was over, King had thoroughly defeated Riggs. Like many hyped happenings, it was anti-climactic. Salaries didn't change overnight, but it was an important figurative victory for women.

It's against this backdrop that we examine elements of *Columbo* feminism where we can find them. Feminism's basic definition is the belief that men and women should have equal rights and opportunities. But many people hate the word "feminism," for a variety of reasons: "An association with strong, forceful, and angry women… [Fear that] men will eventually lose out of power, influence and control… and negative shifts in relationships, marriage, society, culture, and authority dynamics…." As one writer asserts, "Feminism at its core is about choice. Feminists can wear whatever they want. If we cannot choose freely on how to behave, speak, act and present ourselves, then we are moving backwards."[8]

We can roughly distinguish between *Columbo* women who are happy, liberated free spirits (the nude model of *Suitable for Framing*, the Zen-yoga Lisa of *Last Salute to the Commodore*) and those who are seen as strong in character, who have made confident life choices without regret. These women proactively take control of their decisions in a manner more aligned with a feminist ethos. Such ladies could include Eve Babcock and Goldie, and we might add Kathy Goodland (Sandra Smith, *The Greenhouse Jungle*) who makes no bones or apologies to Columbo about her choices.

SUSAN CLARK as Beth Chadwick in *Lady in Waiting*, attired in what all the mod, liberated women were sporting in 1971.

"You still don't approve of my lifestyle, do you? I told you before, I really don't care what you think!" Kathy, you see, has been chumming around with hunky friend Ken while married to the episode's eventual victim, Tony (Bradford Dillman). To Ken, she says, "He's from Homicide… they handle morals now." And while Columbo may, in fact, disapprove of Kathy's lifestyle, it won't bother him as long as it doesn't interfere with his investigation. "You know something, Mrs. Goodland, you're a very unusual person—you're not a hypocrite."

Of primary characters, an interesting feminist discussion centers around Beth Chadwick (Susan Clark, *Lady in Waiting*). In a weird way, her 90-minute story arc can be seen as a glimpse at feminist evolution. Certainly, Beth is a unique member of *Columbo's* Murderers' Row. She begins the episode belittled and verbally abused. When brother Bryce asks, if not for her family name, "Do you think Peter Hamilton would give you a second look?" we feel the pangs of sympathy. But after the fratricide, that promptly changes. Her newfound family freedom is expressed in mod clothes, a fashionable hairstyle, and flashy wheels. But more importantly, in a new attitude. "There's a change in the status quo," she curtly alerts her mother. "Things are different now."

Aside from her move to the head of the boardroom table, she shifts her posture toward Columbo. Unlike other murderers the Lieutenant spars with, the Beth that Columbo meets at the show's beginning is in the traditional female role—powerless and completely without authority. Indeed, her function is to serve coffee to him. But a week after the inquest, Beth commands, "I'm afraid I must insist that you leave me alone!" Throwing her newfound status around, she announces, "I'm perfectly capable of making my own decisions!" She now feels liberated and empowered.

But it is significant that her feminine empowerment is not met with positive reaction from her beau, Peter Hamilton (Leslie Nielsen), who has been portrayed in the episode as the sensible, stolid support for Beth even when she was marginalized. He still loved her. But when decisions like their engagement are taken out of his hands, he feels the relationship's power dynamics shifting, and he abandons her. Beth's sudden feminist progress is a bridge and a mod hat too far.

With the help of her gun, Beth Chadwick climbed the power ladder very quickly. Typically, a woman residing in such a position of authority, with smarts and personal strength of actions and convictions, would be branded as a feminist. Her equality with male power brokers almost guarantees that perception, and not always positive. Indeed, the very title of the episode *Lovely But Lethal* could almost be an anti-feminist neon sign draped around Viveca Scott's pearled neck.

In *Ransom for a Dead Man*, we see Leslie Williams (Lee Grant) as a shark in the courtroom, and bereft of emotion outside it. She relishes being in control over others, as Columbo will tell you after that plane ride. In these qualities, she probably comes as close to a male antagonist as any of the women discussed here. Kay Freestone (Trish Van Devere, *Make Me a Perfect Murder*) guns herself into a promotion that is temporary, but is there any doubt that the strong-willed, confident and aggressive Kay intends on keeping it? It is telling that Columbo compliments her success and ambition. And when exec Flanagan jettisons her, she says, "I'm as tough as you are. I'll survive and you'll want me back."

Tough, yes. But Kay and her female killer comrades also fall into a stereotype that I would suggest might be getting in the way of the popularity of most of *Columbo's* 70s female villains.

Collectively, these women are simply not the same formidable or memorable Rogues' Gallery of baddies as populate the male side. As a guide, we'll turn to the Columbophile Blog. Apart from Abigail Mitchell (Ruth Gordon, *Try and Catch Me*), who resides in both the host's and the Reader's Poll Top 10 Killers lists, female adversaries do not inspire the same level of excitement and admiration among the *Columbo* community. Of Columbophile's Top 28

Seventies episodes, only three feature female antagonists: Abigail Mitchell, Beth Chadwick, and Kay Freestone. Of the remaining 17 lower-end episodes, though, six of the slayers are women. So two-thirds of *Columbo's* Seventies lady killers are in the comparatively worst episodes.

Why? To be sure, some factors will include poor plotting, lazy characterizations, bad Gotchas, uninspired acting, and the usual list of why some *Columbos* don't work and others shine. But perhaps there's a reason that may be focused on the specific gender of the killer, our own stereotypes, and the expectations of a Seventies viewing audience.

Although there will of course be individual exceptions, it is not scientifically inaccurate to note that women's bodies have less testosterone than males, will tend to be smaller in size, generally lesser in strength, and often less aggressive. For countless years, they have been raised in a society that has traditionally valued their nurturing skills over positions of power and authority and reinforced their polite acceptance of this secondary role. Women have tended to be viewed, accurately or not, as being more vulnerable than males. This model of femininity has clearly been in flux in our modern era, but it was much less in doubt in *Columbo's* prime.

Being more vulnerable, it is easier to elicit sympathy for the she-devil. And it is this sympathetic angle to many of the female killers that may be tamping our enthusiasm for them. In 2015, Columbophile produced the "10 Most Sympathetic Columbo Killers." Forty percent of them were Seventies women: Ruth Lytton, Beth Chadwick, Abigail Mitchell, and Grace Wheeler. This percentage is skewed rather high, as women made up only 17 percent of the original Seventies killer catalogue.

The ladies listed here have something usually lacking in the common male murderers—a significant sympathetic backstory. It is more than a mere motive; we understand why Paul Galesko, for example, wants to off his shrewish wife, but we don't have true empathy with him.

And whether man or woman, sympathy is simply not a strong enough motivator for the viewer to embrace the killer as one we love to hate. This villain will draw our compassion, interest, pity and concern, but we can't really pump our fist in the air with satisfaction at the Gotcha (looking at you, Dale Kingston).

Fans will of course disagree on the rankings of Favorite Killers and what exactly makes for a memorable evildoer. But, in general, *Columbo's* women murderers are written and crafted to elicit a degree of sympathy that only a very small number of male antagonists get. This is basically consistent with the stereotypes, societal norms, and viewer expectations of the times.

For those rare occasions when a sympathetic male or female killer is also a significantly memorable one, such as Ruth Gordon's Abigail Mitchell or Donald Pleasence's Adrian Carsini, I would argue that their status as a fan favorite comes as much from the actors playing them as from their storyline.

In the piece "The Psychology of Female Killers: Why Do Women Kill?," Janey Davies asks, "Are we talking about a certain type of woman, or a certain type of crime? Do women that kill all have similar personality traits? Or, are the situations and crimes typical of a female killer?"[9] Davies suggests a variety of types and motives for female murderers, including Revenge, Profit and, more ominously, the Black Widow. These can help us gauge how much sympathy they can expect from us.

As the series' first trigger-happy female, Leslie Williams is arguably the coldest of the bunch, with many qualities of the Black Widow type: "... manipulative and cunning. They plan the murder out meticulously. The Black Widow will always have a close relationship with her victim. We are talking about lovers, husbands or partners."

Viveca Scott is upset with ex-lover Karl, but rather than being a Black Widow, her motive for spontaneously clubbing her chemist is more about wrinkle-free-miracle-beauty-cream profit than revenge. Our sympathy levels for both her and Williams are low.

According to Davies, there are seven different motives for murder, and Nora Chandler's is the one more often associated with men, concealment of another crime. At least, that's the motive for her making a fireball of her assistant Jean Davis (Pippa Scott). Columbophile writes that "Chandler is somewhat sympathetic, especially when set against the ghastly Jerry Parks. But she never shows contrition.... So we must ask: is she as wickedly selfish as her crime would suggest, or is she a tormented soul inside for what she did to poor Jean?" Others may disagree, but I vote option A—she set her personal assistant on fire!

Discounting Lillian Stanhope (Honor Blackman), whose accidental cold cream conking of Sir Roger in *Dagger of the Mind* is hard to take very seriously, the remaining killer ladies are due varying degrees of empathy. In *Forgotten Lady*, Grace Wheeler's (Janet Leigh) degenerative brain aneurism elicits the most sympathy. Next, revenge killer Abigail Mitchell suffocated the man who she believes murdered her niece, and of course we all feel sad for cute little pixie old ladies going to the hoosegow.

Beth Chadwick's primary gains are going to be psychological, not monetary profit. She might lose a piece of our sympathy over the course of the episode, but Columbo has been affected by the encounter, and tells her at the Gotcha that she's "too classy a lady" to shoot him. Is this a ploy to get her to take her finger off the trigger? Perhaps, but I sense that Columbo actually feels pity for her.

Old Fashioned Murder pounds away at wringing the pathos and milking sympathy for Ruth Lytton (Joyce Van Patten). Subtlety is scarce, with multiple "old-fashioned" references, recounting of a lost and stifled childhood, and woe-is-me lamentations to Columbo. Ruth has shot her brother Edward (Tim O'Connor), who runs the dreary Lytton Museum. Her motive for killing doesn't neatly fit into any of Davies' archetypes. Profit? The dishwater-dull museum is a certified money-loser. Revenge? Edward's just being honest about the business. Emotional gain? Ruth is murdering Edward to keep her money-losing way of life where she'll remain an old maid and die unhappy and unfulfilled. Doesn't sound promising, unless she consults with Beth Chadwick for some mod post-murder fashion tips.

Both revenge and profit figure into Kay Freestone's motivations, as she feels wronged by her boss Mark (Laurence Luckinbill). This is a script with more nuanced characterizations and performances. At her childhood shack, she describes her hardscrabble youth and how it shaped her: "You [Columbo] accept things as they are, I try to change them." The goal here is to make Kay a more well-rounded human being, rather than simply a cardboard cut-out villain. When Columbo empathetically says "I understand your feelings" to sympathize with the killer, I think we're supposed to as well, but there are *Columbo* fans who definitely disagree.

Although arguably strong and perhaps even feminists, these Seventies lady killers also often fall in line with the stereotype of the time, as women who are supposed to elicit our sympathy, killers with an empathetic cause. They can be resilient and aggressive like Kay, but unlike their male killing counterparts, their strength is given a motivating reason. This makes these women more interesting people than male slime like Paul Gerard, Riley Greenleaf, or Hayden Danziger, but it doesn't necessarily make them more interesting killers to root against.

Columbo was not a feminist screed. However, as Berzsenyi notes, it had a "relationship to the wider cultural context of the women's movement. Portraying credible women, executives, professionals, lawyers and celebrated performers as killers certainly responds to the country's cultural shifts… toward the empowerment of women and away from being 'put in their place.'"[10] But this was sometimes at odds with the observations of Columbo himself.

COLUMBO (looking at a photo of victim Jennifer Welles): Woman has a beautiful shape, don't you think? Look at those eyes, bedroom eyes.... We've got a girl with a body, money, and a career. Woman like that's gotta have somebody. Eyes like that! But that's me, I'm paranoic. Every time I see a dead body, I think it's been murdered. Can't imagine anyone murdering themselves... especially a young girl like that. Beautiful eyes... but that's me. I'd like to see everyone die of old age.
– *Etude in Black* (1972)

Today, Columbo's musings might be seen as a short step away from fetishizing. 1972 would disagree.

The gender messages provided by *Columbo* echo a culture in a self-conscious transition of social values. In its sympathetic portrayals of female killers, awkward attitudes toward sexy corpses, and its nods to feminism, *Columbo* was a mixed bag on Seventies enlightenment, but on balance fared about as well as any other TV show of the era not starring Bea Arthur.

Other Seventies detectives tried to keep up with women's empowerment. Certainly, *Columbo* was less exploitive than the so-called Jiggle TV of *Charlie's Angels*. But even those busty crime busters may have been slyly promoting a pro-feminist position. Susan J. Douglas, author of *Where the Girls Are: Growing Up Female with the Mass Media*, argues for a more nuanced look at what the Angels were selling.

"The reason *Charlie's Angels* was such a hit was that it exploited, perfectly, the tensions between antifeminism and feminism. [It] pulled off a neat trick: while it reinforced traditional male power through Charlie's voice and agenda-setting instructions, it also tried to pretend that there was no such thing as a patriarchy." Walters acknowledged that it was "escapist rot of the first order," but the ladies were not needy damsels in distress—they were resourceful and self-sufficient, solving their own cases and getting out of their own jams. "In seeking to have it both ways—to espouse female liberation and to promote the objectification of women's bodies—*Charlie's Angels* offered a compromise."

That balance appeared to satisfy the cultural moment. Angie Dickinson's 1974 star vehicle *Police Woman* would at first glance seem to have been more hip to women's lib, but Walters bemoans the character's reliance on male superiors to swoop in for last-minute rescues and the show's reliance on violent Pepper-in-jeopardy rape tropes for plot movement. Dickinson portrayed her cop as smart and tough, but couldn't get around the male hierarchy.

Police Woman was a hit. More feminist-friendly, but largely neglected, was another female cop show debuting that same week in 1974. *Get Christie Love!* starred Teresa Graves as an undercover operative and a dual minority, female and black. She was capable, quick-witted, threw a mean punch, and didn't wear bikinis or rely on her sex appeal. Wisely, producers jettisoned the pilot's flirty and inferred sleeping around with her white male superior (!) in favor of a more independent and empowered detective. The show struggled to last 22 episodes.

In the context of these female fellow law enforcers, it's clear that *Columbo* was not unusual in both advancing the cause of the liberated lady killer, while still expressing the Lieutenant's own skepticism about the movement. It was a delicate equilibrium, but it was one that all other shows of the decade had to negotiate, particularly the cops, and especially those of the fairer sex. In his 1971 Columboverse living room, one can imagine our hero possibly nodding his head in agreement with those veteran ABC newscasters opining about women. But we know that Columbo has a kind heart, is open to change, and values equal justice. He may be a bit slow to recognize the changing times of Women's Liberation, but we have confidence that he'll get there eventually.

3.
Coping with Future Shock

LIEUTENANT DUFFY: Hey, haven't you ever heard of "future shock"? The world's going to hell with itself! Believe me, Columbo, times have changed.

As an expression of Seventies existential chaos, you can't get much more direct than budding futurist Lt. Duffy's assessment of the planet in 1974's *A Friend in Deed*. Would Columbo agree?

Our hero has had a long and complicated relationship with electronics, machines, technology, scientific advances, behavioral control, and adapting to a Brave New World of radical change. From pagers to pacemakers, faxes to floppy discs, robots to remotes, VHS to CCTV, Columbo is forever experiencing—like all of us—future shock.

"Future shock is the dizzying disorientation brought on by the premature arrival of the future."
– Alvin Toffler, *Future Shock* (1970)

It's hard to overstate the sensational impact of *Future Shock*, Alvin Toffler's futurist manifesto ushering in the 1970s with a cold brace of reality about our culture to come. The book dominated bestseller lists and TV talk shows as a true global phenomenon, making Toffler a pop culture celebrity and spawning the catchphrase that eventually made its way into a *Columbo* episode, confirming its mass recognition.

Among other things, *Future Shock* foresaw in various forms: the internet, YouTube, disposable goods, rental products, climate crises, gay marriage,

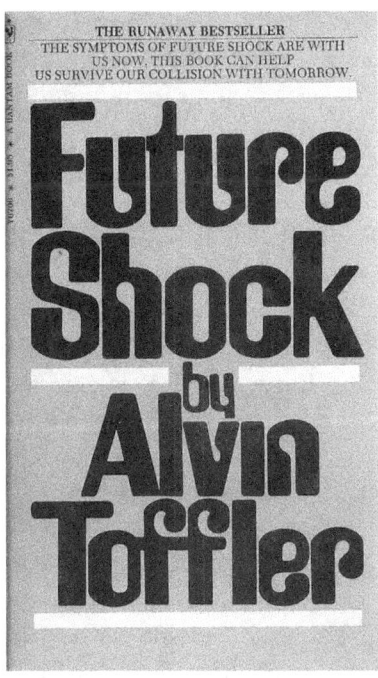

ALVIN TOFFLER'S 1970 bestseller introduced America to the concept of Future Shock, as coping with and adapting to rapid technological changes. Sound like a detective we know?

cloning, home-schooling, email, instant celebrities, interactive media, transient workplaces, telecommuting, virtual entertainment, predictive computer algorithms, and underwater cities. (OK, Toffler whiffed on that last one).

But while prophetic of many elements of today's culture, *Future Shock* also warned of the "shattering stress and disorientation that we induce in individuals by subjecting them to too much change in too short a time." Traditional social foundations would be upset or obliterated, challenging our own sense of personal identity. Structural change was imminent with the transition from an industrial society based on physical labor and manufacturing to a post-industrial, information and service-based economy. "We must search out totally new ways to anchor ourselves, for all the old roots of religion, nation, community, family or profession are now shaking under the hurricane impact of the accelerative thrust."

Toffler coined the phrase "information overload" to describe the massive amount of data, news and trivialities spread by enveloping technology and rapidly expanding mass communication systems. Confusion, alienation and free-floating stress are the results of "the roaring current of change, a current so powerful today that it overturns institutions, shifts our values, and shrivels our roots." *Future Shock* was a fascinating look ahead, as well as a true cautionary tale.

This is the cultural context in which *Columbo* launched its second pilot in 1971, *Ransom for a Dead Man*. Barely eight months after Toffler declared that a "man-machine symbiosis is furthered by our increasing ingenuity in communicating with machines," Leslie Williams transformed her telephone-calling device into a machine that was, essentially, pretending to be a human —her quite dead husband. "Today, they can do everything electronically if they wanted to, I'd bet on that," marvels Columbo to the killer counselor. He then describes a ticket service, "if I wanna take my wife to the ballgame… that's all done by computer. It's really remarkable!"

Six months later, in *Murder by the Book*, it's a mere 70 seconds into our official series introduction to the Columbo character that he's in wonder of elevator buttons "that go off by the heat of your hand." Very early on, as a primary element of his character, Columbo is noticing, interacting and engaging with the same technology that Toffler called "the great growling engine of change."

Toffler's *Shock* and Columbo's shock—simple coincidence? Perhaps Columbo creators Richard Levinson and William Link were themselves, in their own way, futurists who could have shared some of Toffler's views of technology and built this into a Seventies *Columbo* theme.

Computers were already a fact of life in the Sixties and no stranger to television viewers. Although often seen as a *Star Trek* science-fiction anomaly, they made their way into other shows, too. For example, subverting enemy computer systems was a specialty of *Mission: Impossible's* Barney Collier.

In 1967, before their 1968 *Columbo* TV-movie *Prescription: Murder*, Levinson and Link created a new detective show for CBS, *Mannix*. It had a run of eight seasons, but most television nostalgia buffs forget that it was only in the last seven years that Mannix, played by Mike Conners, was a lone-wolf tough-guy gumshoe. In its first season, he was just one of dozens of operatives working for a vast detective conglomerate, Intertect, housed in a gleaming skyscraper with long banks of massive computers used to store and process a mountain of data applied to fight crime. As Link explains in the first season DVD commentary, Mannix was conceived as a maverick investigator trying to avoid becoming a cog in the state-of-the-art Intertect machine. That show bombed.

Desilu Productions oversaw *Mannix*, and its head, Lucille Ball, promised CBS that changes would be made if they'd pick up the show for a second season. Inclined to keep their chummy relationship with the Queen of Comedy, CBS agreed. Ball decided that the show's computer angle was too high-tech, beyond the grasp of the average viewer. Intertect was ditched, and Joe Mannix set out on his own, successfully getting knocked around and knocked out (55 times!) until 1975. Levinson and Link's vision of a computer-driven *Mannix* workplace was an ahead-of-its-time bust. But perhaps Toffler was watching.

Rather than give up the idea of a sprawling detective agency staffed with computer-subsidized, corporatized and privatized private eyes, Levinson and Link brought it back when they conceived the idea for *Columbo's Death Lends a Hand* (initially intended as the first episode of the series). But this time, the computerized set-up wasn't for the public good, but to give volatile villain Investigator Brimmer leverage over his clients. When Columbo gets the company tour, he is startled by the whirring computers with, he is told, "millions of bits of information, all cross-filed and on tape, immediately available. There are more electrical impulses in this room than in your brain."

And while Link and Levinson were familiarizing their *Columbo* viewers with the technological era, Toffler connected the computer pixels to other trends to prophesize, for example, the role of "personal computers programmed to provide the individual with information and to make minor decisions for him. It could store information about his friends' preferences for Manhattans or martinis, data about traffic routes, the weather, stock prices, remind him of his wife's birthday, pay the rent on time, etc." And maybe get those tickets to the ballgame for Mrs. Columbo, too.

For all its warnings of potential angst and anxiety with the coming future shock of constant change, Toffler's book actually tries to provide a roadmap for negotiating this technological revolution. This is not meant to be a bleak dystopian vision. "The super-industrial revolution can erase hunger, disease, ignorance and brutality.... Super-industrialism will not restrict man... It will radiate new opportunities for personal growth, adventure, and delight. It will be vividly colorful and amazingly open to individuality. The problem is not whether man can survive regimentation and standardization. The problem is whether he can survive freedom."

"Future shock—the disease of change—can be prevented," but only with "conscious regulation of technological advance" and the ability of people to understand and embrace this new reality. With the preparation and foreknowledge supplied by Toffler's book, we could adapt to the coming transformations and build a better world for ourselves. Most critically, we can, and must, learn to live with technology.

It appears that this hopeful message didn't make it to Lieutenant Duffy when he exclaimed to Columbo that "the world's going to hell with itself!" Duffy probably saw the uber-dramatic 1972 *Future Shock* companion film, with its cheesy graphics, hyperbolic Orson Welles narration, lurid recreations, and jarring electronic soundtrack from Gil Melle (who also scored *Death Lends a Hand*).[1] As much shockumentary as documentary, this film probably induced for many people *Westworld*-like visions of oncoming robotic mayhem, but *Columbo* had to take a more grounded, reality-based approach to the future.

In his book *Columbo: Paying Attention 24/7*, Professor David Martin-Jones argues, "Columbo's engagement with modernity reassures viewers that if lower middle-class 'everyman' Columbo can master new machinery, anyone can." Devoting much time to the latest gizmos and gadgetry, *Columbo* is "keeping the audience up to speed with ever-emerging new technologies." As new labor markets develop with new technology, "*Columbo* goes out of its way to offer repeated assurances that it is entirely possible to quickly become familiar with very specialized forms of mental labor."[2] The Lieutenant is teaching the viewer how to adapt to change, addressing and challenging responses to future shock.

> "*Computers combine things to make new knowledge at such high speed that we cannot absorb it. They affect not just the things we buy and the things we know, but the things we do.*"
> – *Future Shock* film

Reflecting their increasing prominence in society, computers have a conspicuous presence in Seventies *Columbo*. In *Mind Over Mayhem*, the setting is the Cybernetic Research Institute, where a wide variety of experts in fields like war strategy, chemistry and molecular science apply their collective mental skills to solve the world's problems. This model is also noted in *Future Shock*. Toffler describes the increasingly important role of specialist groups amassing their brainpower to understand and attack potential social issues. "Within a few years, we have seen the creation of future-oriented think tanks.... We might consider creating a great international institute, a world futures data bank." Columbo has some familiarity: "Think tanks… I've read about those in the paper. It's a place full of geniuses, right?"

"Coping with Future Shock"

The K-44 mainframe dominates the sizeable computer room of the CRI. The Institute is run by Dr. Marshall Cahill (Jose Ferrer), who describes the K-44 to Columbo as "ultra-sophisticated, the only one of its kind in the world," adding dismissively, "I don't expect you to appreciate all this." Columbo, having seen powerful computers before in *Death Lends a Hand*, quickly replies, "Oh no, I appreciate it, sir." To demonstrate his adaptability to modern technology, Columbo is trying a newer, more advanced way of taking notes by using a hand-held recording device. Of course, he wouldn't be our Columbo if he didn't shout into it.

Here, the K-44 is designed for war strategy, almost a decade before *War Games*' Matthew Broderick would hear the seductive leading question "Shall we play a game?" And we learn that Dr. Cahill's tacticians have a lot of work to do: "Your retaliatory response indicates a total defeat, with a 75 percent mortality rate for the Western Hemisphere." Yikes, that's bad! The supercomputer is, with Cahill's oversight, clearly in charge. Whether Toffler would view this as a dream or a nightmare is uncertain.

> *"There appears to be no reason why we cannot go forward to build humanoid machines.... If you can define a task and a human can do it, then a machine can."*

The presence of MM-7 at the Cybernetic Institute is significant. The "character" is commonly known as Robby the Robot, and has a long history in movies and TV beginning with 1956's *Forbidden Planet* and including *The Many Loves of Dobie Gillis*, *The Twilight Zone*, *Lost in Space*, and *The Banana Splits*. His/her/its appearance in *Columbo* at a very earth-bound facility reinforces the shift away from looking at automated androids as merely outer-space contraptions. *Future Shock* titles the relevant chapter "The Cyborgs Among Us," and in it Toffler speculates that they could be made "behaviorally indistinguishable from humans."

Our guide to the robotic future is boy genius Steven Spelberg. He has programmed MM-7 with an emotion mode that flips the chessboard when checkmated, and while that's a bit extreme, it certainly simulates a human reaction. He assures Columbo—and us—"Don't be frightened, Lieutenant, it's not a monster!" MM-7 gives a friendly metallic handshake, prompting Columbo to exclaim, "That's the most wonderful thing I've ever seen!" Spelberg channels his inner Toffler when he says, "It can do everything a man can do if you program it…. Everybody can use a robot, Lieutenant. There's a lot of annoying jobs that people don't like to do that robots will be doing someday."

Columbo is curious and open to understanding this new technology. He asks Spelberg if the robot can learn how to housebreak his basset hound, who's along for the visit. Columbo's acceptance of MM-7, and his realization that the robot can both walk Dog and provide an alibi for killer Dr. Cahill, is critical. We should also credit excellent child actor Lee H. Montgomery as Steven, who convincingly sells Spelberg's spiel about warm-and-fuzzy automatons of the future.

> *"In super-industrial society, many tasks will be performed by great self-regulating systems of machines, doing away with the need for bureaucratic organization."*

Some of the glimpses into modernity of the Classic *Columbo* era seem rather quaint and dated today, perhaps none more so than viewers' introduction to the Tricon Delta 2-14 in *An Exercise in Fatality*. Retrieving stored information about a Tricon employee, the scene today feels like a six-minute death march. Columbo appears cluelessly frustrated, the data takes forever to materialize, and the mainframe is almost comically oversized to retrieve such basic information. Today, episode viewers simply fast forward to avoid the aggravation (Irony Alert: using technology to avoid technology).

In 1974, however, there was little fast forwarding, and viewers were treated to a real-time demonstration of adaptation in the Future Shock Era. Explains Martin-Jones, "The noticeable screen time… seems devoted to raising audience awareness of the importance and role of technology in processing information, and the need to get used to the tempo of interaction with new technologies."[3] The scene is clearly episode filler, but not without purpose at the dawn of the computer takeover of bureaucracy.

> *"Technology and science are altering behavior, extending our control over mind and body; we wire the human, and with every new step, the consequences for human life become magnified."*
> – *Future Shock* film

It's probably not a coincidence that several Classic *Columbo* murderers specialize in behavior modification, equating these efforts with villainous activities. Such behavior modification is a form of control, power and authority. Certainly, the specter of loss of individual control of one's actions is a frightening one, and the ability of scientists and behavior specialists to do the controlling is even more alarming. *Mind Over Mayhem* never defines the "Cybernetics" of the CRI acronym, but it's the science of control and communications in animal and machine.

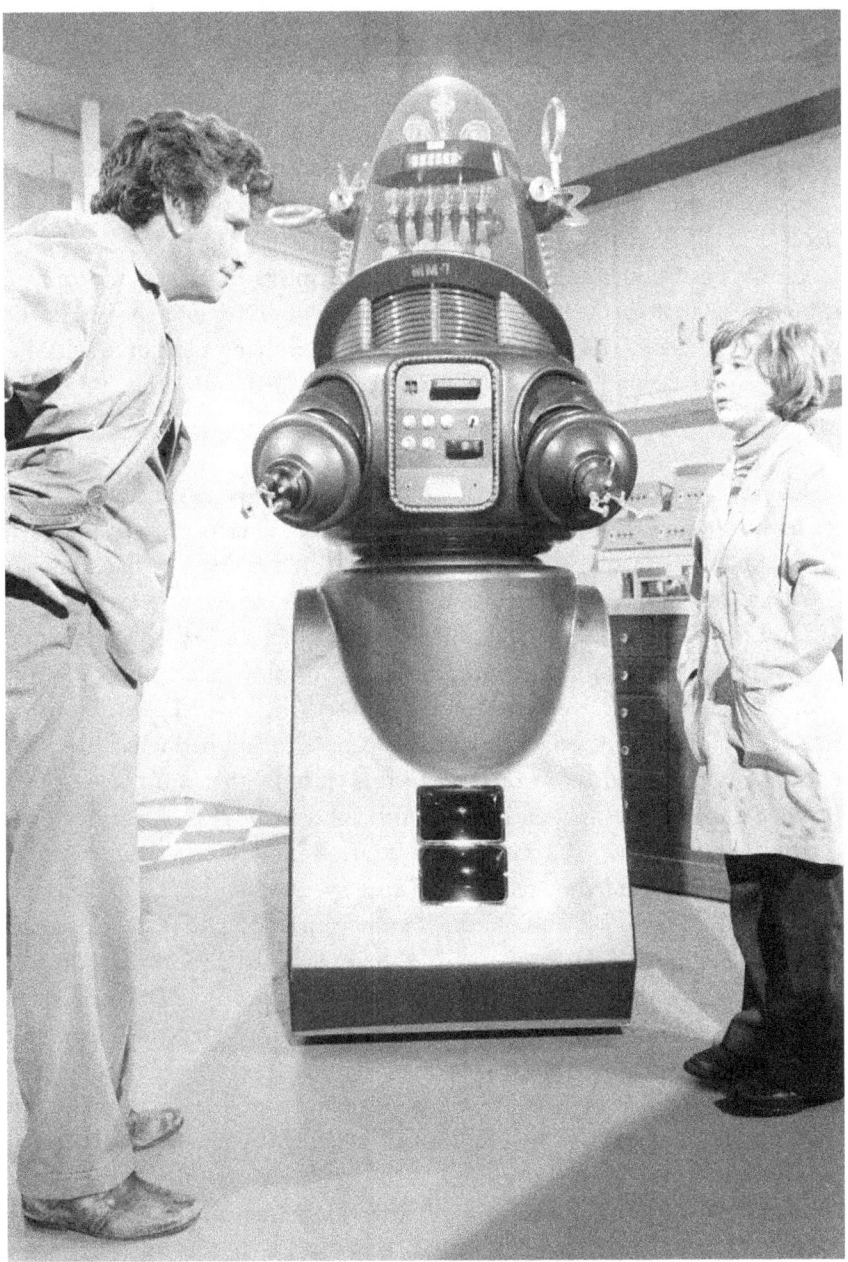

MAN MEETS MACHINE: From *Mind Over Mayhem*, Columbo with Steven Spelberg (Lee H. Montgomery) and Robby, Hollywood's go-to robot.

In *A Deadly State of Mind*, Columbo meets slick psychiatrist Dr. Mark Collier (George Hamilton), whose work is described to Columbo as "concerned with the measurement and manipulation of human behavior, on all levels... Things like peer group adaptability and anxiety catharsis through hypnotic suggestion." Collier's current subject is Nadia Donner (Lesley Ann Warren), and the outcomes of his research will be the foundation for his next book.

Collier's assistant researcher, Dr. Borden, suspects that he is resorting to using drugs that can destroy an individual's will and goose the results he wants for the book. This is a dangerous shortcut implying additional behavior manipulation beyond hypnosis. Collier's lab is filled with rats and guinea pigs, and as Columbo speaks with him, we see prominent rows of wildly blinking computers in the background.

Columbo's been reading a recent Collier tome on hypnosis and admits that it's hard to follow. But the Lieutenant perseveres. He can't prove it in court, but he knows that Collier literally hypnotized Nadia to death by inducing her to take a high dive from her apartment: "You programmed her!"

Dr. Eric Mason (Nicol Williamson) of *How to Dial a Murder* is a behavioral psychologist heading the Institute for Life Control. "Take control of your own space, your own lives, your own responses!" bellows Mason to a room full of devotees. His specialty is training people to use particular words to control emotions and behavior. And in this episode, that word "control" is bandied about quite frequently. "[Mommy and Daddy] took control with control words... Then the words took control! Now I've got the control!" Mason's control is aided by technology. In a by-now familiar *Columbo* sight, Mason studies a bank of ubiquitous *Future Shock* computers, here spitting out needle-graph audience responses on their twist-dial devices to words like "death."

Mason is ostensibly teaching humans how to control their own lives, but having a mass of people simultaneously count down from 100 upon command seems an ironic way to establish one's independence. The doctor contends that "it's not mind control, it's life control... there's a difference." For Mason, it's also cash control—he sure needs it to stock his rare film memorabilia collection. And Mason also controls his killer Dobermans, as Toffler raises the prospect that man is learning to exploit animals with specific training.

> "The ordinary citizen receives messages—mainly from the mass media—that have been artfully fashioned by communications experts... coded but pre-engineered."

In *Double Exposure*, the behavior manipulation of Dr. Bart Kepple (Robert Culp) arises from motivational research. He can control your consumer buying habits. Based on extensive observational data, Kepple (he's rather insistent on being called a doctor) developed a technique of using subliminal cuts in advertising. These subliminal cuts are ultra-rapid visual or auditory stimuli inserted into a piece of film that the conscious mind doesn't recognize.

Authoring such bestsellers as *Human Values Versus Human Motives* and *The Mind-String and How to Pull It*, Kepple's motivations, and his own urge to control, are clear. Indeed, with a little caviar, a tampered thermostat, and some well-placed subliminal images, Kepple controls client Vic Norris right into a bullet's path.

Once again, we find a villain steeped in the technology of rows of TV monitors in his office and on-site to examine others. Columbo observes Kepple's grocery-buying research and marvels, "Isn't this something! Who would believe it? You guys back here with all this hidden equipment are taking pictures of people and they don't even know they're being photographed!" And while Toffler himself doesn't address the threat of bugging and societal surveillance seen here and in *Death Lends a Hand*, *The Most Crucial Game*, *Playback* and *Identity Crisis*, the idea of such personal privacy invasions is Orwellian enough to remind viewers that Big Brother Is Watching, another by-product of *Future Shock*.

Kepple, Mason, Collier… these scientist/doctors are out-of-control control freaks. Columbo may rein in those particular villains, but even our hero can't make everyone in Los Angeles feel safe from future shock's encroaching feeling of dislocation. Says Toffler, "One response to the loss of control is a revulsion against intelligence. Mounting evidence that society is out of control breeds disillusionment with science."

As Martin-Jones notes, one of Columbo's comforting roles is to guide the viewer through this feeling of loss of control in the era of New Technology. "The point is made that the pace of change, and resulting information overload, has become impossible to keep up with. Attention is stretched thin. [But] for Columbo, he can keep pace with modernity. This is quite a reassurance considering that the opposite may well be the reality for many people."[4] Columbo's ability to adapt is one of the keys to his appeal in an era of overwhelming transformation.

> "We are constantly comparing images, associating them, cross-referencing them in new ways, and repositioning them…. Change widens the gap between what we believe and what really is, between the existing images and the reality they are

supposed to reflect."

Every day we get a continual stream of new and updated images to digest, often replacing the knowledge that we already have. But Toffler's focus is on the future shock of potential consequences of constantly changing images. It's not on the potential for media manipulation of those images, which today would be reflected in phony news, Photoshopping, AI manipulation, and deep-fake videos. The blurring of reality (what actually happened) and the invented (what the killer wants Columbo to think happened) is baked into the *Columbo* formula because the show is, after all, about evil villains hiding evil acts.

Media tampering in the form of time shifting is at the heart of *Playback*. Harold Van Wick (Oskar Werner) stage-manages his cameras and video bank to control what and when his security guard will witness, and what gets recorded for Columbo to see. After a time, Columbo realizes that Van Wick's images don't reflect reality, and he is forced to re-examine them, comparing and looking for the cracks in the evidence. He explicitly says that he doesn't know what he's looking for, but he realizes that his perception of the murder is being controlled. Adapting to the demands of technology, closer examination reveals the gallery invitation that proves that Van Wick has manipulated his technology, providing the Gotcha.

In Classic *Columbo*, technology can become an arbiter and alterer of time, through deceptive and doctored recordings that the villains use to help create their alibis. In the final scene of *An Exercise in Fatality*, Columbo makes clear to Janus, and us, how 1974 technology informed his understanding of Milo's alibi ruse. Holding the spliced tape from Gene Stafford's phone call, Columbo explains, "This tape, this is tricky stuff. The other day, I called a fellow, a Mr. Lewis Lacey.... He gets on the phone and says, 'Hello, this is Mr. Lacey.' Now, I get out a whole sentence before I realize I'm not talking to him, I'm talking to a recording! A thing like that makes an impression on you."

To the modern viewer, the use of answering machines to falsely establish time (also used in *Old Fashioned Murder*) may seem old-hat, but what we see in the Seventies episodes was often nascent tech unfamiliar to many viewers, not commonplace. Columbo walks us through the learning process.

In *Fade In to Murder*, Ward Fowler (William Shatner) isn't directly manipulating Columbo, but he is using his VCR to help create an alibi with his go-fer Mark Davis. It's not as sophisticated as Van Wick's multi-camera closed-circuit system, but Fowler is affluent enough to take advantage of the newest tech toy, the VCR, to further his murderous scheme. Because he is stinking rich, Fowler has access to technology that others don't.

This is another feature that *Columbo* underscores about media manipulation—it can be a tool for the wealthy elite. Often, the LAPD simply doesn't have the same technology at its disposal as the 1 percenters, and it's not a level playing field. Columbo hopes his bosses can spring for the telephone machine Leslie Williams has in her office; he has to analyze Van Wick's tapes at the company's lab; Investigator Brimmer's whiz-bang investigative tech far outshines what Columbo works with. *Future Shock* advantage goes to the rich.

> *"Today the pace of turnover in art is vision-blurring.... The expectation that each year will bring a new mode of artists is 'a significant parody... of the accelerated turnover in the avant-garde today.'"*

It was a starry November evening in 1971 when the Columboverse art world of *Suitable for Framing* was breathlessly introduced to the oeuvre of its newest sensation, grumbly Sam "I'm in my commercial phase" Franklin. *Future Shock* was not solely about technology. Toffler foresaw an escalating fragmentation of cultural tastes, choices and values. The art world of the Sixties begat a revolving door of styles, and *Columbo* had no problem poking fun at the baffling variety. The galleries visited in *Suitable for Framing* and *Playback* were sources of confusion for a puzzled Columbo as he bumped into ceiling mobiles or tried to grasp the meaning (and inflated price tag) of sculptures like "Ghost of a Dead Dog."

It's important to note that Columbo was not necessarily mocking the art itself. He simply didn't understand it. As *Playback* gallery host Francine reasons, "We don't explain art, it's something you feel… it's all subjective." *Columbo* viewers who could see paying $4,700 for a kinetic piece like "The Parking Lot" could also be amused by Columbo's skeptical response to it. Viewers who favored the paint-by-numbers landscapes, like he and Mrs. Columbo, were assured that it was OK to mistake a ventilator for a work of art. When Francine says, "Of course, we'll sell that too!" we're not so sure she's joking.

In *Suitable for Framing*, critic Dale Kingston (Ross Martin) is establishing his murder alibi at the art showing for Franklin. There, he chats up a bevy of young ladies to mansplain New Art mobiles: "The meaning of any mobile stems not only from its form, but the relationship between the pieces, which gives it his meaning." A glib one-liner underscores Toffler's point when Kingston then mocks, "And I suppose the relationship between the pieces is really where it's at, isn't it?" A good laugh is had by all.

"Is a future coming towards us that could shatter all our dreams?"
– *Future Shock* film

Columbo is, and always has been, very old school. In *The Greenhouse Jungle*, he doesn't realize that the LAPD stopped using plaster casts for footprints (thank you, Sergeant Wilson). In London, he's learning about New Scotland Yard policing techniques. In *Troubled Waters*, he uses pre-tech methods to identify fingerprints and collect evidence. He's cringeworthy fascinated by the TV monitor test patterns of *Make Me a Perfect Murder*.

Through the Future Shock Era, though, Columbo learns enough about science and technology to realize that it can be used to implement and conceal murderous crimes. With some quick-study and applied learning, he can then turn this new knowledge back against the killer when Gotcha-time arrives. In *Playback*, he examines the videotape to zoom in to find the spot where the gallery invitation sits on the desk. Columbo inserts his own subliminal cuts into a film to trip up Dr. Kepple in *Double Exposure*. He has the killer Dobermans of *How to Dial a Murder* re-programmed to show affection upon hearing Dr. Mason's old kill word.

Throughout the Seventies, everyone was adapting to the products of technological and scientific advances. Television viewers had their own stand-in tech detective. In *Future Shock*, Toffler writes, "The horrifying truth is that, so far as much technology is concerned, no one is in charge." This prompts his question, "Who should be responsible for correcting the adverse effects of technology?" I have a suggestion, but let's first let him figure out how to get those tickets to the ballgame.

4.
Race and Representation

Discussions of *Columbo's* intersections with social culture are examples of the Cultivation Effect. This theory describes the psychological impact that daily media exposure can have on an individual, and media's ability to influence, or cultivate, shifting attitudes and perceptions. On a large enough scale, exposure has the potential to reinforce shared assumptions about society, positively or negatively. And watching a great deal of television may cultivate an imagined reality that does not correspond to actual reality.

An obvious cultivation effect is the wide disparity between the degree of violence encountered in everyday life and the amount of violence seen on television, whether in news or TV dramas. This tends to affect heavier television users, who believe that the world is more hostile and dangerous than it actually is. Another example is the "*CSI* Effect," where a trial's lack of forensic science evidence might influence jury decisions. By this theory, "'television educated' jurors are more likely to exonerate or acquit someone because procedures and techniques they saw in fictional television shows were not used in the case."[1]

Cultivation analysis would suggest examining media for its messages. If pop culture entertainment is sending us messages about ourselves as a society, can we look at *Columbo* to help us learn more about a particular social movement, such as the role of African-Americans in U.S. culture?

On the surface, it might seem a pointless discussion. The most memorable instance of racial issues creeping into the show was probably in *A Friend in Deed*, when Columbo stopped pushy fellow detective Doyle from harassment of a black man who had volunteered at Holcome House, where the late Mrs.

Halperin would be picking up an award. Otherwise, Columbo steered quite clear of overt contact with racial and civil rights issues of the day. It would not be projecting attitudes about race. But that doesn't mean that it wasn't reflecting the American black experience at all. It did, in small ways, if you knew where to look.

What faces do we see in this reflection? If we see diversity in our pop culture, that's an image that reinforces accepting diversity in our society. In recent years, there's been a noticeable increase in interracial and gay couples in television commercials. Visualizing this helps normalize what for many people is a substantial change. It's one thing to read the cold numbers, statistics, demographics and percentages of real-life gay and interracial twosomes, but seeing such couples on screen, even in the context of a commercial or a fictional TV show, makes it more authentic.

Media representation and inclusion gives legitimacy to minority populations and builds a healthy multicultural society. That's the power of popular culture and the cultivation effect. The role of race in *Columbo* may be small, but the role of racial acceptance may be significant.

In *Columbo: Make Me a Perfect Murder*, Amelie Hastie notes that it was a conscious decision for *Columbo* not to have black villains. Per her discussions with William Link, "They [Levinson and Link] felt that television was too replete with representations of African-Americans as criminals. They didn't want to suggest that there were not rich black people in Beverly Hills, but they wanted to disentangle African-Americans from violence on television."[2]

But some have found the lack of black killers in Seventies *Columbo* an affront. "Not having a black actor play the role of a killer was a failure to recognize African-American contributions to TV and film;" "The height of racism here projected by the creators of this program. The theory behind the show is that the major character is 'more' prominent than Columbo and potentially more intelligent in his/her delivery. So the America in which this was first delivered didn't accommodate for a famous AA trying to outwit the sometimes wily Lieutenant;" "He [Peter Falk] never had blacks on his show playing co-star. He had pull, he could've made it happen but he DIDN'T & that was in the 1970's??!!"[3]

Such criticisms (from the Lt. Columbo Forum of the Ultimate Columbo Site) are well-intentioned, but lack the context of Link's desire to avoid stereotyping any black person as a killer. Those commenters are also likely unaware that Levinson and Link developed *Tenafly* in 1973, starring African-American and *Columbo* supporting actor James McEachin.

Eight months after its own pilot movie, the first episode of *Tenafly* debuted as part of the NBC Wednesday Mystery Movie, exactly one day after the TV version of *Shaft*, making them the first dramatic series headlining a solo African-American protagonist. Hastie's book devotes several pages to champion Levinson and Link's portrayal of a middle-class black private detective, where race is a frequent element of the show. Furthermore, they had it written into their deal with NBC that *Tenafly* would have at least one African-American writer.[4]

Beyond the specific argument made by detractors that there were surely rich, black L.A. killers that *Columbo* avoided, there's a broader point being made about African-American representation in the show's universe. The issue is worth pursuing. Its cultural clout allows *Columbo* to be used as one barometer of black portrayal in popular entertainment, even if it's merely to see how many—or even if—black faces are shown populating the monied neighborhoods and establishments of Los Angeles. In sociology, this is called a content analysis, a simple measure that could reveal how well *Columbo* reflected the reality of integration and acceptance, circa 1971-1978.

We have to reluctantly acknowledge that the minorities we find are generally not foreground characters. But that doesn't make the analysis any less valid. As Hastie notes, "The characters are never called explicitly to represent Black identity, but their presence certainly signals the ways in which the series is implicitly entrenched in issues of race and ethnicity."[5]

We'll begin at *Columbo's* beginning, in 1968 for *Prescription: Murder*. It's an inauspicious start. In the opening scene at Dr. Flemming's swanky dinner party, there are exactly two African-American faces—a bartender and a waitress. It's probably and regrettably understandable that for the Sixties, a wealthy power clique dripping in jewels and sporting matching tuxedos at a top-floor dinner bash would have no black representation.

Today, it's easy to forget the social and cultural context in which this TV-movie debuted, a mere six months after 1967's Long Hot Summer of 150 nationwide so-called "race riots." We saw Columbo emerge from Dr. Flemming's bedroom less than two months before the assassination of Martin Luther King Jr., two months before the Civil Rights Act of 1968, four months before Bobby Kennedy was shot, eight months ahead of the Olympic Black Power protests of Tommie Smith and John Carlos, and nine months before television's first interracial kiss in *Star Trek*. The tail end of the Sixties was racially contentious, and the invitation list to the Flemming's formal bash should not be surprising.

Before we continue, let's allow that there will be readers who object to what they may feel are the nit-picky elements of any race-counting exercise. The observations here are merely to see how well *Columbo* reflects an American city becoming more integrated in the 1970s. Unfortunately, we have to concede that we will be limited to discussing the African-American population. Although the Hispanic-Mexican demographic was statistically larger, in the scenes that are described herein, there was no significant representation for Hispanics or Latinos. This includes depictions of the LAPD, which didn't begin substantial hiring of Hispanics until the Eighties and later, with the creation of the 1991 Christopher Commission.[6]

There is, however, a blink-and-you'll-miss-it moment in *A Stitch in Crime* that does acknowledge the wider population beyond Caucasian representation. It's in the opening credits, as Dr. Heideman (Will Geer) is rushed on a gurney into the Los Angeles hospital where he works with evil Dr. Mayfield (Leonard Nimoy). The shot begins in the foreground with a black man in a sling, and two older Asian-Americans are behind him. The camera switches to a Hispanic woman with two young sons, panning to a man with a head wound bandage and a small Hispanic girl. The scene is all of six seconds, and is the clearest depiction of a population beyond white/black in Seventies *Columbo*.[7]

Fast forwarding to the Seventies, there is fortunately more than enough evidence that African-Americans do indeed inhabit the world of *Columbo*. Scanning through each episode's scenes and quantitatively coding those with multiple players in staged settings or on-location, there is clear confirmation of diversity.

Judging from the attendance at his post-murder dinner social, Dr. Mayfield of *A Stitch in Crime* may be wicked, but he at least seems to have a number of African-American friends and co-workers. We view a black doctor, nurses and surgery attendants at Mayfield's hospital. In *Identity Crisis*, international spy Nelson Brenner entertains a black contingent of foreign dignitaries at his own carefree pool party. Earlier, in filming at the Pike Amusement area in Long Beach, there's plenty of racial representation seen during the stroll-along with Geronimo (Leslie Nielsen).

African-Americans may not be many, but they are viewed going to magic shows, on ocean cruises, at publishers' parties, participating in War Room exercises, and waiting in line at the city offices of Building and Safety. They are on Beth Chadwick's inquest jury and at her advertising agency. They attend the hip metro art shows, are on the board of directors at Stanford Chemical in *Short Fuse*, are brainy members of the L.A. Sigma Society, and are seen in the sea of hats at Abigail Mitchell's posh luncheon function.

Those are just a few examples of *Columbo's* ethnic integration. Rewatching these episodes today, we take this diversity for granted. But it's not perfect. We see no black detectives working for Investigator Brimmer, no African-Americans at Veronica Bryce's belly-dancing class, none at Viveca Scott's fat farm, they're not working out at Milo Janus' pricey gym, and they don't hear Salvatore De Fonte's speech at the *Identity Crisis* businessman's luncheon.

We should also note the settings where black faces are not blatantly *over*represented—the downtown housing shelter of *Negative Reaction* and daytime bar patrons of *A Friend in Deed*. And after Dr. Flemming's 1968 glitzy soiree, the most glaring example of African-American waitering happens at Dr. Kepple's pre-murder caviar spread. Unfortunately, the stereotype of black maid and butler servitude is painfully present at the Chadwick mansion of *Lady in Waiting*.

Statistically, African-Americans were 11.7 percent of the American population in 1970, a figure that rose through the decade to 28 percent. Zeroing in on Los Angeles, however, the black populace remained steady between 17 percent and 18 percent.[8] While *Columbo's* representation of black citizens would appear to fall a slight bit short of that, the goal here is emphatically not to play a numbers game that points fingers exposing those instances where *Columbo* might under-represent African-Americans. That's far off the point. It's simply to use Classic *Columbo* as, on balance, a model of pop culture's attempts to address diversity. It does.

And statistics don't inform the whole story. Certainly, there were wealthy black homeowners in the neighborhoods of *Columbo*. But the report "Prismatic Metropolis: Race and Residential Segregation in the City of Angels" examines why this number may not have been substantial. "Residential segregation is, at least in part, a socioeconomic phenomenon. However, studies have consistently shown that black-white segregation does not vary appreciably by economic status: *affluent blacks are just as segregated from whites as poor blacks.*"[9] [Emphasis mine]

Even as Los Angeles' population increased through the Seventies, what the report's authors term the "index of racial dissimilarity" remained exceptionally high. (Their index of 100 is total black-white segregation. In 1970 L.A. it was 91, in 1980 it was 81.[10]) If we're looking at how *Columbo* reflects efforts at integration, the flip side is that it can also reflect the reality of residential segregation.

There's another obvious place to look for black representation, and that's in the Los Angeles Police Department. In 1972, 5 percent of the city's officers were black. This percentage rose only nominally through the Classic *Columbo* decade, reaching 10 percent in 2019. So at most, at any given moment, one in 10 members of the LAPD were African-American.[11]

This figure compares quite favorably with the percentages of black officers at *Columbo* crime scenes and police headquarters. It didn't begin that way. There were none amongst the gaggle of at least nine white officers crowding the *Murder by the Book* search of Jim Ferris' office space. But subsequently, black uniformed officers, detectives, photographers and fingerprint experts were routinely seen in the crime scene foregrounds and backgrounds of Seventies *Columbo* episodes. It's easy today to take for granted the African-American detectives we see at these murder scenes. In the early Seventies, these were casting choices that did not have to be made, yet were.

Regrettably, though, Classic *Columbo* never had a meaningful black role for a crimefighting cohort, ala Sergeant Kramer. One finally appears in the revival's *Undercover*. Waiting until 1994 was a missed opportunity to push this representation envelope, but not the only one.

Substantial black characters were only rarely seen in the series' original episodes. Lawrence Melville, aka Steinmetz's underling of *Identity Crisis* (Otis Young), is a memorable agitated hospital patient, and in *Short Fuse*, Roger Stanford (Roddy McDowall) sarcastically praises David Bucker's assistant Quincy (Lawrence Cook) as "the best combination of chauffeur and private detective in the business."

Two of the better roles went to one actor, James McEachin. In *Make Me a Perfect Murder*, he was projectionist Walter Muirhead, returning to *Columbo* in 1978 after four Mystery Wheel episodes of *Tenafly*. But in *Etude in Black*, he was the rare African-American in a position of more decision and authority, as Alex Benedict's assistant William. Hastie's book notes that the character was specifically crafted by writer Steven Bochco to be "the assistant conductor, a black man."[12]

There are three episodes where race representation deserves a bit more scrutiny. In *Swan Song*, Tommy Brown (Johnny Cash) and the Last Soul Crusaders are a country gospel act whose favorite crowd-pleaser is "I Saw the Light," originally done by Hank Williams in 1948. In the episode, viewers may be mildly surprised to see a full 12-person gospel chorus without any black members at all.

But this highlights a feature of the Southern gospel/country gospel field. Its roots are in Christian music and the traditions of white musicians from the South, also identified as a subgenre of both country and gospel music. The name Southern Gospel was used to differentiate it from what was referred to as Black Gospel, a genre with traditions in the conversion of enslaved Africans to Christianity. The song "I Saw the Light' is itself specifically identified as

JAMES MCEACHIN was always a welcome presence on *Columbo* and other TV shows, playing characters who were solid, reliable, middle-class contributors. *(Photo from Tenafly)*

a "white spiritual," and there are in fact distinct musical differences that developed between the black and white spirituals.[13]

In *Swan Song*, partly filmed at an actual Johnny Cash concert, the audience for "I Saw the Light" looks to be entirely white. Later, Cash and wife June Carter performed the song in 1975 for Dinah Shore's daytime variety show *Dinah!*, where the band and singers were also white.

But the racial composition is different for a song identified as a black spiritual, "When the Saints Go Marching In."[14] This was performed on *The*

Johnny Cash Show in 1971 as a rousing conclusion to a special gospel edition of the program titled "Make a Joyful Noise." Cash was joined by a bevy of African-American artists, including Mahalia Jackson, the Staple Singers, and the Edwin Hawkins Singers.[15] It would appear that the dozen white gospel singers we see in *Columbo* are not a casting decision but a musical one.

Although the fictional Haynes Military Academy was presumably near Los Angeles, The Citadel in Charleston, South Carolina, doubled for the facility in 1974's *By Dawn's Early Light*. It wasn't until 1966 that the all-white Military College became desegregated, and there were never more than two black cadets per class until 1969. In 1971, 14 members of the campus African-American Society protested fans flying the Confederate flag at Citadel football games, while Southern anthem "Dixie" remained the school's fight song, adopted in the 1950s to protest court desegregation decisions.

Despite efforts, the Confederate flag remains on display at The Citadel's Summerall Chapel as of this writing. The South Carolina Heritage Act of 2000 forbids removal of memorials deemed as an honor display, and the confederate banner was gifted to the chapel in 1939. As the school officially states, "The South Carolina Attorney General stated previously that the college was following state law by treating the flag as a memorial that falls under the Heritage Act. If the law changes, The Citadel will act in accordance with that change."[16]

Per David Koenig's *Shooting Columbo*, *By Dawn's Early Light* was filmed at the college during a summer break with 227 cadet non-speaking extras. With The Citadel's minimal diversity in 1974, it will come as no surprise that in the chapel, mess hall, inspection and dormitory scenes, close viewing reveals the presence of precisely one African-American face. *Columbo's* production team most likely couldn't do much about that. [Although why "Dixie" remains in the episode's background band soundtrack for this fictional California school is a mystery!]

But the most racially problematic of all Classic *Columbo* scenes comes from *Ransom for a Dead Man*. Early on, we see villainous lawyer Leslie Williams in court, ostensibly to demonstrate to viewers her brilliance and cunning as a formidable adversary for Columbo. An older black man on the witness stand is testifying to back injuries sustained in an accident, and as the camera pans left, we see an all-white jury. Williams has a whispered consultation with her associate, pleased to tell him, "We have a nice middle-class jury. Their dislike for insurance companies is second only to their distaste for working class people."

Cross-examining the injured man, Williams is quick to ask, "Mr. Crowell, have you ever been on welfare before?" The prosecutor's objection is sustained, but of course, not before the Caucasian jury hears the question, with its blatant insinuation. It's established that the accident occurred from falling down a set of stairs at an apartment house, prior to which the man had been in a café across the street. "In point of fact… you had at least three drinks and no dinner before you left the café and returned to your apartment, and, not being able to see the stairwell steps properly, you fell." The prosecutor objects again: "The plaintiff alleges the stairs were improperly lit." To which Williams immediately snarks, "Although the plaintiff may well have been." This gets a hearty chuckle from the jury, and a sly smirk from the amoral attorney.

As court adjourns, Williams tells her client, "I'll get your insurance company off the hook cheaply this time." She then turns to an older white man and admonishes, "I've been all over that building of yours, and you better start maintaining minimum safety standards or the next time somebody may get killed."

Hindsight opens our eyes to the implicit racial bias in this now-borderline unpleasant scene. Tellingly, the original script for this episode from Levinson, Link (story) and Dean Hargrove (teleplay) made no mention at all of the race of the plaintiff.[17] Somewhere in the production process, it was decided to cast an African-American in the role. With this in mind, I have no doubt that years later, all involved would have loved to have this back for a rewrite. The presence of several black men in the courtroom gallery for this case with an African-American plaintiff supports the strong conjecture that the apartment building is a predominantly black housing unit. That would make the older white male owning the deplorably-maintained building a traditional rich, white slumlord.

In the context of the episode's plot, it makes sense to show us that Williams is an unscrupulous attorney by directly linking her to a corrupt client. Injecting dog-whistle black stereotypes into the questioning might also be defensible if its goal is to show that Williams is a Machiavellian tactician in the courtroom, an opponent whom Columbo needs to heed closely (and stay out of airplanes with).

But couldn't such a purpose also be shown with a case that doesn't bust open a racial can of worms? The episode was several years before presidential candidate Ronald Reagan introduced the lazy, manipulative "welfare queen" stereotype into his speeches, but the intent of Williams' questioning is crystal clear. Add to this the intimation of alcoholism at the café. Being across the street from black housing, the place would also likely have a predominantly black clientele, so the ugly stereotype of the idle, boozing, grifting African-

American is complete.

The jury is composed entirely of older whites who, especially in 1971, would be particularly receptive to this racial labelling, as their quick laughter in response to Williams' quip confirms. Her explanation of their "distaste for working class people" might have been intended as subtle, but in the context of subsequent questioning, doesn't appear subtle at all—substitute "black" for "working class" and that clearly nails it.

That the jury would side with the slumlord is a foregone conclusion after Williams' joke is received so warmly. It raises the question of why the Columboverse prosecutor would let the jury composition become so skewed with affluent-appearing whites on the far side of 40 in a case involving an injured black man at an African-American apartment building.

The answer, of course, is simple. The whole scene reflects the reality and acceptance of 1971 racial stereotyping in the Los Angeles legal system. Accordingly, the scene also reflects the willingness of that era's viewers to accept the entire premise without complaint. In 1971, even intelligent and discerning *Columbo* fans were complicit in concurring with a racial stereotype that would become archaic and distasteful in later years. For television writers at the time, such scenes were not created to actively parade racial hostility. It was, regrettably, just business-as-usual for early-Seventies racial awareness. Williams' scolding the slumlord to literally clean up his act is meant to soften any damage to her character that comes from resorting to racial tropes to prevail.

Again, I recognize that apologists for this scene might argue that it shows how devious and unconscionable a killer Williams is. And sure, that ties into Columbo's Gotcha trick, exposing her lack of scruples in assuming that her late husband's daughter Margaret would stay silent for a suitcase full of cash. But there are any number of courtroom scenarios that could get this accomplished without falling back on racial typecasting. At a bare minimum, the scene is racially insensitive. At worst, it gives us the problematic side of *Columbo's* 1971 reflection upon race, integration and civil rights in Seventies cities.

In at least one instance, an episode's transition from script to screen softened an otherwise troublesome racial stereotype. Earlier, the bubbling-under racial animus of Detective Doyle was observed in *A Friend in Deed*. But this was not a feature of the Peter S. Fischer script of January 3, 1974. Four months before airing, the dynamic between Doyle and Al Como, the volunteer worker from Holcome House, was quite different.

Fischer's description is direct: "Al is mid-thirties, black and very ominous-looking." A patrolman is bringing him to Columbo and Doyle, and Al exclaims, "Keep your hands to yourself, pig." For 21st century readers, this fairly jumps off the script page. Doyle questions Como with, "Where were you at 7:30, fella?" When Como says that he was at Holcome House, Doyle asks, "You can prove that?" and Columbo tells Doyle to let him go. Doyle obediently replies, "Yes, sir."

The filmed version of the scene goes in a different direction. Como is played by character actor Albert Popwell, who is described on his IMDb page as "handsome [and] leanly built," hardly the "very ominous-looking" original casting recommendation. The "pig" line disappears. Como nervously surveys the murder site, realizing what he's just stepped into. Doyle's response is to provoke him with, "Relax, huh? You're making me nervous."

Como says, "The way things look around here, I'd like to get outta here, that's all." Doyle replies coldly, "I bet you would." Thanks to Doyle's microaggressions, Como's attitude is hardening as the innocent man says that he can prove that he was at Holcome House. Again, from sarcastic Doyle, "I bet you can." Columbo, observing the back-and-forth, has had enough. He tells Doyle to let Como go, and Doyle looks about to object, but has no response to the direct order.[18]

The Lieutenant is on the scene to stop the harassment of Como for volunteering while black. In *Columbo: Paying Attention 24/7*, David Martin-Jones notes, "It is as if Columbo reassures viewers that racial profiling by the police is not an issue as long as he is around."[19] Too bad Columbo couldn't be at every Seventies L.A. crime scene.

Columbo began in 1968 at an elegant dinner party and ended in 2003 at a city rave. As you watch *Prescription: Murder* again, it is up to you to decide if it means anything that the fancy dinner shindig of Dr. Flemming's only had black faces as bartender and waitress. At the very least, it was reflecting the reality of African-American visibility in 1968 upper-crust Los Angeles. And the black faces we see at the closing rave of *Columbo Likes the Nightlife* tell us that things were racially much different at the show's farewell in 2003.

There remains no valid sociological study of the Cultivation Effect with respect to Classic *Columbo* and racial issues. We can only speculate that black representation could have played a positive role in the growing acceptance of diversity in the era. *Columbo* was a product of its time, and as with other social issues, the show's significance in pop culture history allows it to hold a unique mirror up to the racial realities of Seventies Los Angeles.

5.
Murder for the Whole Family

WALTER MUIRHEAD: You got any opinions on violence on television?
COLUMBO: Well, I work nights.
– *Make Me a Perfect Murder* (1978)

One of the enduring traits that we learn about Columbo early on is that he doesn't carry a gun. In what was designed as the first series episode in 1971, *Death Lends a Hand*, co-creators Link and Levinson, establish this when Columbo fails to set off the ultra-sophisticated metal detector at Brimmer Investigations headquarters.

Columbo's declaration that he's not packing a pistol gets a bemused chuckle from Brimmer's personal secretary. No doubt, she's well aware that the company's investigators all have them (heck, maybe she has one too). As Brimmer's underling gives Columbo the guided tour, he takes him to their shooting range, where a private eye is getting in some practice time, and is told, "Every one of our operatives is a skilled marksman." But he quickly adds, "Actually, our policy is to avoid the use of the weapon." Whew!

Indeed, guns are almost literally the very first thing we see and hear in the episode's opening credits, as Brimmer himself is blasting away with 12 target practice shots before declaring of the weapon, "This one's as crooked as a dog's hind leg." Those 12 shots were intended to be the launch of NBC's brand new *Columbo* TV series. And those 12 shots are by far the most gunplay we'd ever see and hear in Classic *Columbo*.

With this scene and this episode, Link and Levinson are setting up the contrast of *Columbo* with every other police detective in both the real and fictional world. It satisfies the pair's literary sensibilities, it helps furnish Columbo with a distinguishing trait over his TV rivals, and it provides a contrast to the ongoing violence in the streets of Seventies America. In these ways, the show's statements about guns may rarely be overt, but they do have an intersection with the era's social culture.

Following *Death Lends a Hand*, we discover that not only does Columbo eschew carrying a gun, he actively hates them. He says so, twice, in 1975's *Troubled Waters* and *Playback*. Link and Levinson certainly wanted us to understand that this would be one TV detective who would choose not to do his investigating with a firearm on his hip.[1] After all, *Columbo* was created as more drawing-room mystery than police procedural, and did Miss Marple ever carry a gun?

As we know, this is the Columboverse, so his unlikely decision to go weapon-less provokes barely a ripple in the course of the series among the LAPD (although not entirely unquestioned, as we shall see). Reviewing *Death Lends a Hand*, though, we never get an explanation from Columbo's early character development about exactly why he fails to carry. There's certainly plenty of opportunity to do so as he's told that all the Brimmer operatives are crack shots, and as he marvels at the Brimmer metal detector. But it wouldn't be until four years later that we find out that he actually hates guns.

For that matter, we never get a clear picture of exactly why he hates guns. Is it for personal, practical or philosophical reasons? A check of internet message boards related to the topic will find those who insist that this is a political, anti-gun decision by *Columbo* producers to convince viewers of the moral depravity of gun ownership.

This is never directly explored in *Columbo*. However, extreme online trolling aside, there is at least a grain of truth to this perspective. Link and Levinson were, in fact, no cheerleaders for gun use. Although they were not active in working on *Columbo* after the show's initial season, their story idea for *Death Lends a Hand* did plant the seed for the Lieutenant's lack of a firearm. It was after they left the show, in 1974, when they would collaborate on an ABC TV-movie, *The Gun*.

The movie follows the dramatic path of a freshly-minted .38 caliber special as it changes hands from owner to owner. It was marketed with a press release which looked to publicize the consequences of American handgun use. As the *New York Times* quoted, "Every four minutes someone in the United States is killed or wounded by gunfire. Every three minutes, someone is robbed at gunpoint. A new handgun is sold on the average of every 13 seconds. Used handguns are traded at the rate of one every 30 seconds." The *Times* review, however, was disappointed with the resulting film. "It is oddly muted, as if Mr. Levinson and Mr. Link were mining to anticipate inevitable objections from the powerful gun lobbies. Compromise, in this case, proves counterproductive."[2]

Columbo may not like guns, but he's not entirely uninformed about them. He does confide to General Hollister (Eddie Albert) in *Dead Weight* that he's not a ballistics expert. But he's knowledgeable about caliber converters in *Double Exposure*. He understands the physics of using a .22 in *Ransom for a Dead Man* when he explains to Leslie Williams, "What if he wanted to fire into someone and be reasonably certain that the bullet didn't have the velocity to go through the body?"

The only time that we ever see Columbo shoot a gun, it's for the sound experiment at the Harold Van Wick estate in *Playback*, a test that the Lieutenant reassures a skeptical Van Wick he's done before. In *Troubled Waters*, he knows not to use a pencil to pick up a gun by the barrel for potential evidence, as "the pencil can ruin the grooves, and if you disturb the grooves, it would make a match with the bullet very difficult." [Unfortunately, both he and Captain Gibbons identify this murder weapon as a "British Weatherby," when the Weatherby is an American make, unlike the British "Webley" models].

Perhaps Columbo is simply afraid of guns. In *Playback*, he is carrying out his noise experiment with killer Van Wick, and Columbo asks for the revolver from the officer present. "Is this loaded?" he hesitantly asks, and wonders if the safety catch is on or off. When told it is on, Columbo nervously asks the beat cop to take it off. He suggests that Van Wick might want to put his fingers in his ears. "I can handle it," says Van Wick. "I wish I could say the same," is the reply. We should allow that as with many behaviors of Columbo, this seeming anxiety and ignorance about gun basics and safety protocols may just be a feint to lull the murderer into underestimating him and continue to give him a false sense of security.

Maybe Columbo is embarrassed. He tells Hayden Danziger that he's a bad shot in *Troubled Waters*, and the same to his policeman buddy Harris in *Forgotten Lady*. It's in the latter episode where we learn that Columbo hasn't been range-tested in 10 years, another advantage of policing in the Columboverse. But this time, there is some pushback from Columbo's superiors, who demand that he meet the every-six-months shooting standard, lest he have his license pulled. (Are they aware of this man's ability to solve murder cases?) In addition, Columbo is warned that he could get busted for not having his weapon on him.

With the help of a pricey $5 bribe, Harris will take the practice test for Columbo. And that, seemingly, ends that. In retrospect, however, this subplot ties into the central moral question that Columbo faces in the episode. He knows that Grace Wheeler (Janet Leigh) has murdered her husband, but an inoperable brain aneurysm will kill her in two months, and has rendered her incapable of remembering her role in the crime. He allows Grace's love, Ned Diamond, to cop to the murder instead, and expects that once Grace passes away, he can be cleared. Columbo has chosen to bend the means of justice in pursuit of a noble end, a result foreshadowed by his own bending of the rules on taking his shooting test.

This unique episode is part of an extended run of *Columbos* which aired between February and November of 1975. Of the six episodes in this time frame, four of them had explicit references to Columbo's refusal to carry a gun or his ineptitude in using it. Three of these have been noted above: *Troubled Waters*, *Playback* and *Forgotten Lady*. To this, we can add *Identity Crisis*, in which Columbo affirms that he does not have a gun as he is patted down by C.I.A. spies before a meeting with The Director.

These four episodes in a 10-month span do much to establish Columbo's history, or lack thereof, with guns. Is it a coincidence that these episodes, and almost no others, highlight this character quirk? Looking at an issue embroiling Hollywood and the broadcast industry in 1975, perhaps not. For context, though, we first have to return to the Sixties and the continual sparring over a cultural flashpoint—violence on television.

The late Sixties was prime hand-wringing time for American critics' anxieties about the media's effects upon its consumers, particularly children. This was not a new concern. In 1952, a Senate subcommittee met to discuss the issue, prompted by fears of youngsters imitating action scenes from *The Adventures of Superman*. Two years later, a Senate subcommittee exploring the causes of juvenile delinquency looked to comic books and television for its answer. An exchange between Committee Chairman Senator Estes Kefauver and comics publisher William Gaines is illustrative of the times.

SEN. KEFAUVER: Here is your May issue. This seems to be a man with a bloody ax holding a woman's head up which has been severed from her body. Do you think that's in good taste?

GAINES: Yes sir, I do—for the cover of a horror comic. A cover in bad taste, for example, might be defined as holding her head a little higher so that blood could be seen dripping from it and moving the body a little further over so that the neck of the body could be seen to be bloody.

KEFAUVER (doubtful): You've got blood coming out of her mouth.

GAINES: A little.[3]

The same subcommittee met again in 1964 after three years of study. Comics were out, TV was in. They found that "television programs which feature excessive violence tended to: stimulate aggressive actions among normal viewers, motivate those already under stress to release their hostility, reinforce existing overly aggressive attitudes, encourage imitation of aggressive actions by exposure, produce acceptance of aggression as a 'normal' way of life, and instill the adverse effects of violent scenes which are not eradicated by traditional endings of 'good' overcoming 'evil.'"

The committee specifically cited *The Untouchables* and *Route 66*. They produced statistics showing that between 1954 and 1961, the number of television programs featuring violence and crime during popular viewing hours increased from 16.6 to 50.6 percent. This all sounds quite scientific, but these results were tracked by members and staffers of the subcommittee themselves, hardly impartial observers.[4]

One can trace debate over the issue of media violence back to Greek philosopher Plato, who was concerned about the effects of inappropriate poetry on youth. But instead, we'll jump ahead to 1968, when the issue of televised violence was met with its most explosive furor.

It was years in the making, as events in the United States jelled to create a cauldron of unrest, protest and discord. Disturbing images of the Vietnam conflict had been broadcast nightly to television news audiences, and protests against the war often turned violent. Anti-war clashes were matched with civil rights disturbances in 1967, when the so-called Long Hot Summer yielded over 150 racial clashes in cities across America. In 1968, the Democratic National Convention in Chicago was a focal point for youth rioting and massive media attention. The assassinations of Martin Luther King, Jr. and Robert Kennedy only added to the ugly tone and mounting panic over how to stop what seemed to be an unending, limitless escalation of American violence.

So once again, fingers pointed at television. Being free, available to all, and with only a few channels to choose from pre-cable, the issue was low-hanging fruit for alarmist culture warriors who demanded that networks limit the amount of violence on their shows. The issue was, of course, political catnip. "Hearings on the Mass Media" convened before the newly-formed National Commission on the Causes and Prevention of Violence in October and December of 1968, soon after the February debut of *Prescription: Murder*.

The hearings offer some fascinating sparring between Congressional committee members and television network executives, forced to defend their programming practices in the face of public concerns and spotty "evidence."

First Amendment rights, the free market of ideas, staged news, the Three Stooges, hypnosis research, violence sensitivity, and riot coverage all get attention. Congressman Hale Boggs of Louisiana was a particular antagonist, railing against Saturday morning cartoons and anything resembling "murder, rape, mayhem, sadism, [and] masochism."[5] This becomes a recurring theme.

The disconnect is painfully apparent as one executive, Leonard Goldenson of ABC, tried valiantly to explain to Boggs what a "plot" was.

BOGGS: What do you think about those examples [inserting "broads, bosoms and fun" into a show]?
GOLDENSON: Well, I believe that if it is done just for that particular reason and is not in furtherance of a plot, I would think—
BOGGS: You talking about a political plot, or what?
GOLDENSON: No, a plot of a particular program. I would think it would be definitely wrong.
BOGGS: You mean if this is done just because it had a plot or was an adventure series, it would be all right?
GOLDENSON: Not at all.
BOGGS: That is what you just said.
GOLDENSON: I said I think if there is something in furtherance of a plot, it might be judged in that [way]."[6]

Boggs and his team assembled what they claimed was evidence of violence, which the broadcasters countered was only viewer surveys and sociological opinions. Boggs gave us some insight into his own views, with his spontaneous review of one particular show. "I watched *Gunsmoke* many times. It is a good program. It is all right because the good guy always wins and he uses justice even-handedly. He doesn't use sadism and the other things. And he is a law enforcement officer. Quite a guy, Marshall Dillon, incidentally."[7]

Two shows in particular earned the ire of the committee. One was ABC's *The Avengers*, the British spy series starring Patrick McNee and a series of female partners. The *Christian Science Monitor* created a figurative scorecard that recorded "every violent incident and threat of violence as it was shown" and found that it narrowly edged out the other most offending piece of television entertainment, CBS' *The Wild Wild West*.[8]

Fans of television can immediately spot the obvious similarity between these two programs—they are fantasy spoofs, not to be taken seriously in any way. That subtlety was apparently lost on the committee, whose foremost member Boggs continued to parrot his code words that defined what he wanted to eliminate from TV.

BOGGS: The constant subjection, first to children, of violent scenes that have no connection with morality, that portray murder and mayhem and sadism simply to portray them—
FRANK STANTON (CBS): Let's take it easy. Let's be sure we are talking about the schedule of the CBS Television Network. We don't have sadism in the television network schedule. We have six programs in prime time that have—
BOGGS: *Wild Wild West* does.
STANTON: Then your definition is different than ours.[9]

And the definition of "violence" is key. As one media website explains, "The reality is that we have not yet successfully defined violence and aggression, whether when analyzing the content we consume, or investigating the potentially resultant aggressive behavior. Because individual studies define these notions differently, the goal posts are constantly moving for anyone who is trying to get a big picture look at the situation."[10]
In one definition from the Mediascope National TV Survey, violence is "any overt depiction of a credible threat of physical force or the actual use of such force intended to physically harm an animate being or group of beings." *Wild Wild West* producers, eager to avoid triggering politicos, attached this memo to a shooting script: "Note to Directors: The producer respectfully asks that no violent acts be shot which are not depicted in the script or discussed beforehand.... Most particularly stay away from gratuitous ad-libs, such as slaps, pointing of firearms or other weapons at characters (especially in close quarters), kicks and the use of furniture and other objects in fight scenes."[11]
Throwing a bone to the nay-sayers, CBS cancelled *West* before the next round of committee hearings in spring of 1969. It certainly wasn't because of blood and gore; too much gun-pointing and too many barroom brawls sealed its fate. Two months later, *The Avengers* joined them on the cancellation scrap heap.
With this backdrop, *Columbo* came on the air as a series in 1971. But the issue continued to enflame critics, especially after release of a 1972 report from the U.S. Surgeon General's Scientific Advisory Committee on Television and Social Behavior. The report found a relation between viewing violence on television and aggressive behavior "under certain circumstances." But the report also warned that "the accumulated evidence does not warrant the conclusion that televised violence has a uniformly adverse effect on the majority of children. It cannot even be said that the majority of the children

in the studies we have reviewed showed an increase in aggressive behavior in response to the violent acts to which they were exposed. The evidence does indicate that televised violence may lead to increased aggressive behavior in certain subgroups of children."[12]

In other words, the study was inconclusive. The mere hint of a causal relationship, however, was all that television violence critics needed to hear as they continued to press for changes in programming. The brushfire was stoked in September 1974 with the broadcast of an NBC TV-movie, *Born Innocent*, with Linda Blair. The highly publicized film depicted the sexual and psychological abuse of a teenage girl, showing uncharacteristically graphic content, including a controversial rape scene. Four days later, a San Francisco copycat assault sparked a lawsuit against NBC. The network was eventually absolved of responsibility, but in the heat of the moment, the role of television in fomenting violence was once again in the crosshairs.

Under such pressures, four months later in January 1975, Federal Communications Commission Chairman Richard Wiley forged an agreement with the network heads to limit programs that contained violent behavior, and created the Family Viewing Hour. From 8-9 p.m. each evening, the networks agreed to only show programs suitable to a general family viewing audience. The individual networks, though, would be the ones determining what would constitute inappropriate programming.

It was clearly serendipitous that *Troubled Waters*, with its lead character announcing, "I hate guns," was filming in October of 1974, just before Wiley was hatching his Family Hour plan with the networks. But is it a coincidence that as the Family Viewing Hour continued through the 1975-1976 prime time television season, *Columbo* continued to reference the firearms topic?

Consider that Season 4 of *Columbo* (1974-1975) had aired on Sundays beginning at 8:30. Now, for Season 5, it was bumped to 9 p.m., seemingly in response to fears that the NBC Sunday Mystery Movie might ruffle too many feathers in the Family Hour, if not for *Columbo*, then perhaps for its other, more gun-happy series. For that season, this included the usual *McCloud* and *McMillan & Wife*, but also added Tony Curtis as *McCoy*, a con man who set up elaborate bunco games ala *The Sting* (still fresh in the minds of 1973 moviegoers).

So what was the first episode that *Columbo* aired in this new 9 p.m. time period directly after the Family Hour? *Forgotten Lady*, naturally. Writer Bill Driskill weaves Columbo's gun avoidance nicely into the main murder plot, but one also wonders if it was created as a pointed and specific reaction to contemporaneous events. It's also worth noting that Driskill was the writer

1974's *Born Innocent* starring Linda Blair was the highest-rated TV-movie of 1974. Its controversial shower scene was excised from repeat showings.

behind *Troubled Waters* and *Identity Crisis* as well.

The Family Viewing Hour was under fire almost immediately, and in late 1975, a lawsuit brought by producer Norman Lear and others aimed to bring the policy to court. Lear's *All in the Family* was one of the most affected programs, as CBS was compelled to move it from its headlining spot at 8 p.m. Saturday (back when Saturday nights was a major broadcast evening). The argument of the litigants was that because the policy emanated from the head of the FCC, a government agency, it amounted to unconstitutional government censorship.

This time, hearings were convened in July and August 1976, and Lear was joined by Hollywood heavyweights like former *M*A*S*H* producer Larry

Gelbart and *Star Trek* creator Gene Roddenberry. The Family Viewing Hour had been in effect for almost a year, and Lear called it "nothing more than a smokescreen and a public relations ploy."[13]

Lear described how his *The Jeffersons* was censored by CBS over George Jefferson saying, "Get out of here, sucker!" to get a man to leave his home. "One of the least American solutions [to the violence issue] is the Family Hour, born behind closed doors, pretending to be something it isn't, leaving confusion, obfuscation and censorship in its wake."[14]

There were proponents for the Hour, of course. Said one, "There is much evidence that programs are successful if they offer the audience an opportunity to enjoy itself, perhaps even learn something, and accomplish it all within the boundaries of decency and good taste." Thank you, Mr. Bill Cosby.[15] And actor/director Cornel Wilde gave a plug for our favorite detective in contending that "shows like *Mary Tyler Moore* can be viewed with delight by both adults and children. I think that strong dramatic shows like *Columbo* are possible, too, depending on subject matter and treatment."[16]

Three months later, in November of 1976, Lear was successful, as a federal judge ruled that the Family Viewing Hour was unconstitutional. It immediately became void, but the networks were already into their 1976-1977 programming calendar, so many of those shows stayed on track into the new year. The networks moved forward for the following season, 1977-1978, without the Family Viewing Hour to officially hinder their scheduling. Meanwhile, a *Columbo* episode was filming in August and September of 1977 that would revisit the whole issue and become, in a way, the most violent *Columbo* of all.

In *Make Me a Perfect Murder*, TV executive Kay Freestone (Trish Van Devere) revenge-kills her smarmy boss and lover, Mark McAndrews (Laurence Luckinbill), moving her into his high-profile position at the CNC Network. Her murder scheme involves plugging McAndrews in his office after hours at the exact time that Kay is creating an alibi in the network's projection booth. She is there to screen a new TV-movie for company execs, and the ruse involves her making a reel change while the regular projectionist, Walter Muirhead (James McEachin) is out running an errand for her. Kay rigs the changeover to make it appear that she had to be in the projection booth at the time of the murder, rather than stalking the building's corridors to reach McAndrews and plug him.

In the course of his investigation, Columbo and the viewer learn about cue blips, a circular mark that appears very briefly in the upper right corner of the film to signal the projectionist to change reels. With several reels of film to switch in the course of a movie, the projectionist must be precise and alert to those appearances of the cue blip.

In a subplot, Kay is trying to shepherd washed-up pill-popping former child star Valerie Kirk (Lainie Kazan) through an imminent live on-air musical production, *Valerie!* Although not specified, it seems safe to assume that this family-friendly special would run at an earlier time slot in the evening's programming lineup. Unfortunately, Valerie is terrified of performing live, and self-medicates to the point of being incapacitated. Kay makes a rapid executive decision to replace the *Valerie!* musical extravaganza with the new TV-movie, as "it's the right length." Otherwise, there's no reason for the TV-movie itself to have any significance to Kay's murder plot.

Of course, all of this doesn't make this particular *Columbo* episode any more violent than any of the 44 others in the Seventies library. But the choice made by writer Robert Blees in crafting the TV-movie that fills the *Valerie!* timeslot is very significant.

The movie-within-the-movie is called *The Professional*. The original *Columbo* script rather cheekily sets up the film's premise: "The two-hour film under Kay Freestone's supervision is called *The Professional*, and deals with a man of some intelligence, named Roark, who accepts assignments that are in some countries illegal."[17] He's a hitman. This is never explicitly stated, but rather heavily implied through the visual imagery of multiple guns, Roark's handling of them, and stalking actions.

Several of these scenes are shown to the viewer, and others receive comments from the various executives present at *The Professional's* screening. "Has Standards and Practices seen this yet?" and "Not exactly the Family Hour, is it?" tell us that there's violence or impending violence involved.

Blees' shooting script describes a crucial scene as the hitman apparently prepares for suicide in his seedy hotel room. "Roark sits on the bed in the hotel—touches the pistol—strokes it. He picks it up, caresses his cheek—feels the barrel—its tactile smoothness. Then the barrel slides toward his mouth." It is this scene that projectionist Muirhead observes at the screening after he returns from his errand for Kay, immediately after she has changed the reels following her murder of McAndrews. He comments on this later with Columbo: "The first thing I see [after returning] is some guy blowing his brains out. You think that's right?"

Later, when *The Professional* is run on-air in place of *Valerie!*, Columbo sees the same thing, with an accompanying gunshot sound. Do we know if the movie actually shows "some guy blowing his brains out," or is this just a hyperbolic expression of off-screen action? It's most likely the latter. It's still

1978 network television, after all, and Columbo himself doesn't flinch or show any discernable reaction to what he sees.

The choices here are noteworthy. Blees' script did not at all require that the film-within-*Columbo* be a violent one. The key clue—the cue blip that occurs just before the hitman offs himself—could have easily been supplied in another type of movie. One could argue that it was Muirhead's strong reaction to the scene he witnessed that triggered Columbo's realization that the cue blip placement gave Kay ample time to commit the murder. Or, perhaps, it's an ironic twist where murderer Kay is brought down with a movie about a murderer.

This may be so, but the choice of *The Professional* to be a fictional movie that would challenge the CNC Networks Standards and Practices division also allows for *Columbo* producers to meta-comment on the state and nature of TV violence. Surely, a Columboverse Senate subcommittee hearing would have had a field day with a brutal assassin movie subbing in for a family-friendly musical-variety show. Alternate-reality Hale Boggs would have no doubt called it sadism.

Unlike the titular Professional, Columbo the detective won't be caressing any guns, and *Columbo* the show isn't going to display much in the way of violence beyond, you know, all the murdering. Through the Seventies, some of these are more realistic than others, some are quicker than others, all are bloodless. Those actions are essentially the only moments that weapons are drawn in *Columbo*, and its those drawn weapons that draw the attention of the committees who are counting that as violence.

Rare exceptions would include the officers who rush en masse to collar suspected killer Artie Jessup in *A Friend in Deed*; cops arriving at crime scenes (*Suitable for Framing, Candidate for Crime, Playback*); Suari security in *A Case of Immunity*; and the scripted murder attempt by the hapless actor (Fred Draper) of the latest Lieutenant Lucerne production (*Fade In to Murder*).

Clearly, this figure is lower than the real-life weapons discharges of actual LAPD officers, which totaled 584 instances in the years 1974-1978.[18] And although a full study of television shows not relying on stats from Senate committees would be necessary to confirm, one can be reasonably certain that the *Columbo* count of firearms usage is way below that of other police shows of the era.

One writer has called *Columbo* "A Study in Non-Toxic Masculinity."[19] This description doesn't come from the Seventies, of course. Toxic masculinity is a much more modern descriptor referring to concepts of manliness that perpetuate dominance and aggression, influenced by cultural pressures to behave in a particular way. Columbo's non-toxic masculinity doesn't embody overweening pride or chest-pounding, and "he's not interested in proving anything outside of who committed the murder. He has confidence in his skills but isn't afraid to admit not knowing things and asking for help or clarification." It's about compassion, humility and belief in the goodness of people (sometimes even the murderers themselves). Guns simply aren't a part of his core being. "Guns represent an end that should be avoided at all costs. The real weapons against injustice are kindness and curiosity and empathy."

Those who regard Columbo's choice to go gun-less as a political one are entitled to their opinion. There may even be an element of truth to it. But that's not the point. That's a view shaped more by current events than by contemporaneous ones. In the Seventies moment, Columbo and his creators wanted to take the gun out of his persona and temperament. This would distinguish him from his fictional cop colleagues, and the show from traditional detective/police crime fighting. It might have even served as a subtle pushback to those Senate subcommittee hearings and the Family Viewing Hour. That would be Columbo's way of saying, "Get out of here, sucker!"

6.
Deconstructing Murder and Media

COLUMBO: "[My nephew's] 15 years old, and he sold all his stereo stuff to make 8mm movies. When I was a kid in my neighborhood, we had heroes... DiMaggio, Rizzuto. You know who he's got on the wall? Francis Ford Coppola."

It was February 1978, and *Columbo* was three months shy of wrapping up the Classic Era when he shared that story about his ambitious nephew with CNC Network projectionist Walter Muirhead.

But was it about his nephew? Given the frequency with which *Columbo* has introduced us to a roll-call of relatives who may or may not exist, can we really be sure that the Lieutenant was not talking about... himself? After all, by the close of *Make Me a Perfect Murder*, Columbo is in the production booth commanding the multi-screens and directing the images to convince TV executive-killer Kay Freestone that he knows precisely how she bumped off her smug superior Mark McAndrews. Deconstructing the crime, Columbo has chosen the role of director, itself a position that constructs and, conversely, deconstructs cinema.

Breaking down complicated and well-planned murders has always been Columbo's job, and while that comes as no shocker, it may be surprising to realize just how often Columbo used the camera, television and the language of video and audio composition to assist his crime solving.

Of course, it's just fanciful speculation on my part that perhaps Columbo was talking about himself as admiring Francis Ford Coppola, who did have the acclaimed *The Godfather* and *The Godfather II* on his resume. However, it was a third Coppola movie, one that was nominated for 1974 Best Picture along with *The Godfather II*, that Columbo might have had uppermost on his mind—*The Conversation*.

In this movie, surveillance expert Harry Caul (Gene Hackman) uses an array of recording devices to construct and deconstruct an ambiguous and potentially dangerous tete-a-tete between two lovers. Meticulous perfectionist Harry spends the film trying to piece together the couple's conversation and uncover the crime, or if a crime has indeed even occurred at all. In this context, as Columbo himself has assumed the role of director to take apart and assemble the elements of his own murder investigation, referencing Francis Ford Coppola seems less of a coincidence and more of a tell.

Earlier, we looked at how *Columbo* navigated the Seventies era of *Future Shock*, interfacing with the decade's emergent technologies, scientific and social trends. Whether it was behavior control, computers, think tanks, robots, VCRs, CCTV or simple answering machines, Columbo was there to help familiarize and guide us through the then-modern world.

We noted that *Columbo* co-creators Levinson and Link planted this seed early in the show's run. For *Death Lends a Hand*, they borrowed an idea that failed them in their 1967 *Mannix* series. This was the vast detective conglomerate with banks of massive computers used to store and process a mountain of data applied to fight crime. It was quickly established that technology would be a major theme running through *Columbo*. Through this lens, it's worthwhile to sharpen the focus even more to examine the show's fascination with media technology, particularly the tools of visual study.

Columbo's attention to technology is the most convincing of the themes behind David Martin-Jones' *Columbo: Paying Attention 24/7*. For Martin-Jones, Columbo's "engagement with modernity" helped the tech-shy viewer learn how to adapt to new gadgets. The book's title comes from the surveillance-heavy *Identity Crisis*, with The Director's admonition to Columbo to "pay strict attention," a phrase that Columbo echoes back to superspy Brenner at the Gotcha.

Amelie Hastie devotes a chapter of her book to the Lieutenant's "obsessive preoccupation with gadgetry," a phrase Margaret Meadis uses to dress down her son-in-law Harold Van Wick in *Playback*. Hastie notes that Columbo "is a series that revealed a range of cultural knowledge to its viewers and that understood and taught us about the [television] medium itself... and the relation between murder and television." And "by witnessing the arrangement of murder, enabled by television... we learn how to detect its solution."[1]

I'd go a step further: In deconstructing murder, Columbo (both the

"Deconstructing Murder and Media"

A MAN COLUMBO can admire: Gene Hackman as obsessive surveillance expert Harry Caul in 1974's *The Conversation*.

show and the lieutenant) was often deconstructing media itself, and in deconstructing media, *Columbo* was the first television series to introduce and regularly practice media education.

Today, the theory and practice of media deconstruction is often taken for granted. Usually, it is described as "media literacy," a careful and close analysis of a broadcast or printed communication to understand its deeper meanings and how media messages are constructed. Taking apart a media message can reveal what's below the surface. This includes who created it, the intended audience, point of view, biases, trustworthiness, hidden values, and persuasion techniques.

In their essay "The Past, Present, and Future of Media Literacy Education," authors Renee Hobbs and Amy Jensen describe the practice of media studies "during the 1970s, [when] media literacy education began to be recognized as a critical practice of citizenship... educators, filmmakers, and media professionals began calling for the kind of transparency in media institutions that enables people to 'see how the sausage is made,' challenging the dominant representations presented in the media."

MLE is described as a crucial educational tool. "Learning to analyze news and advertising... distinguishing between propaganda, opinion and information... and exploring the ways in which violence and sexuality are depicted in media messages continue to matter as important life skills."[2] The subject was buttressed by the 1978 creation of the Association for Media

Literacy, which paved the way for more formalized instruction in critical thinking about media.

Practicing media literacy demands a healthy skepticism in analyzing visual and audio communications. The ability to skillfully examine surroundings with a critical eye makes Columbo an ideal avatar for these studies.

Media deconstruction helps us recognize how the message-maker is trying to influence us, the media consumer. Murder deconstruction allows Columbo to take apart the villain's "murder message" and recognize how the murder-maker is trying to influence him, the murder-consumer, to draw the wrong conclusion. The killer has manufactured the how, why and sometimes where of the deed. For Columbo, the careful and close analysis of the killing's little things all contribute to his own critical thinking about the event. This would include matching up the crime scene to the available facts, the scrutiny of a timeline of events, and the reactions of the suspect.

Columbo's "howcatchem" format is ideal for this type of analysis, as it breaks down a murder into the component parts that create the "how" of the crime and need to be decoded by the detective. By contrast, we would rarely see Kojak, Cannon or Baretta use such a technique to learn the truth. (Banacek would combine the whodunit with the howdunit, to lesser effect).

A great example of Columbo's murder deconstruction comes at the end of *The Bye-Bye Sky High IQ Murder Case*. For almost six minutes, Columbo engages brainiac Oliver Brandt (Theodore Bikel) with a puzzle: "Man A wants to kill Man B… it's kind of a minimum information problem, sir."

But of course, this isn't a theoretical conundrum at all, as Columbo walks Brandt through each of the intricate steps required to cover up Oliver's murder of Bertie Hastings (Sorrell Brooke). For this episode, this is required for the viewer as well, as we were not allowed to witness every precise element of the crime. So it's up to Columbo to break down exactly how the automated phonograph arm was timed to touch the clamps which would detonate the squibs, leaving Brandt to step into the Lieutenant's trap by revealing how the red marker was used to tip the mammoth dictionary to the floor, simulating a body drop.

Conveniently for us, Columbo is deconstructing a form of media, the phonograph recording, while he is deconstructing the murder. Oh, and Columbo has also deconstructed Brandt's phony-gold IQ puzzle as well. In total, it's a virtuoso 17-minute dissection. And while not every Columbo murder requires such elaborate unraveling, they do require attention to the details that will unveil how the crime was committed and which of those particulars will nail the killer.

The visual mediums of television and film were the ones most frequently deconstructed in *Columbo*. Of course, this was not the first show to use such technology in the course of crime-solving. In TV's history, you could certainly find a man with a camera—literally, *A Man with a Camera*, starring Charles Bronson in 1958. Photo gadgets of the glamorous spy genre such as cameras hidden in radios, cigarette lighters, and neckties were downscaled for tough-guy crime photographer Mike Kovac, using this basic media conveyance to get the days' hot news scoops.

And fans of *The Prisoner* were familiar with the tools of video surveillance encountered by ex-secret agent Number 6, Patrick McGoohan, as he looked for a way out of The Village in 1967-68. The obvious double meaning of the show's signature phrase, "Be seeing you," would later be invoked by McGoohan for his *Columbo* role of spymaster Brenner in *Identity Crisis*.

But there's an early use of video technology by a TV detective that has a clear *Columbo* connection. In 1965, the pilot episode for *Honey West* was spun off from *Burke's Law*, starring Anne Francis as a sexy tech-savvy private eye. Intended as the series premiere, it had some scenes re-shot and re-scored, and emerged instead as the series' 13th episode, called "The Grey Lady." But as a pilot, it would set the tone for the clever use of visual technology that Honey and her assistant Sam Bolt would employ to fight crime.

In the episode, Honey and Sam look to catch a high-end jewelry thief in the act of burgling a famous diamond from a swanky (for 1965) hotel apartment. To surveil the place, they have a miniature television camera installed—in the room's television! Honey's monitor for the closed-circuit feed is her own TV set. This makes for some meta-level banter, as we see what's going on in the bugged apartment: "A new kind of set… it watches you," "Wonder what kind of rating this show is getting?," "I'm going to spend a quiet evening at home watching television." Sam samples the action from a ground-floor van labeled "TV Service."

Television has here become both the means of watching others, as well as itself the object of watching. Honey's hidden video inexplicably has the ability to sweep around the room to follow people in motion, but that was a common cheat in movies and television at the time. Honey and Sam got the benefit of multiple camera perspectives without the inconvenience of setting up multiple cameras. As we will see in later *Columbo* episodes, the video technology that would help plot crime and uncover it would become exponentially more intricate.

The *Honey West* pilot's link to *Columbo*? While Honey herself, Anne Francis, would later guest on two *Columbos* from the Classic Era, that's not the key connection. No, this 1965 plot where we viewed the law-breaking through video machinery, where technology was complicit in the crime, and where a television set was literally used to catch the crook was written by Richard Levinson and William Link.

As the inventors of *Columbo*, Levinson and Link of course deserve the outsized credit for the show's premise, plotting template, Columbo character, guiding viewpoint, and overall aesthetic. Their early stories and teleplays lay the groundwork for the series. The Levinson and Link take on technology was crucial to *Columbo's* second pilot, *Ransom for a Dead Man*, with a machine expertly rigged to help provide Leslie Williams' murder alibi. Their perspective on Brimmer Associates' surveillance and computerized data informed *Death Lends a Hand*. And television's use as a crimefighting tool, so shrewdly observed in *Honey West*, would be echoed and expanded in their story for *Columbo's* second season debut, *Etude in Black*.

Maestro Alex Benedict (John Cassavetes) doesn't use just any ol' concert to mask his killing of Jennifer Welles. It's a TV production. Twenty-two minutes into the episode, we are introduced to the bank of monitors, varied camera angles, and multiple perspectives that the director uses to create the final televised product. In that live broadcast, there's plenty of foreshadowing, but, because *Columbo* was designed for an intelligent audience, we are not bludgeoned with clues. We see a carnation-less Benedict. We get a glimpse of the orchestra brass section, with future suspect trumpeter Paul Rifkin among them. And although we see Benedict realizing that he's missing his trademark flower, that discovery is, significantly, not part of the on-air transmission.

Episode director Nicholas Colasanto cleverly intercuts the police arrival at Welles' home with the concert soundtrack, seemingly folding this into the actual television production. To close, we see the performance being broadcast on another television, one outside the production booth. It's at the vet where Columbo has taken his new dog, and if Columbo had been paying attention (or, paying "strict attention"), he would have seen the clue to solve the murder before he was even called in to investigate it.

Columbo is showing the viewer how to glean the clues to solve the crime, while at the same time deconstructing what happens during a live television broadcast. Later, we observe Benedict with a slightly different media form, scoring the music for a film. [Side note: Benedict is soundtracking a documentary, apparently about WWII Germany, and as images of Hitler fill the screen, he is conducting in a vertically striped shirt strikingly similar to those of concentration camp prisoners.]

It's not until Columbo is again at the vet when he has a revelation after seeing that the PBS station is replaying the concert on that Saturday morning. "So it's on tape, they got it on tape…. I never thought of that!" Columbo is not a stupid man. Nowadays, in this media-fluent era, we would think, no kidding it's on tape. But remember, in the early Seventies, media literacy as we now know it was in its infancy. The thought simply didn't occur to Columbo.

For the Gotcha, the Lieutenant assembles Benedict, his wife, and various production personnel in the TV studio, massed in front of a bank of four monitors and a vintage collapsable film projector screen. For the coup-de-grace of Benedict, Columbo acts as director. He's not pushing the buttons himself, but he's clearly in charge as he instructs, "This is a film projector… this is videotape equipment. Frank, would you roll the tape?"

We watch Benedict sans carnation, and the tape rolls for 30 seconds until Columbo yells, "Stop!" Knowing what happens as we do, 30 seconds seems an unnecessarily long time to keep that tape rolling, but this is 1972, and for many viewers learning how to deconstruct media, and deconstructing the key murder clue, they may have needed the extra time to process it all.

But Benedict won't concede that he picked up his carnation at the murder scene. Once again, Columbo is ready, and another media form is introduced, newsreel footage of Benedict leaving the victim's house after the murder. Not quite comfortable being the hands-on director yet, Columbo needs a security guard's help in getting the projector started, but soon he barks out, "Freeze!" and the film stops to expose the lie that betrays Benedict and solves the case. *Etude in Black* is certainly not the most complex case to be cracked with media's help, but it was the first.

Of course, television wasn't the only media that Columbo, and *Columbo*, deconstructed for us. In *Negative Reaction* it was photography, with the Lieutenant taken aback by the camera shop clerk's explanation of reverse negatives, then pretending to misapply the technology with Paul Galesko during the Gotcha. Moments away from arrest, Galesko himself is compelled to find the equipment to provide the answer to how photographers can alter their visual messages: "We don't need the original snapshot, the negative will serve the same purpose," he says, grabbing the camera he shouldn't recognize.

Swan Song briefly deconstructs the music medium. Columbo visits a recording studio and recognizes that the "I Saw the Light" arrangement was changed between a soprano and a contralto voice. Speech recordings are analyzed and broken down to deconstruct the alibis of Nelson Brenner in *Identity Crisis* and Milo Janus of *An Exercise in Fatality*. The mechanics of film splicing are critical to *Forgotten Lady*, used to convince Ned Diamond of Grace Willis' guilt.

In *The Most Crucial Game*, a recording that included a radio broadcast was analyzed for its component parts. At the finale, Columbo describes the patience and persistence required in the process: "You know, I listened to this thing, I can't tell you how many times, over and over again, figuring maybe I'd hear something, some sound, an ambulance, a firetruck… that shouldn't be there. Then it suddenly occurred to me—I had it backwards. Maybe there was a sound that should be there, that wasn't." The clock chime gongs, the credits roll, and we see the recording tape unspooling just as quickly as Paul Hanlon's alibi does.

In his amateur media-detective way, Columbo was here giving the viewer a very rough blueprint in the critical thinking of how to take apart a media communication and avoid being fooled by it. There are several episodes that follow where the process becomes more intricate and demands more sophisticated scrutiny.

In *Double Exposure*, a villain once again played by Robert Culp is manipulating media for murder. The Stephen J. Cannell script was based on his college thesis about subliminal cuts in advertising, quick visual or auditory stimuli that the conscious mind doesn't perceive. The guiding tome on advertising at the time was 1957's *The Hidden Persuaders*, authored by Vance Packard. The book included the detailing of an experiment by a market researcher who claimed that a theater flashing quick cuts spliced into a movie of popcorn pictures and "Drink Coca-Cola" spiked concession sales of those items. Years later, that study was found to be a crock. Furthermore, attempts to reproduce it have failed.[3]

But the publicity accorded to subliminal advertising put the National Association of Broadcasters into a panic. They banned the use of the practice in 1958, which Culp's character, Dr. Bart Kepple, explicitly acknowledges in the episode. So, while the effectiveness of subliminal advertising in mass-audience settings such as theaters and television has now been largely debunked, it remained a salient topic in 1973. It also made for a brilliant *Columbo* episode.

The irony here is that even though the purported success of subliminal advertising is shaky at best, the episode is perhaps the best *Columbo* demonstration of the value of media literacy as an instructional tool. *Columbo* forces us to engage with the everyday images that we encounter and consider that they may have been engineered and controlled to produce a message with hidden meanings, values, points of view, and persuasion techniques.

The idea that advertising is created to make us buy particular products was of course not a newsflash to the 1973 viewers of *Double Exposure*. But the behind-the-scenes research, scientific principles, subtle manipulation, and methods of influence were likely eye-opening to *Columbo's* casual consumer.

Kepple's field is motivational research. Author of, among other books, *Advertising and the Motivated Sale*, Columbo notes that Kepple has "changed the course of advertising in just five years!" (the pompous Doc can't help but correct him that it was three years). Columbo and the audience watch as hidden cameras broadcast grocery shopper habits on closed-circuit TV, all part of a massive research effort.

Kepple's own efforts are very hands-on, as we see him splicing subliminal images into the film that victim Vic Norris will be watching, a film showcasing motivational sales tactics. In case we don't get the point, Kepple's narration intones, "We are traditionally a nation of salesmen. But, most importantly, we have advanced salesmanship to a creative art." It becomes Columbo's job to deconstruct Kepple's creative artistry, which has sold Norris on making a trip to the water cooler to get gunned.

Putting the homicide's pieces together, Columbo's takedown of Kepple is a masterclass in both murder and media deconstruction. After reading a Kepple book, Columbo gets a lesson in subliminal cutting from a film editor, and learns how someone predisposed to hunger might want to eat upon seeing a quick cut of a juicy hamburger. "You see [the frame] in your subconscious mind, which is quicker than the eye...."

In a clear nod to the demographics of the *Columbo* audience, the Lieutenant raves to Kepple: "You've invented something I've never heard of... and I'm over 40! Whoever heard of a subliminal cut?" Columbo and his police photographer get busy in Kepple's office, photographing an assortment of pics of Columbo snooping around. Then off screen, Columbo has these images spliced into the same motivational sales film that helped to kill Vic Norris. Unnerved during the film's showing by subliminal cuts of Columbo poking around for a gun, Kepple races back to his office to verify that his calibration converter is still there. It is, and so is Columbo, thus ensuring Kepple's downfall.

"You never would have solved [the murder] without my technique," says a stunned Kepple. He puts the frame of Columbo eyeing a lamp up to one of his monitors, allowing the viewer to investigate the photo at the same time the killer does. It's at this moment that an honest-to-goodness tear actually rolls down from Kepple's eye. The Gotcha, and the lesson in media manipulation, was that good.

Playback revolves around video trickery. The episode immediately sets up an intriguing premise. We know that Harold Van Wick is going to kill someone, but we also see that his mansion is monitored by a security guard viewing multiple closed-circuit TV cameras. How will Van Wick pull it off?

In a deftly-constructed sequence of scenes, the deception is carefully laid out for the audience so we can witness exactly how the finished video product has been manufactured, watched by guard Baxter in the security booth. The heavy use of media technology makes this murder, and Harold's alibi, appear more resistant to cracking than prior cases. How will Columbo pull it off?

Through the Lieutenant's questioning, we learn that the videotaping at Van Wick's is triggered by light, sound and nearby body warmth. Columbo marvels, "I'll be a son of a gun... that's fantastic, absolutely fantastic!" His reaction to these new whiz-bang media toys mirrors our own at the time. Eventually, Columbo realizes that Van Wick is playing him, he just doesn't know how. Figuring that out will require more media deconstruction.

The breakthrough happens when Columbo, never off-the-job, is watching a football game at a restaurant/bar, and a muffed punt gets the replay treatment. But this rerun doesn't just simply show us the same images in slow-motion, as replays did when this equipment was first introduced. By 1975, the technology had become more specific and focused, as we now see a completely different low-level camera angle and an on-screen circle that pinpointed where a player was illegally tripped. As Columbo says later to Van Wick, "That's when it hit me...."

The revelation requires a trip to Midas Electronics to break down the videotaped murder even more closely than the LAPD can. The approach Columbo takes, and is teaching the viewer, is very similar to the method applied in *The Most Crucial Game*, when he listened to audio for the sound that was, or wasn't, there. "I don't know what I'm looking for... a clock on the wall, a watch, a shadow... something that will definitely establish the exact time of the murder." Lining up two shots side-by-side, he tells the Midas technician to freeze each for a comparison, and gives a very specific direction: "Can you zoom in close like they do in the football games?"

At this point, director Bernard Kowalski makes a significant choice by having the scene's point-of-view (POV) and the audience's mirror Columbo's as he pans between the two screens to look for the crucial clue. The camera's tight shots move around to show us, on the videotapes, the entirety of the murder scene. We see what Columbo sees. He doesn't immediately pick it up, but he is modeling for us how to critically analyze a media source.

Inside Van Wick's ultra-modern control room with banks of monitors, videotaping machinery, and connecting cables, Columbo confronts the killer. And by the end of the scene, it's Columbo who is now pushing the buttons.

"Let's make it very close," he instructs, punching up the focus to triumphantly reveal the gallery invitation that seals Van Wick's guilt.

I don't believe that these were haphazard choices made by the *Columbo* team. Lieutenant Columbo has progressed from the cautious klutz who wouldn't start a movie projector in *Etude in Black* to the informed video technician in *Playback*, to the confident control room director of *Make Me a Perfect Murder*. It's a natural evolution for someone who is mastering the art of media breakdowns and showing the *Columbo* viewing audience how they can think likewise.

For *Fade In to Murder*, the video equipment has moved from the security room to the living room, becoming a plaything for Ward Fowler (William Shatner). It's unlikely that many 1976 viewers could afford the $3,000 (over $16,000 in 2024 dollars!) videocassette recorder perched atop Fowler's television, but Ward walks us through how the mammoth media machine will time-shift reality to create his alibi. Van Wick was timeline tampering as well, but he had a bank of security cameras to aid and abet him. Fowler is now showing ultra-rich *Columbo* viewers how they can do the same thing on a single piece of equipment in their living room.

Ward has a Sony U-Matic analog recording videocassette machine, a format first introduced in 1971. The VO-2850 or VO-2860 is a 1974-1975 model[4], advertised for businesses as being "the new concept in communication… ideal for training, teaching, product demonstrations, and messages from management." It's recommended for "Fortune 500 companies to… public schools, in medicine, in cable TV, in government, wherever people must exchange information."[5] Fowler's VCR has not even been marketed yet for home usage, but *Columbo* is clearly fast-forwarding to the future with its inclusion here.

We're learning the difference between media use and abuse. As does Columbo. "It was very brave of you to show me the videotape machine… you certainly like to take a chance," he tells Fowler/Lucerne. But really, what choice did Ward have? The huge contraption was the centerpiece of the TV-video setup right there in his luxury pad. While there's no scene to show us this, one can imagine the techno-curious Columbo immediately asking Fowler what the heck that big box was in his living room. If Columbo had seen this during his first visit to Fowler's manse, he might have divined the killer's fabricated alibi a lot earlier. As it happens, Columbo spends that initial trip to Fowler's place in the expansive hallway, trying to unlock his way out.

As an episode about the television industry, there are more peeks behind the media curtain in *Make Me a Perfect Murder*. In *Double Exposure*, we got a primer on projector film-changing. This time, however, Columbo himself takes the initiative to handle the intricate process and show projectionist Walter Muirhead, and us, that he's more than capable of not just watching, but doing.

There's significant time spent observing the inner workings of a television studio, much like we saw six years prior in *Etude in Black*. This time, it's a botched rehearsal for the upcoming live extravaganza *Valerie!* This is where Columbo gets a mini-lesson on the monitors, personnel and actions that deconstruct a broadcast into its component parts: the director's position, the technical directors console, a line monitor, a preview monitor of what the director wants up next, etc. Columbo is fascinated: "All these screens for just one show.... All these beautiful machines, all these buttons to push... it looks like fun!"

This leads into the most embarrassing two minutes of the Seventies *Columbo* era, as our hero sits spellbound at the console randomly button-pushing TV test patterns, set to a whimsical, silly score. This is clearly time-killer filler, and is not part of the original script. But as ridiculous and awkward as this scene is, it actually serves a purpose. Much like the later reel-changing scene, it foreshadows Columbo's growing poise in taking control of media, rather than allowing it to control him.

Now, 13 years after Honey West concealed a camera to catch the crook, Columbo does the same. His elevator-cam is part of the ploy to trap Kay Freestone with video evidence of her taking what she thinks is the murder weapon. The recorded deception puts Columbo in the figurative director's chair, and by the time he reaches the control room van at the amusement park, he is self-assuredly playing back tape of the gun-in-the-elevator ruse, as well as the scene in *The Professional* that provided proof of Kay's alibi deceit.

Much of this is not in Robert Blees' original *Make Me a Perfect Murder* script. There's no elevator camera, no playback of *The Professional*, no Columbo control of the control board. Instead, the script direction reads: "Like a child playing with his first train, he [Columbo] pushes the button which he saw the Technical Director push the other day." Fortunately, the finished episode more accurately reflects Columbo's stage of proficiency and evolved media intelligence.[6]

Columbo's confidence during the Gotcha is in marked contrast to Kay, who had unraveled moments earlier in front of the 10 TV monitors of the control booth. The sequence is a bizarre riot of Columbo shots seen at skewed angles, negative images, zoom-ins, zoom-outs, color, black-and-white, low-angles, and distortions, all quickly cut while the merry-go-round band organ chirps away and Kay desperately tries to erase the Lieutenant from her screens. The flashy visuals symbolize Kay's chaotic mental state, but also the role that Columbo has in dominating Kay through the very media that she used to control.

Through the Seventies, Columbo learned not to trust the prosperous or the famous just because they were prosperous or famous. Appearances, after all, could be deceiving. And the same applied to media. That bugged recording, that photograph, that promo film, that security camera, that TV baseball game—those appearances were deceiving, and while Columbo was decoding their actual meaning, so were the viewers. We were learning how to deconstruct media.

Columbo's 1989 return immediately gave us two killers skilled in manipulation, a phony psychic and a movie director. And while such trickery would still need to be deconstructed by Columbo, by the time of the Nineties, viewers were becoming much more aware of media's ability to create convincing fakery. Columbo's role as TV fiction's debunker detective, introducing a mass audience to the very concept of media literacy, was in the Classic Era past. In 1975, it takes an extreme video close-up to reveal the barely-visible Grant Galleries invitation that sinks Van Wick. In 1991, anyone with functioning eyesight could see the painfully obvious shrubbery landscaping in the video that dooms Wade Anders in *Caution: Murder Can Be Hazardous to Your Health*. We will later see that, as with the hedges, the media landscape had changed.

7.
Just One More Think: The Psychology of *Columbo*

DR. RAY FLEMMING: Columbo, you are magnificent. You really are. You're the most persistent creature I've ever met, but likeable. You're a sly little elf, and you should be sitting under your own private little toadstool. You say you've been thrown off the case, and yet you have the flagrant audacity to come back here and bother me again. I respect that. It irritates me, but I respect it.
– *Prescription: Murder* (1968)

DR. ERIC MASON: You're a fascinating man, Lieutenant. You pass yourself off as a puppy in a raincoat happily running around the yard digging holes all over the garden, only you're laying a mine field and wagging your tail.
– *How to Dial a Murder* (1978)

From the very first case to its penultimate Seventies episode, from sparring with a killer psychiatrist to a killer psychologist and all manner of villains in-between, *Columbo* has always been about mind games. No matter the adversary, the goal of our unassuming Lieutenant has been to get into the head of his target suspect and pry loose the evidence needed to secure justice. The best episodes would feature a classic battle of wills and, more importantly, a battle of wits between antagonists. No guns, just verbal shootouts with Columbo using psychology as his weapon.

The Me Decade's focus on therapy and self-examination had its roots in psychology. But this branch was dubbed "pop psychology," a less rigorous application of science and scientific method. The expounders of these theories often lacked academic credentials or empirical evidence, instead promising easy answers to difficult problems and feel-good quick-fixes, as long as the price was right.

Many solutions oozed with blissful optimism. This was, after all, the decade of the official *Columbo* series debut in 1971 with Ken Franklin displaying a bright yellow "Have a Nice Day" sticker on his rear bumper. (It's debatable whether or not Ken was being sincere, or simply engaging in killer irony). Summing up an outlook of positivity, Thomas Harris' *I'm OK, You're OK* hit bestseller lists, staying there through 1973. Those validating sentiments were replaced in 1975 by a new bestselling attitude, *Winning through Intimidation*. In prepping readers how to avoid being dominated, Robert Ringer's advice was essentially turning "I'm OK, You're OK" into "Dog Eat Dog."

But no one dominated pop psychology like the cheery, attractive blonde who parlayed her photographic memory into instant fame as a boxing expert on 1955's *The $64,000 Question*. Dr. Joyce Brothers was a ubiquitous fixture of Seventies media, including a monthly piece in the iconic *Good Housekeeping* magazine, a syndicated column in over 300 newspapers, a three-year syndicated TV show, radio host, author and frequent talk show guest spanning over 90 career appearances on Johnny Carson's *Tonight Show* among countless other chit-chats. She is often dubbed the first "media psychologist," bringing personal private issues into the public popular culture, and is credited with normalizing and de-stigmatizing psychology for mass media.

Thanks to Brothers and the proliferation of feel-good self-reflection, psychology was no longer a mysterious or taboo topic. But America's psychology was directed inward, to the self. Columbo's psychology was directed outward, to the killer. His tactics have sound theory behind them. Let's look at exactly what Columbo is doing.

A few minutes of Googling will reveal strategies like The Columbo Technique, The Columbo Method, The Columbo Tactic, The Columbo Strategy, and The Columbo Approach. All are shorthand for essentially the same thing—asking questions. But it's not enough to simply ask some questions and slap the "Columbo" name onto the process. To have real psychological application, we have to know what kind of questions are being asked, and why. And Columbo's actions and appearance have psychological application too. In simple terms, the villain would say that he's annoying, but it's a bit more involved than mere aggravation.

The Columbo character wasn't dreamed up from a Psychology textbook.

But creators Levinson and Link based him on the magistrate of Dostoevsky's *Crime and Punishment*, and G.K. Chesterson's Father Brown, characters who used criminal psychology and knowledge of human nature to solve their cases. The psychology behind Columbo was no mere accident. It was clearly there from the character's origins.

Fortuitously, viewers first see Columbo at work as he pieces together the case against callous and calculating psychiatrist Dr. Ray Flemming (Gene Barry, *Prescription: Murder*). Whether by design or lucky masterstroke, Levinson and Link are immediately able to introduce us to the psychological ploys used by the Lieutenant, as seen through the eyes of Flemming, who can analyze Columbo's moves with clinical precision and tell us all about them.

"You pretend you're something you're not. Why? Because of your appearance. You think you cannot get by on looks and polish, so you turn a defect into a virtue. You take people by surprise. They underestimate you, and that's where you trip them up…. You're an intelligent man, Lieutenant, but you try to hide it. You're a bag of tricks, Columbo. Right down to that prop cigar you use."

A key conversation highlighting Columbo's psychological underpinnings is the hypothetical murder chat that occurs later in the episode, between the detective and Flemming. It's worth noting that director Richard Irving films a stretch of this scene with the two antagonists surrounded in the frame by Flemming's two office walls, floor and ceiling, effectively boxing them in for their lengthy, tension-building verbal joust.

The exchange is purely theoretical, not about any murderer in particular. But of course, they both know that it's all about who strangled the late Mrs. Flemming. They sip their bourbons, comfortably sitting across from each other while the doc calls the crime they're discussing "an elaborate intellectual project," the killer "oriented by his mind… well-educated, too."

They lean into each other closer to refresh their drinks. Columbo chooses that moment to drop a hint: "Like maybe a professional man?" Staring straight at him, Flemming replies, "Like maybe."

Trying to rattle the calculating killer, Columbo speculates that their subject must be insane. Flemming disagrees: "Killing may be repugnant to him, but if it's his only solution, he uses it. That's pragmatism, my friend, not insanity."

Flemming describes someone who plans, calculates, and minimizes risks. Columbo asks (maybe even sincerely), "How do you catch a man like that?" Flemming thoughtfully pauses mid-bourbon swallow to coldly answer: "You don't."

COLUMBO with Dr. Ray Flemming (Gene Barry) in *Prescription: Murder:* "Boy, you've got me pegged pretty good, doctor. I'm going to have to watch myself with you."

FLEMMING: With all your experience, you jumped to the wrong conclusion.
COLUMBO (looks hard ahead); What do you mean?
FLEMMING: I didn't kill my wife.
COLUMBO (pauses): I never said you did.
FLEMMING (coy): But if I killed my wife, and I did say "if," you're never going to be able to prove it.

On paper, this is a perfectly pleasant little tete-a-tete. But while the underlying meaning of the conversation is deadly serious, the surface tone is not contentious. Rarely is there an overt confrontation between Columbo and suspect, certainly never while he's still trying to collect clues. Instead, Columbo looks for ways to relate to the villain as a human being, revealed in his off-the-cuff luncheon speech honoring Abigail Mitchell in *Try and Catch Me*: "Some of the murderers I meet, I even like them too.... Not for what they did, but for that part of them which is intelligent, or funny... or just nice." Being empathetic and respectful, and not arrogant or aggressive, keeps the target from becoming defensive and shutting down. Early on, there will be no direct conflict, no blame cast.

To this end, and to lull the killer into a false sense of security, Columbo does not want to appear to be in the superior position. As Dr. Flemming correctly recognized, Columbo wants his adversaries to underestimate him. In the advantaged power role, the suspect will remain open to talking with him, perhaps giving away a seemingly insignificant clue to the crime. In her book *Columbo: A Rhetoric of Inquiry with Resistant Responders,* Associate Professor Christyne Berzsenyi terms this "antipotency… a façade of cluelessness."[1]

Clearly, Columbo uses his sloppy physical appearance to diminish himself and appear ineffectual. But Peter Falk is also literally of diminished stature at 5'6", and every Seventies male villain is taller than Columbo (in *Try and Catch Me*, Ruth Gordon's 5-foot height cleverly inverts this trope). Not surprisingly, psychologists note that taller people believe themselves more socially dominant, and they feel confident taking personal space away from others.[2]

Physical advantage can take other forms. When Leslie Williams (Lee Grant) first meets him in *Ransom for a Dead Man*, disordered Columbo is bent over in a futile pencil search; in *By Dawn's Early Light*, Colonel Rumford (Patrick McGoohan) reprimands him while stooping for evidence on the school grounds. He'll also endure humiliating physical discomfort from his rivals via plane (*Ransom*), boat (*Dead Weight*), and exercise (*An Exercise in Fatality*).

Before continuing, I should clarify that I believe the behaviors and actions of Columbo to be authentic, and that he is not simply putting on an act to gain a psychological advantage. After all, we see him interacting in similar fashion with innocents and his fellow officers too, asking for a pencil or fumbling around in a sleep-deprived fog.

He'll reveal his more compassionate, less exaggerated character when the killer's not around. We see this in his gentle questioning of Mrs. Ferris in *Murder by the Book* and Mrs. Norris in *Double Exposure*. But Columbo is cunning enough to know how his conduct affects his prime suspects, and if pushing or exaggerating behaviors gives him an extra psychological edge against his adversary, why wouldn't he take it?

Although Columbo's physical appearance is the most obvious way to signal the villain's superiority, this is conveyed in other subtle manners. Often, our Lieutenant is overly deferential to the killer. This can come in the form of fishing for and receiving approval. In *Publish or Perish*, Jack Cassidy's Riley Greenleaf offers Columbo a friendly verbal push out his office door with,

"Listen, I hope you get the men that you're after. If anyone can do it, you're the man. Good luck on that writing... keep that up, that's good." Of course, after a Columbo thank you, there's another question for Greenleaf to clear up. Riley's not getting off that easy.

When Columbo asks for something from the suspect, even an item as trivial as a pencil, a match, or an autograph, he is in the deferential position—the giver is the more powerful of the pair. If not approval or a physical token, Columbo might directly ask for the killer's assistance on the case, as he does of Ross Martin's Dale Kingston in *Suitable for Framing* ("You're the art critic, and I'm going to need a lot of your help.... I suppose you've noticed that already.")

And even if not directly part of the investigation, Columbo may look to the suspect's expertise and authority in a particular area, simply for self-improvement and education. His interests in wines, art, horticulture and the like seem quite authentic, if perhaps embellished. Columbo is too savvy to allow these moments to pass without also using them as ways to feed the pomposity and arrogance of the killers.

As part of this mentoring, Columbo is usually revealed to lean toward simplistic, plebian tastes. This allows the viewer to identify with Columbo's middle class values, and the effete killer will condescend to him. In *Etude in Black*, Columbo heaps praise on conductor Alex Benedict (John Cassavetes):

COLUMBO: I'm Lt. Columbo. I'm a fan of yours, a really big fan. In fact, I just got your latest album.
BENEDICT: Thank you. I didn't realize that you were interested in piano concertos.
COLUMBO: No, no. I'm talking about the album of Strauss waltzes. "The Blue Danube." You know the one I mean?
BENEDICT (with slight disdain): Yes. I'd forgotten that.

For contrast, in *Murder Under Glass*, renowned chili enthusiast Columbo suddenly becomes a knowledgeable connoisseur of multiple food delicacies as he spars with cuisine critic Paul Gerard (Louis Jourdan). The killer is impressed, and has nothing to teach him. Columbo learns about the poisonous fugu used by Gerard purely by accident when he drops in on Paul's dinner party for a Japanese guest. This out-of-nowhere expertise is consistent with new producer Richard Alan Simmons' desire for a more authoritative Columbo, but it's totally out of character for the Lieutenant not to project inferiority against the murderer.

To enhance the superiority of the antagonist, Columbo is not averse to himself playing up the killer's privileged position. As previously discussed, it is one of the most oft-noted aspects of the series that there is a class divide between the rich, high-and-mighty murderers and the humble, down-to-earth, working stiff detective.

What is not remarked upon, however, is the intersection here between class and psychology. Rich, powerful or famous killers personify the superiority complex, and Columbo feeds this—it's exactly what he wants. Columbo himself will deliberately point to the socio-economic standing of his target, in essence, taking advantage of their advantage to remind them of his own insignificance. A celebrated example of this is his visit to conductor Alex Benedict's mansion in *Etude in Black* ("What do you pay in taxes on this place?"). Columbo shares that he makes $11,000 a year, about $69,000 today. That's hardly slave wages, but it's not a princely sum compared to Benedict. And it appears that Columbo has a genuine curiosity about such matters, which is why he'll additionally query non-suspects like lawyer Walter Cunnell (*The Most Crucial Game*) about the price of his shoes.

Columbo's projection of inferiority is also seen in less obvious ways. Something as minor as Columbo's unfamiliarity with fancy soaps ("the ones shaped like little lemons") sends a clear signal to Leslie Williams in *Ransom for a Dead Man* that this is an unsophisticated blue-collar plebeian. Oh, and he'll gladly peel potatoes, too.

If not socio-economic position, Columbo will puff up the celebrity status of the more famous of California's killers to ingratiate himself. It's always a fun discussion debating the accuracy of Columbo's claims about Mrs. Columbo, but count me as skeptical that she's actually a "big fan" of each and every one of the following: Tommy Brown, Alex Benedict, Grace Wheeler, "Detective Lucerne," Abigail Mitchell, Dexter Paris, Viveca Scott, Nelson Hayward, Milo Janus, and Dr. Eric Mason (I'll give you Nora Chandler, as Columbo called home so she could speak with her). Columbo's motive here is to stroke the egos of these murderers to reinforce their stature and fame, just as he highlights others' bank accounts.

Using Mrs. Columbo to assist her husband in this fluffery is another strategic psychological choice by Columbo. Indeed, the whole retinue of extended family members Columbo name-checks—real or imagined or a combination of the two—has a very concrete purpose. Leslie Williams astutely picks up on it: "…The way you come slouching in here with your shopworn bag of tricks. The humility, the seeming absent-mindedness, the uh [smirking], homey anecdotes about the family, the wife, you know?"

All those Columbo relatives and "homey anecdotes" position him firmly as a good family man. But to the more arrogant killers, it could also make him a weak man, revealing a soft domestic underbelly not displayed by a dominant, so-called Alpha Male. Falk himself provided another explanation, saying that Columbo didn't want to confront the villain with his own smarts, so he used "family members" as proxies, supplying the Lieutenant info that could advance the case against the suspect. For example, think of the attorney brother-in-law who supposedly examined Bo Williamson's will in *Blueprint for Murder*. Those seemingly off-the-cuff homey references can really be viewed as yet another way for Columbo to subtly give his antagonist another edge in the show of gamesmanship.

With the killers believing themselves to be on firm footing in the superior role, Columbo then proceeds to unsettle them into making mistakes or admissions that busts their balloons. In intelligence-speak, Columbo employs psyops, psychological operations to destabilize an adversary. This can apply to governments, but also to individuals, as a way of influencing their emotions and objective reasoning. For Columbo, these psyops can take several forms.

One of the most common is the invasion of personal boundaries. This is the science of proxemics, studying the effect of our interrelationships with the use of space. Individual brains have a type of "buffer zone," with neurons that keep track of nearby objects. Violations of personal space have a physical component so we don't bash our shoulder walking through a doorway, but also a concurrent social component as a buffer between individuals. Disruptions of these boundaries create discomfort and tension.[3]

For an exaggerated display of this, watch Columbo's physical interactions throughout *Last Salute to the Commodore* (Go on, I dare you). Mercifully for all, he is usually more subtle, and uses sensory invasions instead. Examples of such would include "excessive noise, smells, poor hygiene, food or drink, and engaging in undesired conversation."[4]

For Columbo, this might take the form of personal questions that hit a little too close to home. Will Dr. Flemming be dining with "ladyfriend" Joan Hudson tonight? "I don't think it's any of your business, Columbo." When the Lieutenant enters a scene coughing, wheezing and sneezing, is he really that sick? More importantly, does it matter? Real or feigned, it's an incursion into the villain's personal sensory space.

But Columbo's most foul assault on the senses were his cigars. Dr. Flemming calls it a prop cigar, but Columbo uses it as much more than a visual crutch. Today's smoking laws have created an artificial buffer zone in public locales, so the impact of cigar smoking may be lost on younger viewers. But Columbo smoked cheap, common, fetid supermarket-bought stogies. So in *By Dawn's Early Light*, Colonel Rumford offers Columbo a Cuban by saying, "Would you like to try one of quality for a change?"

Apart from the stink, the visual cloud serves as another sensory offensive. Observe Dale Kingston trying to inconspicuously wave it away when encountering the Lieutenant at the *Suitable for Framing* crime scene. This was not Columbo merely trying to annoy a killer. After all, his smoking in *Double Shock* annoyed housekeeper Mrs. Peck, and he never suspected her of anything but a bad temper. But its use as a psychological weapon of sorts can't be denied, although Milo Janus might try when he angrily declares, "You can huff and puff on that rotten cigar until next July, and you'll never prove [I'm guilty]." (Spoiler Alert: He does.)

Personal space extends to an expectation of privacy. Such invasions include constant supervision, not being able to take a break, being controlled, and being interrupted. Columbo is an expert at disrupting suspects' routines and private areas, with a long list of these at homes, apartments, restaurants, dinner parties, offices, testimonials, boat docks, gymnasiums, airports, bars, airport bars, solariums, hospitals, grocery stores, stadium skyboxes, beaches, television and recording studios, movie sets, classroom lectures, public parks, dance studios, dressing rooms, fat farms, golf courses, auto shops, construction sites, backstages… and that's just the Seventies.

In therapists' terms, "Proxemics can be deliberately manipulated in the workplace or social arena to send out specific signals to signify the nature of the relationship between the interacting people. Thus, for instance, the dominant person in a workplace relationship has the privilege of entering the less dominant person's space without his permission, but not so the other way around…. Police interrogations often use the strategy [of invading personal space]… to give the officer a psychological advantage."[5] Columbo is simply taking this strategy on the road to fluster his targets.

We see this immediately in our introduction to the character in *Prescription: Murder* when he encounters Dr. Flemming in his apartment. The Lieutenant is already present when Flemming arrives after his trip, and Columbo emerges from the Doc's bedroom (symbol of privacy) to silently slide up behind him. In this way, Columbo cleverly makes the killer seem to be intruding upon Columbo's space, instantly unsettling Flemming using proxemics. Later, Flemming catches Columbo crouching at his apartment door, literally trying to break in on his privacy!

Even more brazenly, Columbo is found asleep (real or faked, no matter) at Dale Kingston's pad in *Suitable for Framing* after the killer critic returns that evening from Murder #2. The Lieutenant had manipulated Kingston into grudgingly providing his apartment key without objection, and the privacy invasion unnerves Kingston, further exacerbated when Columbo violates more personal space by dipping a hand into his art bag to fondle some paintings and presage the classic Gotcha. Finally, Columbo gets a call on Kingston's phone line from the police about the accident/murder that Dale had committed earlier. The pre-cellphone era made for a good excuse to have Columbo reached on a suspect's telephone, but the invasion of personal privacy is an added bonus that through the years we'll find Columbo often taking advantage of.

Most indiscreetly, Columbo had no hesitation showing up at funerals, one of the most hallowed of private occasions. When he does this in *Negative Reaction* to spook Paul Galesko (Dick Van Dyke), he introduces a second sensory invasion when he loudly clicks photographs of the solemn service with the lame excuse of trying to find an accomplice to Frances Galesko's murder. If Columbo had smoked at the funeral, he could have hit the invasion trifecta. Such privacy and personal space intrusions were easy-to-replicate ploys that could be regularly used by Columbo as part of his psychological manipulation of each villain.

Additionally, he occasionally used outlandish stunts to rattle various killers. In *Short Fuse*, Roger Stafford (Roddy McDowall) has used a cigar box bomb in a car to blow up David Buckner. But Columbo publicly dismisses the idea that a bomb was the murder weapon. On a tram ride with Stafford, Columbo pulls out what he claims was the cigar box from the exploded car. Stafford panics when the box is opened, thinking a timed detonation has just been triggered. Stafford's glorious unraveling is all Columbo needs to get his proof of Roger's guilt.

Avid *Columbo* fans will also recognize the closing psychological traps of *A Deadly State of Mind*, *Swan Song*, *Any Old Port in a Storm*, *Negative Reaction*, and others. As Gotchas or set-ups to Gotchas, stunts like these were psyops of a bit grander scale.

While Columbo is employing psychology as a weapon of gamesmanship, he is also looking for holes in the suspect's story of the murder. Columbo assesses what he's seen, what he's been told, and what the crime lab says. When the details don't match, however insignificant, that's when Columbo trusts his gut to tell him that there's something amiss.

In *Etude in Black*, the initial explanation of Jennifer Welles' death seems like a clear suicide. But "little things" immediately disrupt this model: the lack of a clear motive; the gassing of her beloved pet cockatoo; the typed, not hand-written suicide note. Then, it's the mileage on Benedict's car, and the paper placement in the typewriter. The little details start adding up.

When the puzzle pieces don't fit, Columbo begins a process called Motivational Interviewing with a technique of "deploying discrepancies," an approach recommended for therapists instead of a direct confrontation. One mental health course specifically references a particular persistent cop. "With the Columbo approach, an interviewer makes a curious enquiry about discrepant behaviors without being judgmental or blaming. In a non-confrontational manner, information that is contradictory is juxtaposed, allowing the therapist [in our case, Columbo] to address discrepancies between what clients say and their behavior without evoking defensiveness or resistance."[6] Therapists using this approach are breaking down a client's resistance to change, but Columbo uses it to raise awareness of a problem—a discrepancy—with the murder scene or the suspect's remarks or actions.

COLUMBO: Gee, I just can't help thinking though, but... if I was in the hands of kidnappers, and my wife didn't ask me if I was okay, uh... I'd think about that.
AGENT CARLSON: What's your point, Lieutenant?
COLUMBO: Point? No, no, no point. Just that, uh... she's a unique person.

Of course, there is a point, but deploying discrepancies means making it in a civil, non-judgmental way. Leave it to a psychiatrist to figure this out.

DR. MARK COLLIER: You know something, Lieutenant? You're a marvelously deceptive man. You know, the way you get to the point without really getting to the point.

The aptly titled "How to Confront Liars Using the Columbo Method" further explains: "Columbo did not accuse those he was questioning. By taking the responsibility for his confusion, he disarmed the other person—who then would slowly feel comfortable telling him the things he needed to know to solve the crime. The Columbo Method is to present the facts that appear to conflict, give the person the benefit of the doubt, and then ask questions for clarification."[7]

And as we all know, some of most important of these discrepancies are posed to the suspect as seeming afterthoughts, as the conversation is winding down or even apparently over. This comes from *Negative Reaction*, but it could be from virtually any episode: "Uh, one more thing sir, I almost forgot... uh, one more thing that I wanted to check on... um, probably not important. That phone call that Deschler made...." Columbo's presentation is halting and hesitant, almost apologizing to Paul Galesko for bringing up such a small and seemingly insignificant detail, and the presentation helps sell the illusion that Columbo is just doing a job and not, as we know, being a shark.

Outside of the Columboverse, it's not realistic to think that every single crime detail is going to be nailed down tight. But that's not Columbo's fault! "My boss, he won't let me close up this case until I've covered everything. Every loose end's gotta be tied up. Hey, makes you crazy. So that's the problem." (*Swan Song*)

Employing the "one more thing" device, also called the false exit, is shrewd. Levinson and Link didn't initially intend it as a clever psychological trick. It was merely meant to add dialogue to a scene that was written too short. But it brilliantly dovetails with something called the Closure Principle. Simply stated, we seek closure as a release from tension.[8]

Columbo's conversation with the suspect may be superficially friendly and disarming, and the questions phrased indirectly, but it has pointed out discrepancies in the killer's story. This creates tension. The closure of ending the conversation will release the tension, so as the chat gets closer to finishing, the anticipation of this closure—being left alone by that pesky detective—creates relief. So when Columbo circles back and continues the conversation with "just one more thing," the killer's desire for closure leaves him/her open to suggestions that will close the dialogue and end the tension. This is particularly true if Columbo has held back a crucial question for last. "The more 'trivial' a thing is, the more damning it proves. As an application of psychology, it's a superb tactic and it slowly but surely grinds down the criminal's resistance."[9]

Another tactic to defer closure and heighten the suspect's tension is the momentary distraction, where Columbo sets up an important question, then delays asking it, as in *The Greenhouse Jungle*.

> COLUMBO: And the skid marks... I mean, they were really funny... say, what is this thing, sir?
> JARVIS GOODLAND: That is a multi-colored Cattleya bulb from Brazil.
> COLUMBO (inspecting): You don't say... really?
> GOODLAND (waiting): Skid marks, Lieutenant?
> COLUMBO (still inspecting): Huh?
> GOODLAND (exasperated): Skid marks?

Here, we'll break down one of Columbo's seemingly casual interrogations. For this exercise, I've chosen the Lieutenant speaking with Hayden Danziger (Robert Vaughn) in *Troubled Waters*, as it has so many of the classic elements of Columbo's psychology. The dialogue begins as Columbo interrupts Danziger relaxing with a game of quoits, throwing rings on the cruise boat (sorry, ship). They move to the empty restaurant, where Columbo explains why he's checking out previous passengers.

COLUMBO: It's the timing [of the murder], sir... that would suggest a member of the crew or a member of the band. A passenger wouldn't know that—not on the first night, but a previous passenger would. You see?
DANZIGER: That's good thinking, Lieutenant.
COLUMBO: Oh, thank you sir.

Columbo begins by ingratiating himself to Danziger and getting his approval, putting Danziger in the superior position—or so he thinks. Discussion turns to the letter "L" scrawled with lipstick on the victim's mirror, which Columbo long ago dismissed as a phony clue. But instead of pointing out that discrepancy, Columbo uses it as a pretext to ask Danziger about his auto salesmen cruise-mates.

COLUMBO: Let me tell you what's bothering me. The gun was found in the laundry room, so whoever did this had to have had a key to the laundry room.... The criminal had to have had a bunch of keys. Or....
DANZIGER: A master key.

Columbo lets Danziger complete the thought, continuing the impression that Danziger is actually helping the Lieutenant, and is not an adversary. As to who could have a master key? Well, through his extended-family brother-in-law, Columbo has heard of a device.

COLUMBO: He's got a tool. It's called a, uh... a Curtis...
DANZIGER: A Curtis Clipper.
COLUMBO: Right. I knew you knew that. Because he told me that auto dealers, they use these all the time.

Again, Danziger completes the thought, and can't object when Columbo "innocently" remarks, "I knew you knew that," which in another context might be heard as a direct accusation. (He'll use a virtually identical line on the Great Santini just over a year later). Instead, Danziger changes the subject to the receipt for the gun found in pianist Lloyd Harrington's (Dean Stockwell) room.

Danziger and Columbo have been in simpatico, but that changes. The ever-polite Columbo invites his adversary to have a seat, and he starts deploying discrepancies, explaining that the gun receipt is not a tax write-off like Harrington's other receipts. Danziger has no counter: "I see your point." Columbo then sweeps an arm toward the ocean and wonders, "That's the biggest garbage dump in the world. Why didn't he just throw the gun overboard?" Thus begins the trap, which Danziger helpfully steps into by trying to reassert a superior position in the conversation.

DANZIGER (slightly smirking): Lieutenant, I can see you don't know much about ships. He didn't have time. A ship is a much larger place than people think... He had to rush back to the bandstand so he wouldn't be late.
COLUMBO: Yes, that sounds plausible.
DANZIGER: So, he stashed the gun in the nearest convenient place.

Danziger further establishes his expert ship knowledge when Columbo deploys another discrepancy, asking why the gun wasn't simply thrown out victim Rosanna Wells' room's porthole. This time, Danziger does have a counter, and smugly replies that the portholes can't open.

COLUMBO: Oh... Well, you know Mr. Danziger, that's a very good theory. That's probably exactly the way it happened.... (jokingly) You probably couldn't tell, but I've never been on a boat before.

They share a mild laugh as Danziger says he'll "get back to my game," stepping out of the restaurant and onto the deck. The killer "escapes" from the room where Columbo has been ratcheting up the tension with discrepancies, and the final relief of closure for Danziger is palpable. But it's only a brief moment of release, as Columbo follows him onto the deck. He doesn't say "One more thing," but Danziger's exasperated and pained expression tells the story.

COLUMBO (shouting and catching up): Mr. Danziger! About your theory, and it's very good, my problem is I didn't find any prints on the gun.
DANZIGER: He wore gloves.
COLUMBO: But if he wore gloves, sir, why didn't he stash the gloves with the gun in the laundry room?

DANZIGER (thinking): He couldn't have thrown them overboard, because if he had time to throw the gloves overboard, why not the gun too?
COLUMBO: Exactly, sir.

Another discrepancy, and I believe that this is where Danziger believes that he made a crucial mistake. Hayden wants to guide Columbo to fingering Harrington for the murder, but Columbo keeps throwing up roadblocks to this theory, gradually amping up the pressure on Danziger. The Closure Principle applies once again. "In closure, we get to completion, and if there are any gaps left, our minds will helpfully fill them in, like connecting together a dotted line."[10] That's what Danziger does to finally get closure on the discussion.

DANZIGER: Then there were no gloves... don't you see? The gun was found in the laundry room, so Harrington must have used a towel, something like that, not gloves. He threw them both into the laundry room, and nobody paid any attention to the towel.
COLUMBO: That's a very good thought, sir. I'll have to think about that. A towel....

It's useful to help analyze exactly how Columbo is using psychology to engage, bait and snare his victims. And he's not done yet. Later in the episode, he pulls Danziger away from a boat (uh, ship) party to put the kibosh on the towel theory that Danziger thought had wrapped up the case.

DANZIGER: What gloves? I thought we decided that there were no gloves.
COLUMBO: No, not really sir. We just toyed around with that idea, and it sounded good until I checked the hospital. There could be a pair of surgical gloves missing.

Did you notice how both Danziger and Columbo each use the word "we" to describe their theorizing? Even at this late point in the episode, Danziger believes that they are not in opposition. But what was once closed is now open again, and Columbo has the perfect opportunity to employ a variation on brainwashing, that is, putting an idea into someone's head. As one strategy describes, "People like to believe they're clever. We cling to ideas that we believe are ours. The trick is to convince people that your idea is actually their idea... to plant an idea in someone's mind and have them believe it was their own, lay clues without being too obvious."[11]

COLUMBO: Here's my problem. I can't find the gloves. You see, Mr. Harrington did not leave any prints on the gun. That's going to make it very hard for the prosecutor to prove he did it. I gotta find those gloves with the powder burns on the outside because when I find them that's when I can prove why Mr. Harrington's prints weren't on the gun. I don't know why I'm bothering you with this, it's my problem.

By feigning concern over an element of the case, no matter how unlikely or tangential, Columbo uses discrepancies to manipulate his formerly-confident mark into nervously sharing that concern. Danziger becomes compelled to clean up a crime—provide closure—that really didn't need any more attention, and the very act of cleaning it up by creating a new set of gloved powder burns becomes the final proof of guilt.

Of course, Columbo also has an innate sense of human nature and the psychology behind it. When Leslie Williams uses the ransom money of her phony kidnapping scheme to pay off her dead husband's daughter, Columbo applies the finishing verbal blow. "Mrs. Williams, you have no conscience, and that's your weakness. Did it ever occur to you that there are very few people that would take money to forget about a murder? It didn't, did it? I knew it wouldn't! No conscience limits your imagination. You can't conceive of anyone being any different than what you are. And you're greedy. And you believed that Margaret could be bought."

In *A Deadly State of Mind*, Columbo's understanding of psychology allows him to trap Dr. Collier (George Hamilton) at the Gotcha. In a prior scene, Columbo had directly accused Collier of the murder of Nadia and Karl Donner, which puts the doctor nervously on the defensive when the Lieutenant announces that there's a witness who can place Collier at the crime scene. But everyone—Collier, Columbo and viewer—knows that the "witness" was blind. In his haste, Collier had almost run him and his guide dog over fleeing the Donner beach house. How does Columbo use this to his own advantage? It seems an impossible task.

With any obviously sighted witness produced by Columbo, Collier would not have given the game away by saying, "Hey that person wasn't there!" That would be a clear and silly admission of his presence at the scene. The correct response would be, "I wasn't there, so how do I know who this is?"

Columbo doesn't announce that he's presenting a blind witness. Collier, though, assumes that the Lieutenant is trying to trap him with exactly that, since Columbo has already accused Collier of murder and is desperate to put him away. His belief that he is being set up with a manufactured accusation blinds (pun intended) Collier. Provoked by Columbo, the doc grasps at what seems to be an easy way out of the charge by accusing Columbo and his witness of a phony "blind man bluff" charade. In the process, Collier exposes his own guilt. The witness Columbo produces is actually the blind man's sighted brother, who displays no signs of impairment to Collier. Why would the killer say the man is blind, unless Collier was indeed at the scene, where he saw a blind man? That's some seriously twisted double-reverse psychology from Columbo.

Other times, as in *Playback* and *Mind Over Mayhem*, Columbo's antennae go up when a suspect has introduced a new behavior. "When people do something for the first time, detectives always get curious." And he tells Grace Wheeler in *Forgotten Lady*, "From my experience, ma'am, I've discovered that people don't usually forget to do that which they usually do." Columbo has an innate understanding of how the human mind works.

Seventies *Columbo* is a psychology course unto itself. Through countless close episode viewings, we can learn to recognize and appreciate the mind-games and head-tricks that our sneaky Lieutenant uses to peel away his antagonists' lies and discover the truth. We have observed that using the science of proxemics, personal space, psyop stunts, inferiority projection, ingratiation, and planting suggestions, Columbo can dent the confidence of any killer.

For all their combined late-night appearances with Johnny Carson, Falk-Columbo and Dr. Joyce Brothers never sat on the same couch together. That's too bad. In their own way, they were each the decade's most visible figures practicing psychology. Of course, not every interplay between Columbo and killer will use all the elements of Columbo psychology. But the next time you're watching, try to spot when our Lieutenant busts out a few psychological moves on his adversary. It may not be pop psychology, but it is cop psychology.

8.
The Politics of Murder

RILEY GREENLEAF: If anybody was around to write the first genuine bestseller about Vietnam, it certainly was Alan Mallory.
COLUMBO: Is that a fact, really? I was always under the impression that war stories, they all went over big.
GREENLEAF: Only our popular wars. Vietnam… that's plague.

Columbo's reflections of Seventies social issues didn't extend to overtly political hot-buttons. Publisher Riley Greenleaf's profit-driven lament about the Vietnam War might have been seen as political commentary in an earlier year, but by the time 1974's *Publish or Perish* aired, direct U.S. military involvement in the war had ended, for better or worse. Greenleaf's blithe observation about Vietnam's approval ratings was more a factual assessment than political punditry.

As vile as Greenleaf was, though, he knew the book business. Shortly after Columbo collared him for the murder of Mallory, the Vietnam novel *Dog Soldiers* was published, riding critical acclaim to a 1975 U.S. National Book Award. The episode's political leanings were muted, and the harshest commentary was on the war's emotional baggage. The portrayal of psycho killer-bomber Eddie Kane as a loose-screw product of the Vietnam experience would not be the first or last time Hollywood linked war with mental health. It was a convenient, though arguably inaccurate, stereotype.

Nine months later, *By Dawn's Early Light* provided a nuanced view on the politics of war.

WILLIAM HAYNES (to Colonel Rumford): This academy can handle 6,000 boys. This year the enrollment's barely 1,100… Nobody wants to play soldier anymore. The war's over.

COLONEL RUMFORD: It's never over, William. There are too many people set on destroying our country. And that is why institutions like this academy cannot be allowed to die.

HAYNES: You know the incredible thing about you, Rumford? You really believe those cliches.

RUMFORD: What do you believe in, William?

Rumford's point of view is humanized by Patrick McGoohan's restrained and brilliant depiction of a proud warrior defending the necessity of war, at least until the time comes when he can return to tending his rose garden. This was not the snarling, figurative mustache-twirling of Jack Nicholson's Colonel Jessup shouting, "You want me on that wall!" Rumford presents a sympathetic and entirely reasonable argument on the value of combat preparation, marred only by, well, a brutal cannon backfire killing.

In its handling of Vietnam, *Columbo* played it down the middle, or at least, allowed viewers to read their own politics into what they saw. The foreign-affairs issues of 1975's *A Case of Immunity* were more directly pro-West. At the time, relations between the U.S. and Middle Eastern countries were at a nadir. Syria, Egypt and Jordan were retaliating against America with an oil embargo for support of Israel in the Yom Kippur War. The resulting 1973 oil crisis raised prices and sparked a nationwide recession.

In the Columboverse, First Secretary of the Middle Eastern country of Suari, Hassan Salah, is in a power struggle. The boy King and revolutionary Suari students are open to Western influences, as his Majesty explains: "There is a place for tradition, Hassan, but we must learn to live in this world as neighbors. We cannot be blind to the changes happening all around us."

Salah, however, is a fierce Arab traditionalist. Murdering his embassy's security chief and pinning it on the students is a ploy to halt any sympathies to Western values, and perhaps create a path to his own power grab. The King is a Western-curious, friendly, gregarious youth, and he immediately hits it off with Columbo. Salah engineers a double homicide and says things like, "The throne makes the man, not the blood." It's clear who we want to emerge victorious in this clash of civilizations.

The Columbo Phile author Mark Dawidziak calls this *Columbo* episode "a regrettably simplistic treatment of complex and sensitive issues in Arab nations. Hassan becomes the obvious villain because he values traditional

Arab ways. The young King is wonderful because he embraces Western ideas and ideals. There's a painfully obvious message that emerges from this contrast of stereotyped characters: Arabs aren't such bad guys as long as they're willing to act more American. Suari will be just fine if it accepts 'civilized' Western standards."[1]

Dawidziak's is not an unreasonable argument. However, *Columbo* is a TV detective show, not a PBS geopolitical roundtable discussion. Subtlety and shaded distinctions among complicated issues of Middle East-U.S. policy aren't going to be possible while Columbo is stepping on Hassan's Arab robe. America's relationships with hardline dictators around the world have always been problematic, especially when it benefits the United States. Backing brutal authoritarian regimes rather than emerging democracies has had diplomatic, economic and military justifications for many decades. The decision of Columbo to side with a king who doesn't wear traditional garb and likes Western foods may not be so awful in this context.

NELSON HAYWARD: You are voting in this one, aren't you?

COLUMBO (enthusiastic): Oh, I vote, every election, I vote! In our house, you gotta vote, it's a very sacred thing. We sit around the kitchen table, we discuss, and we vote.... You don't have to worry about my wife, she's crazy about you... I'm still a little on the fence, if you know what I mean.

Good luck trying to figure out Columbo's politics. Obviously, we can't read anything into his failure to vote for a killer to represent him in the U.S. Senate. In 1973's *Candidate for Crime*, Nelson Hayward runs relentlessly on an anti-crime platform, which aligns with a "law and order" mentality adopted by late-1960s Republicans like Alabama's George Wallace, California Governor Ronald Reagan and Presidential candidate Richard Nixon. But it was Democratic President Lyndon Johnson who called for a War on Crime in 1965, so political affiliation with this issue wasn't nearly as established in '73 as some might consider it today. Politics aside, the issue is used for Hayward in the episode because of the deep irony of having a candidate for crime prevention be a stone-cold killer himself.

In her book *Columbo: Make Me A Perfect Murder*, Amelie Hastie devotes a chapter to the collaborative writing and producing history of *Columbo* co-creators Richard Levinson and William Link. Their television movies included the previously-noted *The Gun* and other significant productions that were landmarks of the era in their eagerness to tackle subjects that were TV taboos. These included 1972's *That Certain Summer*, the first sympathetic portrayal of a gay couple on the small screen, and 1974's *The Execution of Private Slovik*, a true story about the first U.S. soldier executed for desertion since the Civil War.

Hastie notes that the pair had liberal sensibilities, "a humanism that undergirded everything they originated together. This liberal humanism was spelled out most explicitly in their made-for-television movies... but those progressive politics are part of the foundation of their famous series nevertheless. Appearing during the series original run, the films underscore the progressivism of *Columbo*."[2]

Humanism stresses the value and goodness of human beings; progressive policies endorse reforms that lessen economic and social inequalities. On the humanist front, we can easily accept that this is an overarching theme of both Columbo the detective and *Columbo* the show. The character is clearly one who can relate to a wide range of people, even murderers. We've already documented his comments at Abigail Mitchell's book luncheon: "I don't think the world is full of criminals and full of murderers, because it isn't. It's full of nice people, just like you. And I'll tell you something else. Even with some of the murderers that I meet, I even like them too. Sometimes, like 'em and even respect 'em, not for what they did (certainly not for that), but for that part of them which is intelligent, or funny, or just nice, because there's niceness in everyone, a little bit anyhow. You can take a cop's word for it." That's humanism in a nutshell.

Humanism transcends decades. As for liberal progressivism, though, there's a danger in trying to interpret a 20th century television program through a 21st century lens. For example, Columbo's lack of a gun in the era might seem a liberal choice. But this ignores the history of attempts at gun reform and the role of the National Rifle Association. The NRA had long been an advocate for some form of gun regulation, working with Congress and both Democratic and Republican White House administrations to create gun legislation that would satisfy the crime-in-the-streets fears of their NRA constituency. It wasn't until 1977 that the NRA leadership suffered an internal coup at their NRA convention, and the current no-compromise position on preventing gun reform was adopted.[3] Columbo's dislike of firearms was not the liberal red flag that some might interpret it as today.

On the other side of the political aisle, Columbo's arrests of the L.A. and Hollywood elite might be viewed by some today as a right-leaning populist victory of the working-class hero over the privileged big-city one percenters. Those who want to "own the libs" are free to read this into their satisfaction of seeing genius Oliver Brandt or newly liberated Beth Chadwick get their comeuppance.

To many, the class conflict of *Columbo* is the clearest signal of a progressive objective. "Whether or not the original intention of the creators, these [progressive] politics are most apparent in *Columbo's* emphasis on class structures."[4] While a fair point, it must be repeated that neither Levinson, Link nor Falk agreed with this interpretation of the dynamics of the series. The creators were looking for a clash of styles, not classes, and Falk said that Columbo "had no argument against the rich."

Progressive sensibilities may have been a residual effect of Columbo's crime solving, but were not a primary factor. The takedowns of the rich and powerful were satisfying, but let's face it, they weren't going to do anything to change the economic structure that separated the classes, unless one thought that Columbo would accomplish it monthly, one-bad-guy-at-a-time. *Columbo* created great drama of contrasting styles, and the gratification of bringing down the evil wealthy is undeniable. Whether that's enough to qualify *Columbo* as a progressive show, however, will be left up to individual tastes. Columbo patrolled Bel Air, Malibu and Beverly Hills looking for the social injustice of getting away with murder, not the social inequities of getting away with capitalism.

If *Columbo* had wanted to point in a more progressive or liberal direction, the opportunities were certainly there. While forward-thinking in its use of strong women characters and some liberated awareness, we have seen that there was also some mild pushback to this from characters, including Columbo, who had a hard time wrapping his head around the changing role of women in the Seventies. And although it was reflecting the changing racial composition of the country, *Columbo's* diversity did not extend to black foreground characters as much as might be expected from a series if it had an actively progressive agenda. Racial scrutiny was a blue-moon rarity.

Even the phrase discussed in the earlier chapter about power dynamics, "Question Authority," is murky in its politics. Although traced to Timothy Leary, it's not necessarily a liberal sentiment. Different individuals question different types of authority—religious authority, scientific authority, government authority, and so on. In one explanation of the model, "Each person tends to see some forms of authority as sacred and worth defending, and sees other forms of authority as useless or even damaging. In other words, people piece together their views of what sources of authority are legitimate uses of the word 'authority' based on their experiences. But most people share the commonality of relishing some kind of authority and challenging other kinds."[5]

Columbo's mission is to challenge the presumed moral authority of extreme lawbreakers. That's an equal-opportunity goal, so liberal/conservative politics wouldn't apply. And our hero can't challenge all authority, of course, as Columbo himself is an authority figure, albeit one wearing a raggedy raincoat.

In our current era, it's easy to view moral and social issues through extreme political prisms. A stance on one issue is likely a reliable predictor of a stance on another. The middle ground of centrism is harder to establish. *Columbo's* classic television era certainly saw its share of right/left divide, but those Seventies' *60 Minutes* "Point/Counterpoint" segments were much more genteel than today's shout fests. Zealous politicizing, and laughing at it, was left to *All in the Family*.

Columbo was not interested in staking out positions, just catching the killer. They may have been rich, they may have been famous, and they may have been powerful, but Columbo's "progressive" agenda was getting them out of their mansions and into a jail cell. That was progress enough.

9.
Columbo in the Nineties: A Man Out of Time

One of the unexpected side-effects of the 2020 Coronavirus pandemic and extended lockdowns was the spike in online articles of appreciation for *Columbo*, as binge-watching became more widespread, and people discovered (or rediscovered) how the show could provide some solace in a challenging time. Typical odes praised its ability to be "a cultural outlet to decompress from the daily nightmare… to help maintain just a smidgen of your sanity."[1] Or, "*Columbo* carries a particular nostalgic weight for me because I used to watch it with my father when I was in my early teens."[2]

These unabashed admirations invariably included descriptions of favorite episodes, murders, guest stars, and *Columbo* moments. What, pointedly, didn't they include? Any memories from New *Columbo*. The Nineties era would be glossed over, with perhaps a kindly passing reference to a "slight decline in quality as the seasons passed."[3]

Columbo's TV resuscitation was born out of a misguided attempt by ABC to reap a nostalgia windfall from Seventies icons like Peter Falk, Telly Savalas, Burt Reynolds, and Jaclyn Smith. The network would use these stars to revive the Mystery wheel format that NBC had already been-there-spun-that years before. In truth, the concept had always had more misses than hits, but Falk was game and the price was right.

The rebirth was planned for 1988, but momentarily derailed by a Hollywood writers' strike. This gave more time to build anticipation for the return of one of television's most beloved characters. Executive producer

William Link even hinted that Steven Spielberg was interested in directing the first new episode, just as he had *Murder by the Book* in 1971.

Then, the hyped comeback finally materialized (alas, without Steven) in 1989 with *Columbo Goes to the Guillotine*, followed by three more episodes that year that were met with a resounding and collective… yawn. After two seasons, the ABC Mystery cycle was axed, but *Columbo* survived, now as a series of occasional movies of sporadic airing. Ratings for the entire New *Columbo* venture roller-coastered through the Nineties into 2003 for the *Columbo Likes the Nightlife* finale, never consistently healthy. More importantly, they generated little, if any, of the buzz that provides the fuel for Hollywood relevance, and did nothing to enhance the legacy of Peter Falk and *Columbo*. If anything, it was left tarnished after the overpowering sheen of *Columbo's* Seventies triumph.

The reasons were many, with the prevailing opinion being that overall, it simply wasn't very good. Conventional wisdom would follow that if these rejuvenated *Columbo* episodes had been well-done, they would have resonated with old fans, brought in new ones, and been another smashing success. With quality, there would have been ratings. With excellence, or at least competence, New *Columbo* could have been, perhaps not as popular as Classic *Columbo* of the Seventies, but not ignored in the Nineties.

Don't be so sure.

There's no question that *Columbo* 2.0 was a gigantic missed opportunity. We are right to put some focus on the numerous issues that plagued the show and its quality: behind-the-scenes squabbles, poor judgments by Peter Falk, a depressed budget, low-wattage guest stars, script difficulties, poor acting, run-of-the-mill music scores, and inability to strike the right balance of serious crime-solving, characterization, and humor. A better show would at least have given New *Columbo* a better shot at success.

But concentrating too much on these issues masks the sobering reality that Lieutenant Columbo was simply a relic of another era. *Columbo* reflected the Seventies so well that by the time our hero ambled his way into a new decade, he was an anachronism in this new cultural setting, doomed to insignificance. The cultural forces at play during the revival would not have damaged the show's overall legacy if quality control had been maintained, but those cultural forces definitely conspired to make Peter Falk's return to television and the reception accorded his iconic show anything but a soft landing.

Columbo was an artifact of the Seventies. As merely a continuation of the series, with Peter Falk portraying its eponymous character into the Nineties (and into his 70s), I would argue that no matter how well-done, it was going to have trouble resonating. To see why, we must remind ourselves of the social culture that helped make *Columbo* so popular in the first place.

Let's return briefly to Jeff Greenfield's instructive *New York Times* column of 1973. "The homicide files in Columbo's office must contain the highest per-capita income group of any criminals outside of antitrust law. We never see a robber shooting a grocery store owner out of panic or savagery; there are no barroom quarrels settled with a Saturday Night Special; no murderous shootouts between drug dealers or numbers runners. The killers are rich and white.

"Into the lives of these privileged rich stumbles Lieutenant Columbo—a dweller in another world. His suspects are Los Angeles paradigms: sleek, shiny, impeccably dressed, tanned by the omnipresent sun. Columbo, on the other hand, appears to have been plucked from Queens Boulevard by helicopter."[4]

Josh Spiegel's 2020 critique compares the eras. "Each of the 45 episodes that aired between 1968 and 1978 offered a new opportunity for our ruffled hero to gaze and gawk at how the better half lived in Los Angeles. These episodes—much more than the late-stage revival that aired on ABC—lean heavily into the glamour of the era… and the murderers firmly believe their higher class status is to be flaunted."[5]

Co-creators Link and Levinson had no intention of engaging in class analysis, merely good drama. The decision to heighten the theatrical impact of Columbo's killer conflicts led many pundits to see the class differences as social commentary—not just "get the bad guy," but "get the rich bad guy."

This would be perfect drama in any era, right?

"Greed, for lack of a better word, is good."
– Gordon Gekko (Michael Douglas), *Wall Street* (1987)

For many, those words sum up the ethos of the '80s-'90s Baby Boomer generation. As Scholar in Media and Cultural Studies Siobhan Lyons noted in 2017, "While Gekko's downfall was unambiguous in its message about the toxic culture of Wall Street, the film had the opposite effect, inspiring a new generation of stockbrokers. The ruthless Gekko, despite being the movie's villain, became a sort of cultural hero… and his message of 'greed is good' seems to have only intensified."[6]

Gekko was the money-worshipping anti-hero of *Wall Street*, which premiered in December 1987, a week before the Gekko character's real-life inspiration, Ivan Boesky, was given three years in the pen for securities fraud.

The film's director, Oliver Stone, said, "When I made the movie I thought greed was *not* good. But I learned that people really like money. They like to make money. They will even admire the villain with the money, even when he breaks the law."[7]

For his portrayal of slick and suspendered Gekko, Michael Douglas won the Academy Award, and motivated thousands of young, aspiring executives to become stockbrokers, amoral or otherwise. Gekko was a hero well into the 1990s for a big slice of that demographic pie chart, the Baby Boomer generation.

Baby boomers were born between 1946 and 1964, a total of 76 million people that by 1990 would encompass the 26-44 age range. This vast group was prosperous, economically and politically influential, and represented 46.5 percent of employed Americans as the Nineties began.[8]

Baby Boomers' economic values differed significantly from prior generations. One study notes, "Boomers, motivated mainly by prestige and work accomplishments, are more materialistic.... This generation eagerly adapted to credit spending and traditionally spent more than the previous generation on housing and retail purchases."[9] Another observes, "The Baby Boomer generation loves material goods and capitalist consumerism. Raised during a time of prosperity and economic growth, Boomers were avid consumers of new products and technologies."[10]

For this generation to spend money, they had to make money. And Gordon Gekko was their spiritual teacher and advisor. As one self-described boomer blogger laments, "We took what we wanted without regard to what it would cost others... We have behaved as the greediest generation...."[11]

Whether you agree or not with these characterizations of Boomers, the fact is that this was the generation that was making many of the household television decisions of the era. Those viewers put a New *Columbo* movie into the Nielsen-rated Top 25 just 10 (out of 24) times. It makes some sense that in the context of a powerful demographic of Gekko-idolizing boomers, Columbo's takedowns of the rich and fabulous might not hold the same sway that Jeff Greenfield waxed poetic about in 1973.

Perhaps instinctively realizing this, Executive Producer Richard Alan Simmons' plan for *Columbo's* return was to create murders that played off villains' professions and not their bank accounts. As noted by David Koenig in *Shooting Columbo*, it was the characterization of the killer that was to be emphasized more than clever clues. And although Simmons was jettisoned after the 1989 season, the trend toward less threatening villains continued. This was even after a viewer survey that "found the murderers too likeable.

THE POPULARITY of Michael Douglas as Gordon "Greed is Good" Gekko in 1987's *Wall Street* didn't bode well for *Columbo's* 1989 return.

They wanted their villains cold, calculating, unremorseful and unsympathetic. They wanted them to bully Columbo."[12]

Bullies have or project power. And this appears to be one area where New *Columbo* went astray. Maybe Boomers were not as keen on locking up a Gordon Gekko, but without a powerful adversary, Columbo had nobody to challenge him. So these *Columbo* episodes had our hero up against a psychic, a dentist, college kids, a sex therapist, an artist, a playboy, a nightclub owner, and a race horse breeder, among other lessers. Who among those could threaten to pick up a telephone and hit speed-dial to take Columbo off the case? Organically, as part of the plot, the Nineties murderers were usually affluent, but the vibe was often different than it was in the Classic Era. There were fewer bullies and authority figures.

Columbo wasn't punching up in weight class as much as he did in days gone by. Earlier, we noted that sociologist Lilian Mathieu's "Columbo: Class Struggle on TV Tonight" offered insight into why the Seventies social culture may have provided the breeding ground for *Columbo's* popularity. The ideals of the youth generation of the Sixties were often in conflict with older authority types over the Vietnam War, civil rights, gender issues, free speech, and the sexual revolution. Columbo's opposition to the opulent symbols of power and influence struck a chord with these TV consumers in the Seventies.[13] This was lacking in the Nineties.

But less viewer appetite in putting the Nineties wealthy away didn't necessarily mean less enthusiasm for law enforcement. The difference was in the cultural environment between eras. This was reflected in the evolving changes through the decades in television shows' depictions of the police.

There was a time when Westerns thoroughly dominated television. The genre depicted the values of a post-WWII America, which professor Christyne Berzsenyi (*Columbo: A Rhetoric of Inquiry with Resistant Responders*) describes as "an expanse of frontier thinking… moral conflicts between good and evil, hero and villain, passing on an American code of ethics akin to fairytales."[14] But the format became oversaturated and tired.

In the Sixties and Seventies, the detective/police drama/procedural rose to prominence, replacing the dusty sagebrush settings with urban environments, but retaining the basic cultural values of the showdowns between right and wrong that had made the Western popular. Those moral conflicts were now the domain of the sturdy cop-on-the-beat or the brash private eye. The year 1968 saw the debut of *Adam-12, Hawaii 5-0, Ironside, Mannix* and *The Mod Squad*. It was also Columbo's first appearance in *Prescription: Murder*.

Through the Seventies, countless more crime busters shared the small screen with Columbo. But Columbo did not share their standard cop tropes, and his underdog status gave him an edge. Cannon and Kojak could nail the rich crooks too, but they didn't inspire *New York Times* columns by Jeff Greenfield. It was this combination of qualities that helped make *Columbo* successful in the Seventies—the little lieutenant besting the venal, vain villain.

And although a cop, Columbo thrived comfortably in a niche that producers Levinson and Link did not intend to be for cops at all. In their traditional mystery format, police realism was surrendered in favor of smart banter and clever plots. Columbo's refereeing of those enduring moral conflicts between good and evil had been polite and genteel. No violence was required.

Columbo returned to the airwaves on February 6, 1989. Producers betting on the rumpled Lieutenant's relevance had no way of realizing that just over one month later, on March 11, 1989, a new police show would debut that better mirrored and shaped its era. The expectation was that the drawing room mystery that impersonated a cop show could repeat its success for the next generation of *Columbo*. Little did they anticipate the first generation of *Cops*.

In the early Nineties, America was at Peak Crime. In 1991, for every 100,000 people, there were 5,856 felonies, 716 violent crimes, and 9.8 murders.[5] Gallup opinion polls reflected this with a belief that criminality was rising. Between 1989 and 1993, anywhere between 84-89 percent of people feared increased crime.[16]

Public unease over this issue is nothing new. But into this period of amplified lawbreaking and corresponding fears, the Hollywood writers' strike provided opportunity for a new type of program that promised and seemed to deliver an exciting weekly documentary on actual, effective policing in America. It was Reality TV.

Cops was birthed out of economic uncertainty. The 1988 writers' shutdown that inconveniently delayed *Columbo's* return to television was forcing the industry to become creative. With no new scripted shows forthcoming, and no sense of how long the strike would last, the Fox network finally took a chance on a concept that had been pitched but turned away several times before. With no writers, no high-priced talent, and no lack of crime to exploit, *Cops* was cheap and instant programming.

The format was simple. Audiences were taken on exciting ride-along missions that shunned re-enactments and used real footage of police busting up drug deals, prostitution rings, and other unsavory crimes in cities across the country. Video and sound teams recorded the so-called "unfiltered" action and reactions from the cops on the scene, a morality play that gave viewers the sense of instant justice. It burnished the overall police image, as departments from coast-to-coast volunteered to show off their effectiveness in the face of the national crime wave.

Cops delivered ratings, perhaps not on the #1 order of a *Cheers* or *Roseanne*, but a dependable vessel for servicing an appealing Adult 18-49 demographic. The cinema-verité style was unique, attention-getting, and it worked. And while the scripted TV cop competition was scarce, the most acclaimed police dramas of the Nineties, *NYPD Blue* and *Law & Order*, shared a quality with *Cops* that was now clearly lacking in our disarrayed detective.

There was an affected, heightened realism to these Nineties police dramas that made them appear much more relevant to the modern television consumer. In the Seventies Columboverse, weak Gotchas could be excused if the ending was convincing to the killer, Columbo and the viewer. But now, *Law and Order* could show us the depressing reality of what would happen to those cases. Maybe D.A. Jack McCoy could get a grand jury to indict the proverbial ham sandwich, but even he would toss away the table scraps provided by Columbo if the case turned on a pair of inside-out panties like 1990's *Murder in Malibu*.

Overall, post-1989 saw 24 *Columbo* episodes inconsistently airing with varying viewership and minimal at best cultural impact. *Cops* was a constant, spawning 1,000 episodes in its lifetime, and in a single week might be seen in syndication 69 times across the country.[17]

Socially and culturally, the show came along at the right time, just as *Columbo* had in the Seventies. Overall, the era saw a generally positive impression of the police. From 1993-1999, the institution earned anywhere between 52 and 60 percent of "Quite A Lot/Great Deal Of" confidence in Gallup polling, with only one in 10 professing "Very Little" confidence. Respect for officers saw similar results.[18]

The problem was that people had little trust in the justice system as a whole. In polls from the same period, "Quite A Lot/Great Deal Of" confidence in criminal justice percentage plummets to between 15 and 24, with "Very Little/No Confidence" hitting as high as 49 percent. A 1992 question asks, "Do you think the criminal justice system in this country is too tough, not tough enough, or about right in its handling of crime?" 83 percent were adamant that the criminal justice remedy in America was not tough enough, and a microscopic 2 percent felt it was too harsh. This question was asked between March 30 and April 5 of 1992; it was three weeks before the verdicts in the Rodney King case would be handed down.[19]

In March of 1991, 25-year old black motorist King was stopped by white Los Angeles police officers after an eight-mile high-speed chase through the city, and subsequently subdued with batons and a stun gun. King had been drinking, and resisted arrest. Police responded by battering and breaking King's cheekbone, skull bones, and ankle. In another, pre-tech era, this would likely have gone unnoticed. But the violent encounter was filmed on a camcorder by an L.A. resident, released to local media, played and replayed constantly, and the outrage resulted in four of the officers being charged with using excessive force.

To some, the American justice system itself seemed to be on trial. On April 29, 1992, three of the officers were acquitted, and a mistrial was declared for the fourth. King's initial resistance to officers was cited as a determining factor. There were no African-Americans on the jury.

Immediately, Los Angeles became engulfed in riots, with over 60 people dead and more than 2,000 injured. To many in the black community, the case became a red-hot symbol of the brutality endured for years at the hands of white law enforcement. Famously, King himself captured much of the Nineties social climate by pleading during the unrest, "Can we all get along?"

Into this cultural moment, with television newscasts across the country continually looping this episode of seeming police brutality, *Cops* episodes affirmed the no-grey, black-and-white-only judgments of its own videotaped officers. *The Guardian* completed an extensive content analysis of 846 half-hours of *Cops*, separating the reality of police work from the fiction that the program presented as facts. "The cops on the show are, statistically speaking, extremely good at their jobs. Segments on the show end in arrest 84.4 percent of the time. (That number reflects a change over time, from 61 percent back in 1990 to 95 percent in the most recent season.) In *Cops*' world, law enforcement officers are so effective, it's basically a given that a crime will end in an arrest."[20]

In actual experience, this arrest percentage is greatly exaggerated. But the Gallup perception that the criminal justice system was ineffective and skewed to the criminal was widely held, and *Cops* provided a simplified and comforting scenario.

"The observational style seemed to show the police as the thin blue line holding back the violence and chaos of American inner cities," said Zoe Druick, a professor of media studies and cultural theory. "The show drew a line between police and criminals, using the observational format to suggest that we could simply see who was good and who was bad in the situation... *Cops* therefore also implicitly suggested that courts were irrelevant. You could see with your own eyes who was guilty—the very ones police came for."[21]

Bypassing "irrelevant" courts might have seemed an attractive option for those Americans who watched with disbelief as O.J. Simpson was acquitted for the 1994 murders of Nicole Brown and Ron Goldman. The 11-month "Crime of the Century" trial blanketed television and aroused deep racial divisions between those who felt that Simpson was railroaded ("If the glove does not fit, you must acquit!") and those who were convinced that Simpson got away with it.

Although we can speculate on the answers, there was no Gallup polling after the Simpson trial asking if the criminal justice system was soft. But for some of that 83 percent of 1992 America that felt that the justice system was going light on criminals, *Cops* might have been served another purpose. *The Guardian* analysis noted, "Over and over, *Cops* shows officers acting in violent, abusive, racist and potentially unconstitutional ways. This can include anything from repeatedly tasing suspects who are in custody, to prying open a suspect's mouth with a flashlight in search of drugs. Rather than critiquing this sort of behavior, or even presenting it neutrally, *Cops* portrays it as good policing."

The show's cops-eye-view format compelled its audience to identify with the police, with minimal context for the crimes they encountered. There would be little sympathy for those whose activities were soundtracked at the start of each episode with the suspects' de facto theme song, "Bad Boys."

Cops was a comfortable fit into the decade, but the show did its own influencing of the social fabric by continually reinforcing and perpetuating its own negative stereotypes about crime and criminals. *The Guardian* found that "the world portrayed on *Cops* is not like the real world. There are about four times more violent crimes in *Cops* than in reality. And three times more drug arrests."[22] Minorities were over-emphasized as criminals. The civil rights group Color of Change claimed the show's producers "have built a profit model around distorted and dehumanizing portrayals of black Americans and the criminal justice system."[23]

The exaggerations shaped what one study described as "a very particular vision of criminal justice." In "*Cops*: Television Policing as Policing Reality," Aaron Doyle writes, "*Cops* and similar programs form part of the context for increasingly punitive 'law and order' policies. These include 'three strikes, you're out' legislation, a prison population explosion, the rebirth of chain gangs and the renewed rise of punishment by death.

"In 'law and order ideology,' society is seen to be in decline or crisis because of spiraling crime, specifically violent street crime of the underclasses. The answer is tougher crime control. Due process and civil rights are part of the problem, because all right-thinking people know criminals are guilty. Police themselves are not too soft; instead they are held back by others, such as liberal politicians. The answer is partly more police, and police who can get tougher. Intertwined with the notion of a soft system is an Us and Them mentality: crime is a problem of evil or pathological individuals who are a Them, less human than Us."[24]

Lower classes comprised the "Them;" white collar and corporate misconduct was definitely not on the radar of crimefighting reality TV. As we've observed, there was much less appetite in the Nineties to go after America's Gordon Gekkos. *Cops* both mirrored this mentality and fed it in a manner that Doyle described as "mutual reinforcement. Like many media products, *Cops* is not exactly 'preaching to the converted,' but more preaching to those who lean that way—reinforcing fear of crime and law and order views among people already pre-disposed to them." Culturally speaking, a graying lieutenant in a shabby raincoat driving a beat-up clunker simply didn't stand much of a chance for relevance in the *Cops* universe.

The good news is that Nineties violent criming significantly declined through the decade, and people's perceptions of the frequency of felonies declined with it. But *Cops* had by then established a cultural foothold through its frequent network and syndication viewings, while *Columbo* puttered along with an inconsistent schedule of movie airings into the early aughts.

Cops aside, the variety and quality of television offerings had already started changing after *Columbo* first ended in 1978. In this transition period between Old and New *Columbo*, 1981's *Hill Street Blues* was fresh, innovative and the acknowledged standard for police shows. Others would follow.

By *Columbo's* second wind in 1989, the sloppy cop was already a piece of history from a different era. Through the Nineties, its episodes could be judged against exciting and innovative network and cable fare like *Oz, ER, West Wing, The X-Files, The Sopranos,* and *Twin Peaks.* New *Columbo* no longer owned the Quality trademark. In fact, it lagged well behind. In that environment, *Columbo* 2.0 was bound to falter. If you squinted, you could still see signs of value, but for those who grew up with the Classic Era, they were faint traces of what once was.

Such laments were unimaginable in February of 1989, as the *Columbo* true believers eagerly anticipated the return of their favorite disheveled detective. ABC felt the same way. In an early show of good faith, the network debuted the series return during February Sweeps. This was one of four periods during the year when the ratings provided by Arbitron and the A.C. Nielsen Company would determine local advertising rates. TV sales executives could charge advertisers more money if they could prove that more people were watching their station. This ongoing tradition meant that networks loaded up particular weeks in February, May, July and November with special programming that they were certain would draw a big audience.

For ABC, that included *Columbo*. The cover of *TV Guide* for February 4, 1989 blared "Get Ready for a Hot February!" Inside was an article co-written by Peter Falk promoting the arrival: "Rumpled and Ready—Columbo Returns! What You Can Expect from Him Now." The title alone fairly invites the reader to comparison-shop with Classic *Columbo*.

As befits a *TV Guide* article, it's not long on words. However, it does spend extended effort to assure everyone that this is, absolutely, your father's *Columbo*. "*Columbo* isn't going to change. I liked it just the way it was and that's how it's going to stay," proclaims the star. "When Columbo comes back on the job, he's gonna be just the same as always. He asks questions. He thinks about the answers and asks more questions—until there's that one last thing he needs to ask to solve the case. That isn't going to change." A more perfect description of the anti-*Cops* could not have been written.

"Making sure the show would be exactly the same after a 10-year absence wasn't easy.... The world's changed a lot since then. More guns, bombs, missiles—they're making too much progress," lamented Falk. "I guess it's true that the world has changed around Columbo in the last decade. Styles of clothes, models of cars. Now there are personal computers and no-smoking sections. But Columbo will keep doing things the way he's always done them."[25]

It is prophetically ironic that Falk noted the changed popular culture in the most superficial way possible, never recognizing the actual sociocultural changes that would make it difficult for New *Columbo* to gain traction. Perhaps it was a sign of the times that on their Sweeps cover, *TV Guide* had photos of Robert Duvall in *Lonesome Dove*, Billy Crystal, bikinied Catherine Oxenberg in the TV-movie *Swimsuit*, a photo from something called *The Sex Tapes*—and instead of Peter Falk, it was Burt Reynolds promoting *BL Stryker* for the ABC Mystery Movie.

After its *Columbo Likes the Nightlife* 2003 swan song, the Lieutenant didn't evaporate from collective memory. He never lost his status as a Seventies icon or his towering place in the annals of detective fiction. The show did, perhaps, take a hiatus from popular admiration, although the debut of the Columbophile Blog in June 2015 established a welcoming community for its millions of worldwide fans.

Unfortunately, it took a global pandemic in 2020 to bring *Columbo* back to relevance during a trying time. The opportunity to binge-watch while shuttered from the outside world inspired the many online appreciations and recommendations that spiked interest and raves for the shambolic Lieutenant. And the social culture that made *Columbo* a sensation in the Seventies but less relevant in the Nineties came full circle to bring the Classic Era of the series back to popular attention.

Although it could not have been forecast at the time, Columbo's takedowns of the Seventies elite proved to be very morally comforting in 2020s, when the divide between the haves and have-nots grew even greater than it had been 50 years prior. Gordon Gekko's status as a money-grubbing antihero to the generations had passed. As Spiegel wrote, "The last few months of our lives have, among other things, shone a bright, unfeeling light on the class inequities in our country. Billionaires keep getting richer, while the unemployment rate soars and joblessness floods the streets. There's little actual victory to be seen against the rich, so we have to take the victories we can get in popular culture."[26]

The need for equal justice provides another reason for *Columbo* to impact us now. Traditionally, television shows promoted the view of law enforcement as the ultimate authority, above reproach, and their vision of right and wrong and how to police it was churned out nightly in what critics labeled "copaganda." Clearly, *Cops* was a proud proponent of this, but the history of this formula reaches far back to *The Untouchables, Dragnet, Adam-12*, and continued through the decades with *Hawaii 5-0, Kojak* and scores of others. New generations of viewers were discovering that *Columbo* went against the grain of this strain of lawman.

And once again, contemporaneous police events with an accompanying presence of video evidence impacted the cultural environment. In May 2020, cameras captured the sight and sound of George Floyd pleading, "I can't breathe" as Minneapolis officers kneeled on his neck or otherwise restrained him for over nine agonizing minutes. A wave of massive protests immediately swept the United States.

The April 2021 guilty verdict for Derek Chauvin in the Floyd murder trial highlighted the policing issues that had been plaguing U.S. law enforcement for some time, and the concept of equal justice today remains a slippery subject. But a dialogue had begun. "The Black Lives Matter movement has rightfully initiated a re-evaluation of crime shows and the harmful role they have played in making (anti) heroes out of violent, regulations-dodging cops. Columbo relies exclusively on observation, deduction and psychology, which gives his police work an abstract quality: Visual signifiers of law enforcement are largely invisible, whether they are uniforms, patrol cars, police stations, and jails or, most important, guns."[27]

Calls for re-examining the effects of copaganda crime shows on social discourse did produce a major casualty. *Cops* was canceled in 2020 before its 33rd season debut on the Paramount network. Although subsequently re-imagined as a streaming program, the cultural environment had now conspired to turn *Cops* from a Nineties social phenomenon into an historical leftover.

Meanwhile, *Columbo's* anti-copaganda stance thrived once again. "*Columbo* is a representation of cops, not as they actually are, but it's an idealized representation of what cops should be.

Columbo doesn't bother sex workers. He doesn't arrest petty criminals. He leaves a lot of people alone, because they're not hurting anyone and he doesn't care. He's a walking avatar for the ideal of what an actual community-driven policing service could manage. And this is despite being largely nonviolent, refusing the use of guns and coercion."[28]

Not being weighed down by the aggressive tropes of the traditional cop, Columbo is free to dispense justice on his own terms, and his sense of integrity and lawfulness drives his actions, arrests and their consequences. In today's world, this provides a further element of comfort and was another prominent theme running through the pandemic appreciations: "There's a bit of wish fulfillment in seeing this humble public servant walk into sumptuous mansions and make jerks who think they're above the law finally face the consequences of their crimes."[29]

In an era of social media trolling and posturing, fake news claims, "alternative facts," defiant doubling down, and attempts to obfuscate the truth, the simpler Seventies of *Columbo's* universe provide a moral clarity and calming influence, as author Dana Schwartz explains. "The pleasure of *Columbo* isn't in knowing the ending… it's in briefly inhabiting a world where everyone agrees on a clear set of rules. When the murderers are outsmarted, they politely turn themselves in… There is an elegance in their defeat, an acknowledgment of a game well played, and an understanding that there's no point any longer in making a fuss."[30]

Recent political events have many concerned about the possible damage to the public trust that is so critical to American democracy. In such a world, writes one, "I've been leaning hard into *Columbo* lately because of how certain the triumph is…. [Today] scores of criminals… will likely not be held accountable for their crimes in any way whatsoever."[31] *Columbo* fans, just don't think too hard about what happens when the Lieutenant's cases go to court in the Columboverse without the certainty of producing convictions.

COLUMBO: I'm just another cop. My name's Columbo. I'm a lieutenant.
JOANNA FERRIS (distressed, walking away): Oh, I think I'd better get back…
COLUMBO: Look, wait a minute. Let me tell you something… you look very tired to me, and I think you had a terrible experience in there, and I think I ought to drive you home. Let's call it a night. I think you've answered enough questions…. I'll bet you haven't had anything to eat…

Leave it to an L.A. cop—but certainly not "just another cop"—to help provide a measure of salve for our post-pandemic angst and collective frustration. Just as he did for the newly-widowed Mrs. Ferris in *Murder by the Book*, Detective Lieutenant Columbo is ready to whip up an omelet for all of us.

Cultural forces can shape perceptions. The failure of *Columbo* in the Nineties helps verify that it was a significant product of the Seventies. But even when not quite suited to the times in its second run, Classic *Columbo* episodes remained ingrained in the memories of older demographics and newly-discovered by the younger. The popularity of *Columbo* endured.

Fortunately, *Columbo* is uniquely suited to *our* times, as many have discovered and are still discovering. We see that a hero can indeed bring down the rich and famous to mete out justice, while we're stuck in an era where the moral compass to determine right from wrong is hopelessly demagnetized. To our rescue, riding a sputtering junker, comes a disheveled everyman with one good eye and a taste for chili. All things are possible in a time where we need escapist entertainment and, yes, comfort. Columbo carries a beacon of humanity in our sometimes-inhumane surroundings.

IV.
Columbo and Popular Culture: Crossing the Cultural Streams

In *Columbo: Make Me a Perfect Murder*, Amelie Hastie aims to examine Columbo intertextually. (Don't be scared, it's not as intimidating as it sounds). Her working definition: "In contemporary media studies, intertextuality has come to mean that any individual text, whether an artwork like a movie or a commonplace text like a newspaper article or a billboard, is part of a larger cultural discourse."[1] In academia, text is anything that conveys meaning to us, not necessarily a literal text of just words. A TV show, a painting, a map, or an advertisement is as much a "text" as a book.

So, as Hastie notes, when we watch *A Stitch in Crime*, for example, we are likely to associate the actors Leonard Nimoy and Will Geer with previous similar roles. Nimoy's Dr. Mayfield has some cold *Star Trek* Spock in him; Geer's Dr. Heideman, the folksy and friendly Grandpa Walton. When we see Laurence Harvey play a chess master in *The Most Dangerous Match*, 1973's viewers would associate the character with famous contemporary chess genius Bobby Fischer. We are referencing the different texts of separate news items and TV shows.

When Dr. Spengler cautions his fellow ghostbusters, "Don't cross the streams!," that's literally the opposite of what happens intertextually when we sample any media. Cultural streams get crossed all the time. Movies, books, television, Tik Tok, music, graphic novels, video games, you name it. There are multiple ways to make connections and meaning between different cultural works. So when we watch *Columbo*, we can intertextualize: with another fictional detective, with an iconic movie auteur, with a Peter Falk film fantasy, with rap music, with a prolific guest star, and even with—heaven forbid—Mrs. Columbo.

Columbo's intersections with popular culture extend to its connections with other media and other characters, both within and beyond the decade of the Seventies. So let's cross some streams.

10.
The Legacy of the Thinking Detective

Crime pays because crime sells—in magazines and books, movies and television, true crime and fictional. From Marlowe to Marple, Spade to Spenser, Chan to Charles, and Hammer to Hardy Boys, the list of popular crime-busters and their crime-solving methods is a long and distinguished one.

In this famous lineage, Columbo and Sherlock Holmes each belong in the class for cerebral investigators, keen intellects using incisive observational skills to solve the crimes likely to go unsolved by conventional officers. While Columbo and Holmes are not the only "thinking man's detectives," their cultural prominence and worldwide fame set them apart from the now-stodgy Ellery Queens and Nero Wolfes of the literary sleuthing set.

No intersection of the Columbo character with popular culture can avoid the long cape-and-deerstalker shadow of Mr. Sherlock Holmes. Peter Falk himself has invoked the Holmes name in describing his eponymous show and character: "Columbo is an ass-backwards Sherlock Holmes. Holmes had a long neck, Columbo has no neck; Holmes smoked a pipe, Columbo chews up six cigars a day...."[2] What makes Columbo and Sherlock stand out among the detecting crowd?

Holmes' worldwide popularity is untouched. Guinness World Records lists him, by a wide margin, as the most portrayed literary human character in film and television history. For all of Columbo's fame, it was Arthur Conan Doyle's creation of Holmes that pretty much invented the modern practice of fandom. When Conan Doyle wrote Holmes into a plunge from Reichenbach Falls in 1893's "The Final Problem," the unprecedented outcry from readers of *The Strand* magazine forced the author to resurrect the character years later (lucky for Conan Doyle, nobody had viewed an actual Holmes corpse). According to the BBC, "The public reaction to the death was unlike anything previously seen for fictional events. More than 20,000 *Strand* readers canceled their subscriptions, outraged by Holmes' premature demise. The magazine barely survived."[3]

In *Troubled Waters*, Columbo inexplicably whips an iconic Holmes-style magnifying glass *out of his pants pocket* to examine the murder weapon. This would seem a curious choice to make for a tourist cruise carry-on item, but the magnifier, so closely aligned with our image of the great Victorian Era detective, is very apt. Let's pull out our own figurative lens to observe and analyze the two famous sleuths for ourselves.

The physical traits of the pair are almost polar opposites. In the first Sherlock Holmes work, *A Study in Scarlet*, his chronicler Dr. Watson describes him: "His very person and appearance were such as to strike the attention of the most casual observer. In height, he was rather over six feet, and so excessively lean that he seemed to be considerably taller. His eyes were sharp and piercing… and his thin, hawk-like nose gave his whole expression an air of alertness and decision."

The 1887 novel depicts his distinctive attire, often consisting of tweed suits, frock-coats, "and occasionally an ulster." The frock was a formal, long-sleeved coat with a knee-length skirt cut just above the knee with a back center-vent; the ulster was a daytime overcoat with cape and sleeves. Watson also describes "a long, grey travelling cloak and a close-fitting cloth hat" in the fourth short story, "The Boscombe Valley Mystery."

It's in this work that illustrator Sidney Paget first conceived of the now-familiar deerstalker cap to adorn Holmes' head, although Conan Doyle himself gave no such specific description.[4] Paget's precise and evocative drawings accompanied Conan Doyle's short stories of *The Strand*. They created the distinctive interpretation of Sherlock Holmes that has remained in most movie and television adaptations, and contributes to our immediate minds-eye image of the detective.

The visual contrast of Sherlock with Columbo shouldn't be too hard to picture.

The character qualities that make Columbo so appealing are as easy for us to recall as his disheveled appearance. Among other attributes, the Lieutenant is unassuming, unimposing, respectful, humble, self-effacing, and deferential. Holmes is not.

Their presence at investigations can give us a few clues to their temperament, as Falk himself noted for Mark Dawidziak. "I remember being very impressed by Sherlock Holmes. He'd show up, and everybody would turn to him for the answer. I thought it was important in the opening of *Ransom for a Dead Man* that no one turn to me for anything. I was just a local. I wanted to be ignored.... Nobody wanted to know this guy's opinion. There's a lack of pretension. You expect something quite different from a great detective. [Columbo] arrives and, instead of people turning to him, their attention is on this major kidnapping. What's he doing? He's looking for this engraved pen that he's dropped. That's a nice quality... it's a humanizing thing."[5]

As Falk explained, Holmes often expects to be the center of attention, even—or especially—when at an official Scotland Yard crime scene. In *A Study in Scarlet*, he is literally between competing Inspectors Lestrade and Gregson as they vie for his favor at a particularly bloody murder tableau.

HOLMES: It reminds me of the circumstances attendant to the murder of Van Jansen, in '34. Do you remember the case, Gregson?
GREGSON: No, sir.
HOLMES: Read up on it—you really should. There is nothing new under the sun.

After a close examination of the dead man by Holmes, he allows Gregson to have the body carted away.

HOLMES: Is there no circumstance on which this whole case appears to hinge?
GREGSON (offended voice): I have said all I have to say.

Watson notes a chuckle from Holmes, who is about to make a remark when Lestrade enters with news of a discovery in the adjoining room. Lestrade proffers his explanation of the evidence, prompting Holmes to "ruffle the little man's temper by bursting into an explosion of laughter."

Gregson and Lestrade defer. Holmes and his magnifying glass inspect the scene, as he "chattered away to himself under his breath the whole time, keeping up a running fire of explanations, groans, whistles and little cries suggestive of encouragement and of hope. For 20 minutes or more he continued his researches, measuring with the most exact care the distance between marks which were entirely invisible to me.... In one place he gathered up very carefully a little pile of grey dust from the floor, and packed it away in an envelope."

WOMEN GO CRAZY for a sharp-dressed man: Artist Sidney Paget originated the classic Holmes look.

The Scotland Yarders "watched their amateur companion with considerable curiosity and some contempt." They eagerly look for Holmes' opinion. Instead, he says, "'You are doing so well now that it would be a pity for anyone to interfere.' There was a world of sarcasm in his voice as he spoke."

Over the course of each of their series of episodes and stories, Columbo and Holmes would subtly shift these crime scene demeanors, Columbo becoming a tad more authoritative over the years, and Holmes a bit less of an ass. But these behaviors do help illustrate the differences between the two.

Columbo's relatable humanity and kindly nature is as natural and lived-in as his raincoat, plain for all to see. We know that Columbo is an empathetic everyman. For the reader to make any emotional connection with Sherlock Holmes, however, something more was required—a partner. Dr. Watson is not exactly a sidekick, but his presence serves as a foil for the London sleuth. More crucially, his friendship with Holmes and his narration of their adventures humanizes a character who would otherwise be stiff, cold and unrelatable. As for Columbo, when the second season opened, NBC's request for a sidekick was answered by producers with Dog.

Columbo appears to be out of his element when pursuing the rich, coddled and famous killers who populate the fancy neighborhoods and private communities of Los Angeles. While he looks and acts out-of-place in Alex Benedict's *Etude in Black* mansion, for example, we know that his persistence in the face of wealth and power results in justice prevailing despite the many advantages afforded his antagonists.

Unlike Columbo, Sherlock Holmes is much more comfortable in the orbit of affluent Brits as well the assorted royalty who occasionally pop up in his adventures. Hobnobbing with higher-ups isn't limited to London, as Holmes encounters others of Europe's pampered and privileged. But Holmes also takes many a case from what Dr. Watson calls "the poor folk," and, like Columbo, he treats them with respect and solace. At least, as long as their problems are a worthy challenge. Holmes' targets are often upper-crust, well-regarded, or protected by their status. This is not to the exclusion of other villains, but Holmes favors no class, as long as his own sense of justice is met in the end.

But because Holmes is a private for-hire investigator and Columbo is a public-sector police detective, their justice endgames may not always be the same. Columbo only once let a killer off the hook (*Forgotten Lady*), but the fates were going to be cruel to the terminally ill and brain-diseased Grace Wheeler anyway.

Holmes exhibits more flexibility in how he dispenses justice, especially in a handful of cases after his timely resurrection from Reichenbach Falls. "The Adventure of the Bruce-Partington Plans" and "The Adventure of Charles Augustus Milverton" showcase some warrant-less breaking and entering. In "The Five Orange Pips," he explicitly announces, "I shall be my own police." And in several exploits, Holmes concludes by waving off the perpetrator from facing Scotland Yard at all, after concluding that the crime was justified in avenging a heinous wrong. The backstories for such rationalizations usually involve noble causes, odious blackmail, doomed romances, hidden secrets, or damning betrayals (Ex: "The Adventure of the Abbey Grange," "The Boscombe Valley Mystery").

Columbo was never an action series, and Columbo's physical skills seem to be limited to falling down a hillside (*The Greenhouse Jungle*), falling from a tree (*Forgotten Lady*), and some sweaty cycling at Milo Janus' spa. By contrast, Sherlock Holmes' physical abilities are a complement to his mental acuity. He is an expert at singlestick, a martial art using a wooden stick as a weapon. He has strength, athleticism, swordsman skills, and training as a boxer and martial artist (bartitsu). Unlike Columbo, Holmes is adept with the pistol he sometimes carries. He is also a master of disguises, skillfully impersonating a venerable Italian priest, an elderly woman, and an old master mariner, among other guises. Columbo was underwhelming *Undercover*.

Their methods of case-solving differed. As we observed earlier, there is a very real psychological foundation for how Columbo parries with the killer as he pokes and prods to get the villain to incriminate himself. The science of proxemics examines how Columbo's specialty, personal privacy invasions, are used to unsettle a target; he expertly feeds the killer's superiority complex and projects his own inferiority; he rarely looks to pose an intellectual or physical threat to the killer; he'll lull the baddie into a false sense of security before closing in for the kill. Psychology is applied to the enemy.

Holmes' psychology takes a counter approach. Columbo never wants to intimidate, but Sherlock is an imposing figure, both physically and intellectually. And, unlike Columbo, Holmes has a degree of notoriety, thanks to the writings of Dr. Watson. In one of the rare short stories written from Holmes' perspective, the detective himself states clearly, "I have found it wise to impress clients with a sense of power." ("The Adventure of the Blanched Soldier")

Much of Holmes' psychology is in how he thinks and uses observation to solve the puzzle, and not necessarily in his interplay with the suspects. Exceptions would include his relentless hounding of arch-nemesis Professor Moriarty in "The Final Problem," and his cat-and-mouse with the beguiling Irene Adler in "A Scandal in Bohemia" (as Watson wistfully notes, "To Sherlock Holmes, she was always the woman").

The two each have a healthy degree of skepticism when they approach a case. They have open minds. They recognize vital facts, even if they do not immediately piece together their significance. For Columbo, this would bug him incessantly until he could tie up the "loose ends." For Holmes, this was the proverbial "three-pipe problem" that required complete isolation while he sorted through the possibilities. In the books, it was in Holmes' "brain attic" where he developed his theories; in Steven Moffat's modern *Sherlock* updating, this was Holmes' "mind palace" where he retrieved relevant facts.

Do great minds really think alike? Columbo and Holmes certainly had parallel approaches in their reasoning. Conan Doyle's real-life model for the Holmes character was forensic surgeon John Bell, whom Doyle studied under at Edinburgh University in 1877-1878. Doyle's autobiography says of Bell, "He was a very skillful surgeon, but his strong point was diagnosis, not only of disease, but of occupation and character. I had ample chance of studying his methods and of noting that he often learned more of the patient by a few quick glances than I had done by my questions. Occasionally the results were very dramatic. I used and amplified his methods when in later life I tried to build up a scientific detective who solved cases on his own merits and not through the folly of the criminal."[6]

In the second Holmes novel, *The Sign of Four*, Holmes specifies "the three qualities necessary for the ideal detective: the power of observation, that of deduction... and knowledge, which [can] come in time." Let's review how Holmes and Columbo share these traits.

For both detectives, the devil is in the details. Columbo is bothered by how the shoelaces are tied, the weight of the luggage, the bullet hole placement in the victim's dress, the missing clock chime, the unscuffed bedroom slippers, or the turned-off light in the murder room. For Holmes, it might be the useless bell rope, the ventilator shaft that doesn't ventilate, or the bed clamped to the floor ("The Adventure of the Speckled Band").

In "A Case of Identity," Holmes explains the practice of observation to Watson. "You did not know where to look, and so you missed all that was important. I can never bring you to realize the importance of sleeves, the suggestiveness of thumbnails, or the great issues that may hang from a bootlace. Now, what did you gather from that woman's appearance? Describe it."

Unlike in those Basil Rathbone Sherlock movies, Watson was actually no slouch. He provides a lengthy and finely-tuned description of the client who had just paid them a visit at 221B Baker Street. Holmes' reply is withering: "Pon my word, Watson, you are coming along wonderfully. You have really done very well indeed. It is true that you have missed everything of importance, but you have hit upon the method... Never trust to general impressions, my boy, but concentrate yourself upon details."

Holmes' powers of observation were stretched to such an extreme that he could reliably spit out an instant biography of someone he just met simply by discerning the arcane trivialities of their outward appearance. Columbo couldn't do that, but would surely concur with Sherlock when the Great Detective says, "It has long been an axiom of mine that the little things are infinitely the most important." Events that may be seemingly self-evident, like the apparent suicides of *Etude in Black* and *Forgotten Lady*, are anything but to Columbo, once he considers the crime scene details. Holmes has a thought to cover that, too: "There is nothing more deceptive than an obvious fact." ("The Boscombe Valley Mystery")

Holmes decried guessing. Without details, he was reluctant to speculate, lest the evidence get twisted to fit a hypothesis. In "The Adventure of the Second Stain," Holmes would repeat one of his truisms: "It is a capital mistake to theorize in advance of the facts." Once the facts are collected, the deductions can begin, which may lead the investigator to an unexpected result. "How often have I said to you that when you have eliminated the impossible, whatever remains, however improbable, must be the truth?" (*The Sign of Four*)

Details drive the deductions. As British philosopher John Gray explains, "The type of reasoning Holmes uses—sometimes called abductive reasoning—can't offer certainty or any precise assessment of probability, only the best available account of events.... Holmes notices things other people don't, and then, using a mental agility that involves creative imagination... comes up with hypotheses he tests one by one.... It's not cold logic but a clairvoyant eye for detail that enables him to solve his cases. Holmes has the knack of knowing where to look, asking the right questions and crafting theories to account for what he has found."[7]

Columbo has a similar way of thinking, which might be best summarized with a statistical model that social science dubs "Posterior Predictive Checks." This is the comparison between what a model predicts would happen in a particular situation and the actual observed data, which will tell if the model is inadequate to describe the data. "The goal... is to drive intuitions about the qualitative manner in which the model succeeds or fails, and about what sort of novel model formulation might better capture the trends in the data."[8]

Columbo would never offer such a smarty-pants description. He'll simply observe a scene, or listen to a killer's story, and, using the available facts, gut-check how well that story produces the ending—the death that is being investigated. If a particular explanation is not very good at producing the ending, Columbo will look for other stories that are better.

The Jesse Jerome murder scene in *Now You See Him* is a perfect demonstration of the PPC model. Columbo can't fathom the supposed chain of events that led to Jerome's shooting. "How does a man get shot in the front but land here?" he wonders, pointing to an area away from Jerome's office door. Columbo quickly paces the rooms, his index finger to his lips, his hands to his temples, literally walking through numerous scenarios, from door to body outline, body outline back to door. "Suppose Jerome comes from the office, opened the door...." He spitballs three different "Suppose" situations, exasperated, saying "I don't understand how this happened." But finally, he sees the light: "The murderer opened the door! Jerome hears the door open, now he comes walking forward to see what happened. The murderer sees him, shoots him from the front, and the body falls just where we found it. That I understand!"

The third quality for Holmes' ideal detective is knowledge. Holmes' natural intelligence is clearly in his DNA, since his brother Mycroft is even smarter, though lazier. But Holmes diligently learns about anything that could give him a crime-solving edge. Some of his specialized areas of expertise include code-breaking, cryptanalysis, tobaccos, latent bicycle prints, gunpowder residue, poisons, geology, tattoos, music composition, and chemistry. He continually hones his reasoning skills with his obsessive attention to detail.

[Sherlockians may counter that in the debut novel, Holmes famously professed ignorance that the earth revolved around the sun. To which, I propose that Holmes and his new flatmate were just getting to know each other, and Holmes was likely yanking Dr. Watson's stethoscope. Conan Doyle never expected to be writing an entire series of Holmes mysteries, and if he had, it's doubtful that he would have immediately set limits on his protagonist's abilities. In any event, there is zero mention in future stories about a ceiling to Holmes' knowledge.]

Columbo and Holmes each share an innate curiosity about their surroundings. Sherlock may appear to know just about everything under the sun, but even for him, the search for knowledge continued. "Education never ends, Watson. It is a series of lessons, with the greatest for the last." ("The Adventure of the Red Circle") And over the course of the Seventies, Columbo learns about wine, food delicacies, advertising, horticulture, art and more, thanks to the wisdom conferred by particular killers-of-the month.

Columbo also has natural intelligence, as noted by both psychologist killer Dr. Flemming in *Prescription: Murder* and Sigma Society brainiac Oliver Brandt in *The Bye-Bye Sky High IQ Murder Case*. But Columbo's work ethic had a bit different nose-to-the-grindstone focus than Sherlock's. He tells Brandt, "In school, there were lots of smarter kids. And when I first joined the force, sir, they had some very clever people there.... But I figured, if I worked harder then they did, put in more time, read the books, kept my eyes open, maybe I could make it happen. And I did." Holmes worked smarter, but Columbo worked harder.

The *Columbo* inverted mystery format itself provides a crucial difference in how we perceive the two detectives. In the inverted mystery, Columbo and the audience know who did the murder deed, so the goal is to collect the clues that would establish guilt. The viewer tags along. Columbo digs, he questions, he speculates, he learns, and most of it is transparently in the open for us to observe. We see the observation and deduction process as it unfolds in "real time." Our job, as alert viewers, is to detect which clue(s) will pin the crime on the villain. The mystery for us is in how Columbo will establish that guilt, not in establishing whodunit.

This is not the mystery we join when Holmes is on the case. Most often, Sherlock is prowling the scene alone in his thoughts amidst Watson and others, who wouldn't dare interrupt the master investigator while the game is afoot. Holmes might deign to bestow Watson a vague comment or question to send up a flag that a particular point may be of interest, knowing full well that Watson will either interpret the clue incorrectly or miss the point entirely. As do we. Which is fine by Holmes, because it allows him to show off his masterclass detecting skills at the story's conclusion as he Holmesplains it all.

Contrast that with Columbo's approach. In *A Matter of Honor*, he's dropped into a case while on break in Mexico, helping Comandante Sanchez probe a death at the ranch of famed ex-matador Luis Montoya. The victim had been gored in the ring by a bull, an action which the audience knows was induced and facilitated by Montoya. Columbo, and presumably the viewer, knows nothing about bullfighting, so his ignorance is shared by us as he asks for clarification on key items and their functions: the muleta, picks, and a lance. The Lieutenant telegraphs to us the importance of these bullfighting clues, providing the breadcrumbs that will be followed as Columbo pieces together the killing.

A Sherlock Holmes mystery would approach it differently. Pages would be spent on the backstories for victim Rangel and his son, Hector. Holmes would do his inspection of the scene, but he would likely already know the particulars of Spanish-style 1726-era modern bullfighting. Conan Doyle's stories frequently invoked foreign, and therefore "exotic" means of death by poison, strange animals, and the like, all of which Holmes grasped, but Watson and the neophyte reader did not. Bull goring would be no different. At the close, Holmes would reveal all, perhaps with a dramatic flourish of his own muleta.

This is not to say that one approach to the Tale of the Murderous Matador is better than the other, just that they would be different. One is all-seeing and all-knowing, the other less so, but nonetheless successful. There's certainly storytelling space for each.

Off-screen and off-page, the development of stories in the Holmes and Columbo canon share a common frustration in that they were hard to plot. It was a frequent lament of Peter Falk, particularly in the later years, but also one of Arthur Conan Doyle, who felt the pressure of cranking them out regularly for *The Strand* magazine. Close readers will recognize recycled elements in the first set of Holmes stories after rising from Reichenbach Falls in 1903, *The Return of Sherlock Holmes*.[9]

There was an eight-year break between Holmes adventures after Conan Doyle killed off his creation. If one were of a cynical bent, it might be said that both Conan Doyle and the ABC network brought back each of the detectives for reasons having to do more with commerce than art. And, as many *Columbo* fans are disappointed by the quality of episodes in passing years, so too are Sherlockians eager to debate whether or not Conan Doyle actually wrote some of the later stories himself, the quality is so slipshod.

We can all point to our least-favorite Seventies *Columbo* clunkers and acknowledge that not all episodes were gems. So too, you'll find plenty of ho-hum Holmes among Doyle's earlier narratives. But even in the lesser-lights of the Holmes library, one can find strong writing quality in the characterizations, atmosphere and setting descriptors of each short story. Likewise, the high-grade production elements of the Classic *Columbo* era helped mitigate any issues when plots and gotchas might come up short.

Columbo and Sherlock Holmes have been at this detecting thing for quite awhile now. Their popularity is undeniable. Their legacies are secure. But for the future, one wonders if we need Columbo to develop the superpower that fuels Sherlock Holmes and keeps him relevant across generations—the power of regeneration.

The first Holmes novel, *A Study in Scarlet*, was published in 1887, and since then the character has traveled in and out of the public domain in the U.K. and the U.S. A property in public domain may be used by anyone without restrictions. Otherwise, a property's copyright protects it from being used by others without permission and/or compensation. Without detailing the copyright intricacies here, the character of "Sherlock Holmes" had been almost completely in the public domain for many years and of free use for anyone wishing to adapt it. Thus, Stephen Moffat's *Sherlock* and the American TV series *Elementary*.[10]

On the other hand, as of this writing, the rights to the Columbo character have remained in dispute for years, keeping any development of another *Columbo* series in limbo. Many fans are pleased by this, not wanting to see a bungled sequel, reboot or reimagining that they believe would sully the good Lieutenant's name and reputation. To this I would say, be careful what you wish for.

As a legacy popular culture icon, Holmes already has a clear advantage, originating as a written work. Although the illustrations of Sidney Paget gave readers an early visualization of the classic Holmes look, readers' freedom of imagination has allowed many actors to essay the role in their own style through the years. Personally, Basil Rathbone, Jeremy Brett, and Benedict Cumberbatch have all been favorites. New actors are engaged, new plots are concocted, new technologies are applied. In this way, new generations of

Sherlock Holmes fans have been allowed to spawn and spread the legacy.

Not so with *Columbo*. And for many, it's Peter Falk and nobody else. An advantage to being a written work is that Sherlock Holmes doesn't age (noted exceptions being a handful of unsuccessful stories from his retired beekeeper era). A revolving door of actors keeps the character fresh and ageless. I would argue that we have already seen what happens when we don't allow anyone else to be Columbo, and unfortunately, it's called Nineties *Columbo*. For Classic *Columbo* devotees, it is sometimes painful to watch Peter Falk displaying the familiar effects of time on this earth as Older Columbo works a case.

Without regeneration of the character, years from now Falk-as-Columbo will be trapped in amber, adored by a certain generation of fans, but in perpetual stasis without fresh interpretations. If the same had been allowed to happen to Basil Rathbone in 1946, would the legacy of Sherlock Holmes be what it is today?

The Reboot-or-Not argument is a familiar one to *Columbo* fans. Mark Dawidziak, author of *The Columbo Phile*, argues that it can be done. "Nothing's ever going to touch Peter's performance, but if a character is truly a great character, then it should be able to be played and reinterpreted by other actors," he said. "It all comes down to how it's done. I think the Columbo character is strong enough and vibrant enough to be brought back…. If Hamlet's a great character and he can be interpreted and reinterpreted by many different actors, why can't Columbo? If Sherlock Holmes can be played by a lot of different actors, why can't Columbo? And I think Peter might be one of the first to say that, because he was an actor himself."[11]

> DET. CHIEF SUPT. WILLIAM DURK: Holmes… Sherlock Holmes was, I suppose, our most famous detective. But I'm sure you noticed on your visit to our new file section at the Yard why he wouldn't even qualify these days. No, no. In our modern police—
>
> COLUMBO (not paying attention): Those fish and chips are greasy, but they're sure good! What were you saying, sir?
>
> – *Dagger of the Mind* (1972)

Columbo's jolly jaunt to London, *Dagger of the Mind*, is generally not among the favorites of *Columbo* devotees. It's very stereotypical and campy, but some would argue that's precisely the point of a fun homage to Britain and its grand tradition of the intellectual parlor mysteries that Levinson and Link based their lieutenant on. The episode has many of London's tourist attractions box-checked, as Columbo runs around snapping pics of everything from Big Ben to Tower Bridge to a Buckingham Palace changing of the guard to the Houses of Parliament.

So of course, we get a Sherlock Homes reference. Yet, it's not made by Columbo. And when Scotland Yard official Durk makes the remark walking along the Thames, the distracted Columbo's not even ambling alongside him to notice. For Peter Falk, who had such a familiarity with how his character compared to Holmes, this seems a tad curious. My own explanation is that while Falk the actor could make that comparison, Columbo the character never would. Columbo's modesty would prevent him from even uttering the name of the most famous fictional detective of all time.

Holmes, of course, would have no problem acknowledging the plaudits. Fans of the two detectives wouldn't have it any other way.

11.
A Hitch in Crime

Today, we barely notice any intertextual difference between a movie and a television show. Technological advances in size and picture quality have heightened the visual medium's home consumer experience, and watching from the living room couch is no longer a squinting exercise. Television came of age being called the "idiot box," the "small screen," and the "boob tube," now-archaic descriptors of how we watched everything from *ALF* to *Zorro*. It wasn't until Columbo's 1968 debut that sales of American color TV sets surpassed black-and-white models.

The quality divide between movie and television productions used to be unmistakable. No longer. Actors, directors and behind-the-screens personnel are shared. Netflix films are nominated for Academy Awards. But during most of television's history, and certainly in the Seventies, theater features were clearly perceived one way, TV series another.

There was one exception to this rule. Steven Spielberg, director of the first *Columbo* series episode *Murder by the Book*, immediately recognized this special quality, as he was told to make his show "look like a feature film.... That was my first experience with episodic television where the producers were encouraging me to make shots, whereas other television producers would beg me not to."[1]

What helped make *Columbo* different than all other television series of the time was its "connective tissue," the superior production elements that held an episode together while Columbo was in relentless pursuit of the killer. These features would include the scripting, direction, music score, sets, costuming, locations, supporting actors, camerawork, editing, guest stars, and the overall ability to strike the right balance of serious crime-solving, characterization, and humor. Minus commercials and the difference in screen size, it was a cinematic experience.

In movie parlance, many of these elements create the *mise en scene*, the on-camera components seen by the viewer that are controlled by the film's director. *Columbo* mastered these elements on Sunday night television. And in the theater, the undisputed master of the cinematic *mise en scene* was also the Master of Suspense, Alfred Hitchcock. This shared quality of Hitchcock and *Columbo* is not the only one. Columbo's genesis—and *Columbo's* excellence—have their roots in the rich Hitch history.

"One of television's great contributions is that it has brought back murder into the home, where it belongs."
– Alfred Hitchcock, *National Observer* (1966)

The throughline from Hitchcock to *Columbo* begins in March 1960. As chronicled in an Emmys Hall of Fame tribute and by Mark Dawidziak in *The Columbo Phile*, *Columbo* co-creators Richard Levinson and William Link were aspiring writers at the University of Pennsylvania's Wharton School of Finance and Commerce when they made their first literary sale to the *Ellery Queen Mystery Magazine*, winning a Best New Short Story award in 1953.[2]

But it wasn't until several years later, after their Army service had been completed, that the pair sold their next piece, titled "May I Come In." Featured in the March 1960 issue of the *Alfred Hitchcock Mystery Magazine*, its title was changed to "Dear Corpus Delecti," and was the first of a number of Levinson-Link mystery and crime stories purchased by *AHMM* over the next nine months that helped keep the writing pair solvent as they looked to break through in Hollywood.

As Levinson describes it, "May I Come In" also almost introduced the world to a now-famous police lieutenant. "[The story] contained the alibi for the crime," noted Levinson in Dawidziak's book. "It ended with a knock on the door, right before the entrance of a police officer." Per Dawidziak, "Had the officer made an entrance, it would have been Lieutenant Columbo." In this telling, Hitchcock's magazine would be remembered as merely the tease to the first appearance of perhaps the most popular and celebrated detective in television history.

This is a memorable account, but it's not quite correct.

Don't take my word for it. It's right there for the reading in "Dear Corpus Delecti," as found in *Hitchcock's A Choice of Evils* short story collection. The brief tale does indeed set up killer Charles Lowe's alibi after offing his wife Vivian, and the mechanics—the disguised girlfriend, the reliance on Lowe's maid to find the body, the airplane argument—will all be very familiar to *Columbo* fans.

But as Lowe cockily returns from his weekend getaway/alibi, he is met outside his apartment door by a police lieutenant, the one that Levinson claims never appeared in his story. Lieutenant Fisher of the 45th Precinct, "a slight, insignificant little man," delivers news to Lowe that serves as the story's twist and brings the narrative to its end, just as Lowe is entering the apartment murder scene and Fisher asks, "May I come in?" The appearance of the Lieutenant amounts to only 255 words, but that's 255 more words than we have ever known about this clear Columbo prototype.

Levinson's mistaken recollection of his own landmark fiction, with its first glimmer of a Columbo-like character, might be seen as inexplicable. Was it a foggy memory? There were several iterations of the Columbo origin story, so it is certainly possible that in his re-telling of the tale years later, Levinson simply conflated them. It began with a short story, became an hour-long TV teleplay, then expanded to a stage production (with rewrites), and finally the 1968 movie. Certainly, Levinson could be excused for an innocent mix-and-match of the details.

Perhaps there is a speculative answer to be found by considering a more straightforward connection to Hitchcock and his magazine—money. 1960 *AHMM* issues contain a standard phrasing: "Copyright 1960 by HSD Publications, Inc. All rights reserved. Protection secured under the International and Pan-American copyright conventions." Although authors generally keep ownership of the copyright in their works after publication, they also often enter into an agreement with the publisher that gives the company license to publish without violating the author's copyright. The precise terms of an agreement of this type would determine how exclusive or non-exclusive that simple "All rights reserved" phrase actually is.[3]

Levinson and Link were keen on leveraging their writing talents into the television world. An opportunity presented itself with the 1960 Hollywood writer's strike, which prevented filmed shows from accepting new scripts. However, a loophole allowed writers to submit material for live events. "Dear Corpus Delecti" seemed ideal for this task. The pair would need to expand their short story and provide the killer with a challenging adversary.

Obviously, the finished television product, *Enough Rope*, shared its DNA with the *AHMM* blueprint. There wasn't much getting around that. But if there was a hint of the Columbo character itself being created under an

AHMM copyright, then perhaps clever lawyers at HSD Publishers might, in theory, retroactively try to claim a chunk of the monetary windfall due Levinson and Link for their seminal creation, beyond the one short story. To be clear, this is just a hypothetical, but it's tempting to ascribe to it the name switch from Fisher to Columbo and Levinson's subsequent disavowal of the character as being relevant to "May I Come In."

Interestingly, the Hitchcock TV programs had first dibs on the rights to film any stories from the Hitchcock magazine property, according to a 1964 article in the *Palm Beach Post*.[4] "The disappointing factor was, we never met Hitch at that point," said Link many years after. "They guarded him; he was rather a private man."[5] Alas, ironically, "We learned later that the *Prescription: Murder* stage play had been submitted to Hitchcock and he had turned it down." A missed opportunity for *The Alfred Hitchcock Hour* became a prestige anchor show for NBC.

So whether or not any of Levinson and Link's changes to "Dear Corpus Delecti" would have staved off a copyright claim on the Columbo character was rendered moot for lack of interest. Scant weeks later, the scribes transformed Lt. Fisher into Lt. Columbo, and expanded their story to a live television presentation for the *Chevy Mystery Show*. It was July of 1960 when *Enough Rope* premiered, and thus was born the very first official appearance of Lieutenant Columbo, as played by competent journeyman actor Bert Freed. But the co-creators had no intention of letting it be Columbo's last appearance.

Less than 18 months later, the stage adaptation, now titled *Prescription: Murder*, began a six-month run in America and Canada, with the role of Columbo essayed by Thomas Mitchell (Uncle Billy of *It's a Wonderful Life*). The play's life was short, but the audience response to the Columbo character confirmed his popularity and viability as a leading man. In February 1968, Levinson and Link used the TV-movie version of *Prescription: Murder* to mark the debut of Peter Falk as Columbo, and a television icon was created.

Columbo's humble beginnings as the afterthought to an *Alfred Hitchcock Mystery Magazine* short story isn't the only Levinson-Link-Hitchcock connection. In 1961, they began writing for the *Alfred Hitchcock Presents* anthology show, contributing two scripts for the 30-minute TV suspenser, followed by five titles for *The Alfred Hitchcock Hour*. One of these, "Dear Uncle George," would feature a jaded, snarky advice columnist who murders his cheating wife and spends the rest of the episode trying to pin it on her lover. The killer was played by Gene Barry, five years before he would be cast as the more cold and calculating Dr. Ray Flemming of *Prescription: Murder*.

The roles are different, but Levinson and Link's cross-pollination between their Hitchcock products "Dear Corpus Delecti" and "Dear Uncle George" is an intriguing one.

Years later, the two writers did eventually meet the legend over a three-hour lunch. Hitchcock was frustrated trying to find a suitable book to adapt for an upcoming movie, so it was perhaps at that meal that Link and Levinson recommended a 1972 novel about a clairvoyant looking for a missing heir, and a kidnapping team who ransom their victims for diamonds. On Levinson and Link's suggestion, Hitchcock adapted *The Rainbird Pattern* into what would become his final movie, 1976's *Family Plot*.[6]

Levinson and Link's early experience with the mystery and suspense auteur was fortuitous timing. It also probably helped raise their profile, a convenient by-product of Hitchcock's brilliant branding. Long before the age of social media influencers and brand management awareness, the Hitchcock name and image were associated with quality chills and thrills. The director, who worked in sales and marketing before his film career, stoked this linkage through the frequent cameo appearances in his movies, and lending his name to print and television spread Hitchcock's fame and ubiquity.

While his primary contribution to the *Alfred Hitchcock Mystery Magazine* was simply allowing his prestigious name to be used, the print venture reinforced his visual image as well as his penchant for black humor. *AHMM* covers featured him posing with guns, hangman's nooses, and black crows; decapitated, knifed, mastering a guillotine, and as Sherlock Holmes and a cannibal chef.

But Hitchcock didn't just farm out his name for a few extra bucks in his television projects. He expertly heightened his cultural profile with his creative participation and active efforts in these ventures, directing 17 episodes. Thanks to television, the corpulent Hitchcock silhouette became instantly recognizable, as did the musical theme associated with his shows, 1872's "Funeral March of a Marionette." He appeared on-camera to open and close every episode with short pieces that often had nothing to do with the story, but highlighted a wry wit that became another weekly exercise in self-promotion.

Hitchcock's successful branding is significant for its elevated platform showcasing writers and providing opportunities for young talent to thrive. Noted authors who would contribute to the *Alfred Hitchcock Mystery Magazine* over the years included Ed McBain, Donald Westlake, G.K. Chesterton, and Robert Bloch. Hitchcock's TV shows featured works by Roald Dahl, Eric Ambler, Ray Bradbury, and A.A. Milne.

With American pre-cable TV audiences focused on just three networks, Hitchcock's shows were Top 25 ratings successes their first four seasons, and solidified his status beyond cult to mass-appeal. Hitchcock properties were far from the only outlets for suspense stories in the Fifties and Sixties, but it's a decent bet that Levinson and Link's association with Hitchcock didn't hurt in fast-tracking their breakthrough efforts. This was the power of "branding by association," far predating today's practices of social media commenting, tagging other users, and following influencers.[7]

Hitchcock's successful branding had another notable upshot. It helped to solidify him as the gold standard in thriller directing, The Master of Suspense. In his acclaimed biography of Hitchcock, celebrated French director Francois Truffaut defines him as "the most complete film-maker of all... not merely an expert at some specific aspect of cinema, but an all-round specialist, who excels at every image, each shot, and every scene. He masterminds the construction of the screenplay as well as the photography, the cutting, and the sound-track, has creative ideas on everything and can handle anything, and is even, as we already know, expert at publicity!"

This mastery of all elements of filmmaking is sometimes described as "The Hitchcock Touch," and when other directors create their own movie magic, it is often complimented as being "Hitchcockian." In examining the craft of Hitchcock's directing—the scripting, music score, sets, costuming, locations, supporting actors, camerawork, editing, guest stars—we can observe the high-quality parallels to the production of every episode of Seventies *Columbo*.

It's a cliché to say that Hitchcock has influenced every film director in his wake, but not hyperbole to say that *Columbo* may be the most Hitchcock-influenced program in TV history (well, excepting those Hitchcock shows). The many, heralded specific elements of Hitchcock's cinematic genius are well-documented and beyond the scope of this chapter. The bottom line is that Hitchcock's signature style as a director was to emphasize the visual unfolding of a story.[8] *Columbo* treated the varied elements of visual storytelling in a similar manner. If you're rewatching a striking *Columbo* scene, it likely has many of the same ingredients utilized by the Master of Suspense.

"I always try to tell a story in a cinematic way, through a succession of shots and bits of film in between."
– Alfred Hitchcock

Of course, for outstanding *Columbo* directing, nothing beats a great murder scene. The Columbophile Blog does a thorough job summarizing the

ALFRED HITCHCOCK'S gallows humor was a feature of his *Mystery Magazine* covers.

very best *Columbo* killings, including those executed by Leslie Williams, Dale Kingston, Carl Brimmer, Alex Benedict, Paul Hanlon, Barry Mayfield, Riley Greenleaf, Milo Janus, and Eric Mason.[9] All of these slayings benefit from superb direction, deft editing, and chilling music scores. For our purposes, though, let's go back to the very beginning for a different *Columbo* death to detail.

The *Prescription: Murder* homicide (dir: Richard Irving) was no doubt quite shocking for much of its 1968 audience. Dr. Flemming is having what sounds like a casual chat with his wife Carol, but his tone belies what we, the audience, sees and knows—Flemming is building up to the moment when he will be choking the life out of her. He slips on the thick gloves, deliberately hides his hands behind his back, and slowly, cautiously approaches her from the rear. The seconds tick off, the suspense escalates, and he moves to strike.

But it's a false start to the strangulation, as Carol unexpectedly turns to face him.

This releases the viewer's tension, but the pause is a brief one. Moments later, now shutting the balcony doors, we see the back of Carol's head in close-up, and Flemming's hands suddenly leap into the frame. Immediately, the Dave Grusin music score amps up and the telephone rings. Amidst the competing sounds, quick cuts show rear views of Flemming's chokehold, closeups of his sweaty face, the ringing phone, Carol's hands grasping at the curtain, and finally, her limp hand crashing to the piano keys for a final off-key note.

It's all very compelling, with a clear Hitchcockian air. Notably, director Irving doesn't linger on the violence of the strangulation, but intercuts it with close-ups of the consequences of the violence. Television standards of the era kept bloodshed off the small screen, much as The Hays Code regulated movies between 1934 and 1968 to limit profanity, nudity, suggestive sexual acts, and graphic violence. To work around The Hays Code, Hitchcock often suggested violence without explicitly showing it. Famously, the shower scene in *Psycho* does not show Norman Bates' knife cutting into Marion Crane. *Columbo* directors would take a similar what-you-don't-see approach to many of their murder scenes, maintaining suspense even while eliminating the most gruesome ingredients.

Directorial flair was a driving element signaling the early *Columbos* as high-quality showcase television. Irving helmed the second pilot, *Ransom for a Dead Man*, with another distinctive murder scene. (And while the creepy dissolve of Lee Grant's eyes to auto headlights might seem dated today, it was pretty cool in 1971). The next filmed outing was *Death Lends a Hand*, with the killing and post-murder cleanup reflected in Robert Culp's shades (dir: Bernard Kowalski). In this episode, the eyeglass-reflecting violence is reminiscent of a prominent technique in Hitchcock's *Strangers on a Train*.

Twenty-four directors helmed the original set of 45 *Columbos*. Discussion of these directors usually begins and ends with that one kinda famous Spielberg guy from *Murder by the Book*, which is a shame, because there are plenty of highlights from the remaining 23 directors throughout the Seventies run. They include Hitchcock TV director vets Norman Lloyd, Harvey Hart, Boris Sagal, and Alf Kjellin. Even without the Spielberg name, many *Columbo* moments—murders and otherwise—have the stylish panache, imagination and excellence to give *Columbo* a top-quality movie sheen in the Hitch tradition, which no other television program was even attempting.

Consider Beth Chadwick's eerie imagined fratricide of her brother 10 minutes into *Lady in Waiting*. Or the opening credits horror-mad scientist vibe of *Lovely But Lethal*. Or the foreshadowing of twins in *Double Shock* when Lisa opens the bathroom double doors and the room resembles a negative-positive photograph. The psychedelic chess nightmare in *The Most Dangerous Match* resembles the bizarre Salvador Dali design for Gregory Peck's dream sequence in Hitchcock's *Spellbound*.

Again, this is not to imply that the great directorial flourishes of Classic *Columbo* are steals or have a direct link to Hitchcock scenes. But what they do have is a link to the elevated quality of movie-making that Hitchcock was consistently achieving.

Hitchcock movies were also acclaimed for their ability to weave superb music into their narratives. He didn't write the scores, nor was he alone in using soundtracks effectively. But Hitchcock films usually featured distinctive music highlighting the visual story he was telling, providing atmosphere and tone, creating emotions, supplying psychological cues to the audience, and reinforcing or foreshadowing plot points. Marion Crane's *Psycho* stabbing set to Bernard Herrmann's slashing arrangement gets the most attention, but there are many more iconic scores to underscore the on-screen action. Roger Thornhill and Eve Kendall skirting the noses of Mount Rushmore in *North by Northwest* is a good place to start, but there are countless more.

The practice of marrying murders with exciting and distinct music was a conspicuous component of *Columbo* soundtracks of the Seventies. Listen for the unique elements provided by series composers like Billy Goldenberg, Dick DeBenedictis, and Gil Melle as they score the stylish killings. Waterphone effects, eerie electronics, dissonant strings, multi-tracked synth effects, exotic percussion instruments, and more are all designed to create mysterious, suspenseful, and unnerving experiences. No other television program was putting death to music in this manner, as Hitchcock had achieved in his films.

As for *Columbo*'s inverted mystery format, where the audience knows who the perpetrator is, Levinson and Link have noted that author R. Austin Freeman first introduced the concept on the printed page in 1912. But they have also acknowledged the format's antecedent on the big screen. "The only person who did it in a couple of movies was Hitchcock, like in the picture *Rope*. You see the beginning, they kill the professor [sic], they put him in the wooden trunk.... [Hitchcock] had done it a couple times, but that wasn't on television. Television was totally fresh, and I think it shook people up."[10]

The other Hitchcock film Link was likely referring to is a much clearer parallel to the *Columbo* mystery template. 1954's *Dial M for Murder* has so many of the inverted "howcatchem" characteristics and character similarities that it sparks questions as to its conscious or hidden influence on Levinson and Link's *Columbo* formula.[11]

Beginning as a stage play written by Frederick Knott in 1952, the basic elements to the inverted mystery setup are already there. After its introduction as a filmed BBC "television play," the production had a strong run in London's West End and on Broadway, and Hitchcock then showed how effective the proto-*Columbo* format could be on-screen when he adapted it in 1954.

Hitchcock himself, ironically, was somewhat dismissive of the venture, remarking, "I just did my job, using cinematic means to narrate a story taken from a stage play. I could just as well have shot the whole film in a telephone booth."[12] But The Master's touches, especially the suspenseful murder-with-a-twist scene, properly embellished Knott's dramatic plot points. And audiences responded, making it his most commercially successful movie since 1946's *Notorious*, earning $2.7 million.[13]

As would befit a *Columbo* episode, the viewer watches smooth and calculating ex-tennis pro Tony Wendice (Ray Milland) plot to kill his wealthy and unfaithful wife Margot (Grace Kelly) to sustain his comfortable London lifestyle. When the plan goes awry, Tony switches gears to frame her for premeditated murder.

Along the way, Tony is visited by the deceptively affable Scotland Yard Chief Inspector Hubbard (John Williams), a smoker carrying a crumbled rain mac, asking observant questions that Wendice is able to fend off, like any good *Columbo* villain. Hubbard persists with subtle suspicions, even at one point uttering, "Just one other thing, sir...." Through an elaborate ruse, as part of a cat-and-mouse between killer and cop, Hubbard finally cons Tony into giving the game away.

Dial M's Inspector is more polished and nattily attired, but his psychological strategies foreshadow the ones to be used later by his more sloppily-garbed lieutenant descendant. Apologizing for having a few more questions for Tony the day before Margot is to be executed, Hubbard is overly deferential: "I'm sorry to have had to bother you;" "It was only a routine matter, I didn't want to disturb you;" "Do you mind if I smoke?" He feigns forgetfulness with "Did I say that?," and plays along with Tony's fanciful tale about going to the dog track while Margot is locked up: "I know how it is, it helps to take the mind off things." Not suspecting that he is being set up, Tony literally walks into the trap through his own apartment door.

Credit goes to playwright Knott for penning the clever screenplay that Hitchcock closely hewed to. In fact, Knott stayed with Hitch during the movie's production, and the two fiction schemers formed a friendship.[14] But

"A Hitch in Crime"

THE "HOWCATCHEM" FORMULA on screen: 1954's *Dial M for Murder*.

it was the famous director who ensured *Dial M's* inverted-mystery success for the masses, a success replicated years later by Levinson and Link's *Columbo*.

An interesting thought experiment wonders if, before he passed in 1980, the Master of Suspense himself set aside a Sunday night each month to catch the latest *Columbo* killing. Since the program was a Universal Studios production, and Hitchcock was the third largest shareholder of Universal's owner MCA, it's no doubt likely that he was very familiar with Levinson and Link's iconic creation, or at least its bottom line.[15] One imagines the legend comfortably leaning back in a reclining chair and putting his feet up, like millions of others across the country, to enjoy the latest *Columbo* murder as it was telecast into his home, right where Hitch himself said all good murders belong.

12.
Columbo Gets His Wings

The intertextuality between Peter Falk the movie actor and Peter Falk the TV star was never more apparent than in a 1987 German movie that has a heavy *Columbo* connection.

It's been hailed as one of the best films of the Eighties, one of the Top 1,000 movies of all time, and one of the greatest 100 foreign language pictures ever made. It's been described as a "quintessential arthouse film," "a postmodern masterpiece," "a singular cinema souvenir of a moment in culture and Western history," and "a cinematic experience unequalled in its originality and beauty." The film is *Wings of Desire*, and as unlikely as it might seem, Columbo—both Peter Falk and his iconic detective character—was integral to its success. What in the world is Columbo doing in a largely black-and-white German-language film fantasy about invisible angels in Berlin at the end of the Cold War?

To be clear, there is no crime-solving at the Berlin Wall, no "One more thing" (or *"ich hätte nur eine Frage"* auf Deutsch), no search for a pencil, no Peugeot, no hard-boiled eggs. *Wings of Desire* chronicles two eternal observer angels, Damiel and Cassiel, who watch over the city of Berlin, hearing the thoughts of its lonesome and isolated human souls, providing a palliative comfort of hope to the despairing. As invisible witness to humanity without ever being able to experience being human, angel Damiel decides to shed his immortality for corporal existence after observing a lonely trapeze artist and falling in love. Peter Falk appears as… himself, but notably, as an ex-angel himself. In the film, Falk has discarded his own immortality to become an actor, recognized and referred to as "Columbo" and "Lieutenant." *Wings of Desire* plays with this intersection of Falk the person and Columbo the persona, capitalizing on the global recognition of each, as "Der Filmstar" helps Damiel through his transition.

Wim Wenders wrote and directed *Wings of Desire*, one of several acclaimed films of his career, noted for a mix of both narrative and documentary features. For the latter, he has been nominated for three Academy Awards, and won Best Director for *Wings* at 1987's Cannes Film Festival. Wenders is not a hired hand. He is considered an auteur filmmaker of the "New German" wave of directors, with a unique and personal cinematic style and thematic focus for his pictures.

WIM WENDERS (on the inspiration for *Wings of Desire*): As I walked around Berlin, I saw angels all over, as monuments or sculptures or reliefs in public places, more than in any other city. I was really looking for a story that could help me tell the city's story. Eventually, my night reading being populated by angels, and the angels I photographed and encountered all over the city, led me to the realization that I wouldn't find any better characters for my project. So I started to come up with a story that had guardian angels as protagonists. The more I thought about it, the more I thought I was crazy. But the idea opened so many possibilities to look into so many different lives, because these angels could be anywhere. They could cross the Wall. They could meet anybody and be perfect witnesses of life in Berlin. I finally had a point of view that was all-encompassing. Not that I really believed in angels, but I liked them as a metaphor.[1]

Without a full-blown analysis of *Wings of Desire*, we'll note that the film touches upon a number of possible themes identified by critics: love and loneliness, the progression and blessings of life, a celebration of humanity, idealization of childhood, and a call for German reunification. Certainly not for all tastes, the movie nonetheless has been able to strike a chord of melancholy reflection about life's significance with many filmgoers.

In *Wings of Desire*, Falk has a relatively small but recurring appearance. As himself, he is an actor making a movie near the Berlin Wall about an American detective in WWII Germany, searching for a client's brother's missing son. This is barely established in Falk's throwaway dialogue: "The brother's dead, the family's lost, find the kid." The fiction of Falk interacting with fellow actors portraying Nazi officers allows Wenders to arouse the unpleasant memories of Germany's past, an overt act by the director, who intended *Wings of Desire* to use the geography and history of Berlin to model the human experience.

Roaming Berlin in his preparation for the detective role, the Falk character encounters Damiel and intuits the angel's presence. This is the first hint that Falk may not be all that he appears. Wenders has described Falk's role as being one who seduces the angel into crossing over to flesh-and-blood humanity.

The Falk character speaks to the invisible Damiel ("I can't see you but I know you're here") and offers his hand in friendship as a "companero." Sensing Damiel's desire for human existence, Falk describes some simple earthly pleasures ("There's so many good things") such as warming ones hands, drawing and "to smoke and have coffee—and if you do it together, it's fantastic."

Falk's role as conduit between angels and humans is now regarded as an essential element of Wenders' narrative. And yet the character, and who would play it, were never considered part of the original story conception.

WENDERS: Peter's part was never scripted and came as an afterthought. We were already shooting for two weeks, when my assistant Claire Denis and I were brooding again one night in front of our walls with photographs and scene ideas. I said to Claire: "Don't you think these angels take themselves too seriously? Don't you think we're lacking some humor in this production?" She nodded. That night, we came up with the idea of an "ex-angel" who would have gone through the exact experience that Damiel was going through, a man with a "sixth sense" for any angel who'd be tempted to make the leap. And that night, we came to the conclusion that Peter Falk was the ideal cast.[2]

WENDERS (casting Falk): We needed a figure who wouldn't take themselves too seriously. We wanted someone known—we thought, wouldn't it be great if it was somebody everyone would recognize? The idea of a former angel would be so much more thrilling if it was someone we all know… here was some tenderness in Peter Falk, and something very convincing, a friendliness and gentleness in his whole persona, and I figured it would translate into him being a former angel really well.[3]

WENDERS (on Falk's popularity): Rarely a shoot was so much fun as those days with Peter Falk. Everybody recognized him, of course. As soon as you stood in the street with him, people showed up from everywhere. Pizza bakers came running out of their pizzerias, their hands still full of flour! Buses stopped! I never saw anybody deal with his fame so generously and kindly. Peter Falk shook everybody's hands, smiled at everybody, gave everybody an autograph, had everybody spell their funny German names, had his picture

"Columbo Gets His Wings"

ACTOR PETER FALK as ex-angel Peter Falk in Wim Wenders' *Wings of Desire* (1987). His appearance here may have helped trigger the '90s *Columbo* comeback.

taken with everybody, no exception. And everybody walked away happily: "I met Columbo!" We really had found an ex-angel![7]

In the movie-within-the-movie, the search for truth by an American detective played by Peter Falk purposely evokes his universally recognized television counterpart. Although Wenders is here commenting on the warm and gentle nature of Peter Falk, the description could just as easily apply to his signature Columbo character.

The director knew that the commingling of Peter Falk the person, Peter Falk the character, and the popularity of the fictional Columbo were all key to *Wings of Desire's* success. The role works in the film's context, not because of Falk's prior characters in *It's A Mad, Mad, Mad, Mad World* or *Husbands* or *The Cheap Detective* or *A Woman Under the Influence*, but almost entirely because viewers felt warmly about that disheveled, disarming detective. The notion of intertextuality—viewing Peter Falk as Columbo somewhere other than in a *Columbo*—was essential to making Wenders' high-concept story resonate with filmgoers.

Peter Falk (about filming in Berlin): Columbo, everybody knew him—it was fantastic! The German people connect with that character, and maybe that's why Wim even thought of it. I guess they have such an affection for that character, that he would be a good ex-angel.[5]

Writer/critic Casey Jarrin explains, "He's an unassuming Everyman detective who could be anyone and no one.... He is recognizable yet relatable: he doesn't want to look like or be anyone in particular. Looking into a full-length mirror, his inner monologue proclaims: "I want to look anonymous... melt into the crowd."[6]

Wings of Desire's 1986 production capitalizes on Columbo's world-wide common-man appeal, even as the classic series run had petered out in 1978 and the revival was still over two years away. In the movie, teens passing Falk wonder if he's the famous TV detective ("Isn't that Columbo?" "Don't think so... He wouldn't be out here in this muck."). Later, the trapeze artist with whom Damiel falls in love meets Falk and addresses him, twice, as "Lieutenant."

Falk's function, as a former angel, is to bridge two worlds, the spiritual and the physical. The value in giving up angelic existence for human existence must be convincing to both Damiel and the viewing audience. As critic/professor/short-film creator Richard Raskin notes, "Falk is also, in our eyes, the guarantor of the rightness of Damiel's plan. And this is what tips the balance for us, in favor of Damiel's becoming a mortal. Falk can do this because he has a special status for us. He enjoys our confidence because we know him as Columbo and as the actor, Peter Falk. For the first time, we can feel, without reserve, that what Damiel is giving up to become a mortal is more than counterbalanced by what he will gain.... Damiel will never regret becoming a mortal, since Falk, 30 years after his own transformation, radiates fulfillment and well-being."[7] Falk, particularly Falk-as-Columbo, is the convincer.

On set, Falk's acting style perfectly matched Wenders' directorial style, which for *Wings of Desire* meant working without a script.

WENDERS: Peter understood exactly what he was supposed to do. The part wasn't written. And that's why he accepted the role. I got him on the phone in the middle of the night... Peter laughed for a while and said, "You are making a movie and you're calling me to tell me that I should join you because there is an unwritten part? What is it?" I said, "An ex-angel." He laughed for another long while and then he said, "I'll do it. I do my best work this way."[8]

FALK: There's an eternal tension between freedom and order... That feeling is something that affects me all the time too, where you want to break out of the lines, but you have to be very wary. There has to be some kind of a form, or construct within which you have to operate.... I love Wim. He's wide open.

He's not anxious, not fearful. If something tickles or interests him, he'll go for it. Real loose.[9]

Columbo viewers familiar with the stories of Falk's on-set script changes and dialogue-tinkering will no doubt nod in recognition. Wenders' wish to incorporate his star's real personality into the film allowed for scenes created around Falk's penchant for sketching, his search for the proper hat to wear in his detective role, and improvising the inner monologues of his ex-angel character. Falk truly inhabits the ex-spirit persona, which means that Columbo does too. Perhaps unsurprisingly, Falk wandered away from the *Wings of Desire* film set one day, only to get lost and need Berlin police to fetch him to return to work.

FALK: It never occurred to me that *Wings of Desire* would play in the U.S. I was wrong, and thank the Lord for it. It not only played here, it was immensely successful. I can't tell you how many people were affected and delighted by it.[10]

The acclaim for the film and Falk's contribution to it may have had an added bonus. Veteran Hollywood scribe Dominic Patten of *Deadline* firmly believes that it was "thanks in no small part to Wim Wenders' *Wings of Desire*" that the *Columbo* revival was green-lit by ABC. Since last appearing in first-run U.S. television episodes on May 13, 1978 in *The Conspirators*, it would be almost 10 years until anyone in America would hear the name "Columbo" uttered again by any new screen characters. The resonance of the role had proved enduring, and, like an angel given a chance at another life, *Columbo* would return to the TV screen in 1989.[11]

In *Wings of Desire*, Falk offers a final piece of advice to his angel counterpart that sounds as if it could have come directly from the lips of his most famous character.

DAMIEL: I want to know everything!
PETER FALK: You need to figure that out for yourself. That's the fun of it.

13.
The Curious Case of *Columbo Takes the Rap*

TOMMY BROWN: You got a good ear for music.
COLUMBO: Well, I'm Italian, you know.
– *Swan Song* (1974)

As country gospel singer Tommy Brown discovered, Columbo is a music fan. If you believe him, he saw Tommy render that big hit "I Saw the Light" in concert, digs Alex Benedict's album of Strauss waltzes, and is familiar with all the classical superstars that Mrs. Columbo enjoys, "like whatsisname, the guy who wrote 'Marriage of Figaro.'" Intertextually, though, some matches of *Columbo* and music were just not meant to be.

Many *Columbo* viewers are familiar with the tale of the first stage version of the character, 1962's *Prescription: Murder*. Evolving from a short story to an hour-long TV production to a stage play, the role was finally owned by Peter Falk in 1968, as the production was made into the TV-movie that launched a detective icon. But even hard-core *Columbo* buffs have likely never heard of the second and final stage iteration of the Lieutenant, written years after the end of the Nineties series. For many, the very existence of another *Columbo* play is surprising. Why is this production not a part of the *Columbo* legend?

After all, *Columbo Takes the Rap* was written by the co-creator of *Columbo*, the celebrated William Link. The classic character is unchanged, but in a modern backdrop, investigating a rap star's murder. It hits the classic formula notes—no *Undercover* shenanigans here. It didn't try to introduce us to a young Mrs. Columbo, it didn't give the Lieutenant an eager sidekick, it wasn't set in Tucson or Topeka.

The play was performed at the inaugural International Mystery Writers' Festival in Owensboro, Kentucky in 2007, where it was described at the time as a big success. Then, on July 11, 2007, the *New York Post* breathlessly told its readers, "LT. COLUMBO SOLVES B'WAY." It described how the play would be touring the United States in anticipation of a run under the bright lights of Broadway. The founder of the Mystery Festival, veteran stage producer Zev Buffman, proclaimed, "I must consider it a contender."[1]

Link himself was effusive about the discovery of the "new" *Columbo*, a Chicago stage actor named Norm Boucher. Peter Falk was not considered for this. "I love Peter, but he's a bit long in the tooth [80]," explained Link. He added, "Norm was so good, Peter would have been jealous."

The following day, on July 12, the "Columbo on Broadway" headlines blared through theatre media: *Broadway World, Playbill, NY Tix*, even *TV Guide*. And then… nothing. The play managed to make it to the Vertigo Theatre in Calgary for a three-week stint in 2008, with someone else entirely as the star. That's it. No American tour. No published script. No acclaimed kudos for a new Columbo actor. No Great White Way. *Columbo Takes the Rap* simply disappeared. What happened?

Norm Boucher is now a voice talent coach at Acting Studio Chicago. He has filmed roles on *Chicago Fire* and *Chicago PD*, as well as two Super Bowl commercials among others, and has been on the stage extensively in the Chicago area. Widely touted post-Mystery Festival as the "next Columbo," Boucher has a unique perspective on the *Columbo Takes the Rap* saga.

"It was important to Ron [Parson, play director] and Mr. Link that I not do Peter Falk," Boucher told me in a telephone interview as one of the Acting Studio plays was being staged nearby. "It was me doing my New York Guy. They showed the crime first, then the lights went out, then they come back on, and there I am in the raincoat and the cigar, and I would get big entrance applause. Now, I know that they were applauding for the raincoat and the cigar. But of course, I happened to be standing there. It was the best entrance I've ever had."

"There was such a good template already that I didn't feel like I had to add much of anything," says Boucher about bringing his own personality to the role. "As long as you have a cigar in one hand, a notepad in the other, scratch your head, and ask, 'one more question'… otherwise just stay out the way. It would be a disservice to do anything other than be that Italian guy from New York. It wasn't a personal spin so much as trying to keep up with the—what's a good way to put it—the intricacies of his mind."

Boucher's ability to inhabit the role was certainly noticed by William Link, who was part of the audition process and a presence at play rehearsals. Link was very flattering in his praise for Boucher on a 2008 DVD commentary for the pilot episode of *Mannix*, of all places. [Levinson and Link created the original *Mannix* concept, sold it to Desilu Studios, then hustled off the project with their pilot re-written and the original concept watered down and tossed out entirely for Season 2. But they got their check!]

In noting the hope for a national rollout of *Columbo Takes the Rap* on the DVD, Link said of Boucher, "I have a new Columbo who's terrific, nothing like Peter. Forty years old, a little paunchy, losing a little bit of hair, charming, very clever, brilliant actor."

So what about the national tour and Broadway fame? "They did dangle that carrot in front of me," says Boucher. "The way I caught wind of it, it came out in the *NY Post*, then Regis and Kelly were talking about it on their show. I certainly got excited because that would have been a big ticket for sure." But rather than get word through anyone in charge that the plans were scrapped, Boucher simply didn't hear anything else about it. "My heart beat fast for just a minute, and that was the last I heard of it."

Ron O.J. Parson was the director of *Columbo Takes the Rap*, and helmed Boucher's appearance in *Arsenic and Old Lace* at Chicago's Court Theatre. Parson was in regular communication with William Link, and his own take on the story mirrors Boucher's. "Oh yeah, they had big plans," Parson told me. As for why the play didn't leave Owensboro, "I wouldn't know. William and I talked about the *NY Post* thing—it might do this, it might do that—but then, it fizzled out. Norm figured they wouldn't come to him, they would come to a star, and I figured they wouldn't want me to direct, they would have gotten one of the majors to direct, so I kinda lost touch with it." Parson won the Director's Angie Award (named after Angela Lansbury) for *Columbo Takes the Rap*. That was the end of his involvement. "And you move onto the next thing."

Says Boucher, "I can't begin to assume what was on their minds, but I think that they [the play producers] wanted someone who was a name to play Columbo, whereas the way Mr. Link and Ron were talking about it at the beginning they wanted me, a relative unknown to play Columbo, then perhaps put in a star as the rap artist." Alas, festival creator/producer Buffman passed away in 2020 without leaving Boucher or *Columbo* fans an answer.

Parson has been in-demand, directing countless plays in regional theater across the country, now concentrating on his role as an acclaimed artist in residence at Court Theatre. He has fond memories of his unexpected association with *Columbo* history. "Zev Buffman was the producer of the festival, and he had William Link's people call me, which freaked me out because I'm not on the internet. But Mr. Link said they had been watching me online, and he thought I would be a good person to direct his play."

"So they sent it to me, and it was intriguing because I was a *Columbo* fan. We became friends and he told me all the stories, the whole history of *Columbo*. He told me some of his favorite episodes, and I told him some of mine. He wanted to do something contemporary and hip-hop was becoming popular, and he thought this would be a good story, and it was. We had fun doing it. We stayed in touch for awhile. I admired him so much, and I was so honored to actually know William Link before his death. He loved what I did with the play, and that was good enough for me."

Fortunately, the play's production has not been totally lost to 2007 posterity; there is a video proof-of-life that can help us visualize *Columbo Takes the Rap* on stage. Kentucky Educational Television (PBS) captured the preparations for each of the six plays being presented at that first International Mystery Writers' Festival, conceived by Buffman as a launching pad for brand new mystery plays. The IMWF was hyped as a big deal; founding festival members included William Link, Sue Grafton (the Kinsey Millhone "alphabet mysteries") and Ira Levin (*Deathtrap, Rosemary's Baby, The Stepford Wives*). Ed McBain of "87th Precinct" fame contributed a script (hopefully it turned out better than his Nineties *Columbo* adaptations).

Over the ensuing years, the success of the Festival would ebb and flow, with financial issues eventually sinking the endeavor in 2013. But KET was there to document the very first fest with a fuzzy behind-the-scenes peek at walk-through and dress rehearsals, plus actual stage performances of *Columbo Takes The Rap*.[2] We get a glimpse of the plot machinations, what Columbo-in-the-round looks like, and Boucher's comic timing, which results in an oddity for *Columbo* fans—belly laughs from the viewing audience. Certainly, we know that *Columbo* has humor, but hearing a room full of hoots after a Columbo line is definitely a new experience.

The video also lets us see Columbo interacting with a whole new set of individuals largely untouched in the 69 television episodes—black characters. As director Parson explains to viewers, "Not that it's based on Biggie Smalls and Tupac, but it has a lot of similarities in its rivalry. The record producer [villain] is trying to pit one against the other." Seeing our hero interact and adapt in the rap milieu is absolutely unique.

But was it also a missed opportunity? The murderous record producer is white. We know that William Link never used a black villain in the TV show, not wishing to contribute to the perception that African-Americans were criminals. But for *Columbo Takes the Rap*, it's 2007, and seeing a white person as the protagonist in the rap world may appear incongruous. The actor playing the killer, George Keating, seems at least obliquely aware of this in the KET video. "I play Carson Luck, a high-powered record producer of rap music, of all things…I don't know how much he knows about rap."

I was curious if Parson had his own thoughts on the play's casting, as a black director. "I didn't even think about that," replies Parson. "I wasn't thinking about race in the play…. It wasn't something that I thought about back then. He [Link] wrote the play about rap, to show the way producers control that world, and ironically, a lot of them are white. But maybe now, with the world as it is, it might be something to think about and talk about dramaturgically."

"But I will say that William Link was very progressive." Parson points to Link's creation (with Richard Levinson) of *Tenafly* for the NBC Mystery Wheel starring *Columbo* supporting actor James McEachin. Laments Parson, "America wasn't ready for *Tenafly* yet."

Judging by some of the play's lines we see delivered in the KET video, *Columbo Takes the Rap* directly acknowledges at least a few of the more famous tropes that have become attached to Columbo through the years: "That dude is a bigger con artist than me," says a rapper of Columbo, and later, "Man, you told me you were gonna take off that damn raggedy raincoat!" The villain holds a gun on Columbo at the finale, and as the Lieutenant makes evidently yet another Mrs. Columbo reference, the killer wails, "My God, you are still at it!"

While these might be fun self-referential moments, it is actually jarring to hear Columbo try to talk his way out of the bullet end of the producer's gun by saying, "You're a rich guy, you've got the best defense lawyers money can buy…chances are you can still beat this in a trial!" Even allowing for the weapon being pointed at him, this is like Columbo spilling the beans to at least half the Seventies killers on how to sidestep the traps the episode writers laid for them.

"If you're on a drug tip, don't be a Dumbo/Police investigate like Columbo if they think you're sellin' jumbo…"
– Kool G Rap, *Rikers Island* (1990)

Through the years, there have been multiple *Columbo* references in rap

NORM BOUCHER as William Link's hand-picked Columbo in *Columbo Takes the Rap*, on stage at the 2007 Mystery Writer's Festival in Owensboro, Kentucky.

music. It certainly doesn't hurt that "jumbo" is slang for a marijuana joint filled with crack cocaine. It seems like it might be easier to meld Columbo into rap than rap into Columbo.

Officially, it's a mystery why *Columbo Takes the Rap* failed. Unofficially, it could have been the sheer incongruity of the mix. It could have been the scripting of Link without Levinson. It could have been the fear that Peter Falk was the only possible Columbo. It could have been a gut sense that time had passed the character by. Whatever the reason, it seems unlikely that *Columbo Takes the Rap* will ever again see the light of day. Its fate remains, for now, as the red-headed stepchild of *Columbo* works, a member of the Columbo family that he won't even use for an invented "homey anecdote" for Leslie Williams.

It's now been many years since *Columbo Takes the Rap*, and Norm Boucher is good-humored about his brush with Columbo fame. "I really did have a blast doing that. The only downside was, I actually started getting a taste for cheap cigars… stinky White Owls, just the worst." My relaying of Link's *Mannix* DVD praise for Boucher's work was, in fact, the first that he had heard of it. Quite appreciative, he harbors no animosity toward William Link about the play's Broadway come-on ("He could not have been a nicer guy") and referred to him respectfully as "Mr. Link" throughout our conversation. Boucher still catches a lot of *Columbo* episodes in the Chicago TV market, and thought that *Columbo Takes the Rap* "did a great job of modernizing the world Columbo lives in."

As for today, Boucher says, "Anybody's who's waving a check around, I try to show up." Many actors have played the Columbo role in touring productions of *Prescription: Murder* across the globe since its San Francisco debut in 1962. But none of those men have the very rare distinction of playing the Lieutenant in William Link's second Columbo production. *Columbo Takes the Rap* remains a unique and largely-forgotten curio in the Columbo universe. What might have been one for the Broadway footlights instead became a Kentucky footnote.

> COLUMBO: Carnegie Hall and Nashville—they don't mix.
> – *Blueprint for Murder* (1972)

14.
The Debacle of *Mrs. Columbo*

It was February 26, 1979. That Monday evening, NBC set aside two hours to eagerly premiere a new mystery program with a familiar name as part of its massive prime-time overhaul of lackluster shows, in an effort to reverse the network's dismal ratings and woo back fleeing advertisers. Viewers watched, as the show that debuted that night captured 34 percent of the national audience and ranked 18th among all prime-time programs that week. A Top 20 finish was surely a sign of success to come, right? NBC executives were no doubt in a celebratory mood that evening.

Any celebration was short-lived. The show's next broadcasts came in 45th, 59th, and 56th. It limped along for nine more episodes, dragged out into Fall '79 with a surprise renewal. Desperately trying to fool viewers into sampling an episode—any episode—there were three program name changes, and one character name change.

This program has since been described as "perhaps the most infamous TV mystery series ever made,"[1] the show's distaff namesake called it "disgraceful," and no less than the program's actual star said, "I wouldn't be the least bit surprised if everyone said, 'Uggghh.'"[2] This was *Mrs. Columbo*.

And *Kate Columbo*. And *Kate the Detective*. And *Kate Loves a Mystery*. With Kate Callahan. Any way you Kate it, the show was a bomb.

The dustbin of failed and ludicrous television series is littered with hundreds of hare-brained ideas, from *My Mother the Car* to *Manimal* to *Homeboys in Outer Space*, but *Mrs. Columbo* elicits a particular stream of venom from the many who adored Peter Falk and *Columbo*. Apart from the heretical thought of visualizing the heretofore unseen Columbo missus, the very concept of

Mrs. Columbo strikes a nerve, even decades after its 1979 debut. For many, this is the ultimate example of inane, cynical network executive arrogance in stealing the name of a popular departing show and slapping it onto a young and attractive female lead, contemptuous of the intelligence of its television audience and driven by sheer greed.

The premise of *Mrs. Columbo* envisioned the character as a writer for a penny-saver weekly local, who would somehow get involved in solving crimes while her disheveled detective hubby was out of town or otherwise unseen and unavailable. The show's opening credits leaned into the Columbo mythology (Dog, the Peugeot, a moldy ashtray cigar) so we wouldn't mistake the identity of her invisible husband. Here's the official NBC biography: "She's a lady in perpetual motion. She is always trying—and somehow succeeds—to juggle the conflicting demands of being a mother, a freelance detective, part-time student, writer for a weekly newspaper, and wife of a policeman."[3] Oh, and she takes home-schooled French lessons, acts in school pageants with her 10-year-old daughter, and is a thorough housewife. Really, what can't Mrs. Columbo do?

This time, our intertextual goal is not to engage in mean-spirited sniping, but to present the brief story of *Mrs. Columbo* in the words of its participants and relevant onlookers, from conception to cancellation. This oral history is collected from a variety of video interviews, books, online audio sources, and American/Canadian/U.K. magazine pieces. Some of the saga you may know, some of it may be new. The evolving viewpoints of its star, Kate Mulgrew, are especially enlightening. And it all just might give some fresh perspective on how the maligned Mrs. C may have helped chart a path to success for another more famous amateur lady sleuth five years later.

It started with Fred Silverman. As the newly-crowned President of NBC in June 1978, it was Silverman's final call on what to do with *Columbo* after its seventh season. The network was in perpetual crisis mode, with a small handful of shows that anyone deemed watchable. Of course, *Columbo* was one of them, which would seem to make it a lock for more mystery crime solving. But this was a special case. Technically, the show was never officially canceled. Unofficially, the show was simply not renewed.

PETER FISCHER (*Columbo* writer, story editor 1974-1975): Silverman got rid of one of the network's jewels. Maybe he didn't like the financial arrangement. No question it was expensive, but NBC didn't have a whole lot going for it. But *Columbo*? I know Peter was disappointed by his cancellation, but also ambivalent.… Rightly or wrongly, Peter took his time doing the shows, and he once took 30 days to film a segment that was scheduled for 14. No network or studio can operate like that. And then there was the matter of money. Falk never worked for peanuts.[4]

PETER FALK: I wanted more time to do other things, but that was only part of the reason. *Columbo* just wasn't that important to the network anymore. When we were part of the [Mystery Movie] wheel, *Columbo* helped nail down Sunday night. Five or six movies weren't as important to them. On its own, *Columbo* was no longer life and death to the network.[5]

For whatever reason, *Columbo* was no more. And Fred Silverman needed to remake the network, quickly. He had done exactly the same thing in years prior at CBS and ABC as Head of Programming, where his list of successes was truly prodigious. He championed or developed, among many, *The Mary Tyler Moore Show, All in the Family, The Waltons, M*A*S*H, Kojak, The Love Boat, Charlie's Angels, Happy Days, Roots*—in effect, an entire generation's television memories. *Time* magazine gave him a 1977 cover story proclaiming him the "Man with the Golden Gut." Silverman's gut managed to create many more hits than misses, sometimes in unconventional ways.

FRED SILVERMAN: I had always thought that kids in a haunted house would be a big hit, played for laughs, in animation. [I] developed a show with Hanna-Barbera, and there was a dog in there, but the dog was in the background; it was much more serious.... [CBS President] Frank Stanton says, "We can't put that on the air, that's just too frightening." I booked a red-eye and I couldn't sleep. I'm listening to music and as we're landing, Frank Sinatra comes on, and I hear him sing "Scooby-do-be-do." It's at that point I said, "That's it, we'll take the dog, we'll call it Scooby-Doo."[6]

DEAN HARGROVE (*Columbo* Producer/Executive Producer 1972-1974): Silverman's instincts were quite amazing. The thing about Fred is, he'll have 20 ideas, two of them will be brilliant, two of them will be pretty good, and then there's a descending scale down to not very good at all... and he would pursue all of them with the same enthusiasm. That was part of his genius.[7]

Silverman's arrival at NBC came during a disastrously low ebb for the network, and new series ideas were needed, pronto.

SILVERMAN: I didn't understand how bad the situation was over there; it was the decay of a company. You had to start from the ground up. There was something I had learned not to do, just ad-libbing shows, getting them on the air quickly, "bim bam boom." But the schedule was so weak in September, we had to get out of those shows as quickly as we could.[8]

Silverman's fast-tracked timeline for NBC's turnaround meant that certain key details of a show's development might be missed. He impulsively green-lit the variety show *Pink Lady and Jeff* after seeing a photograph of a Japanese singing duo, who he paired with rising comic Jeff Altman. It was only later that he found out that those Pink Ladies spoke no English. Oops.

Over the years, one of Silverman's tried-and-mostly-true programming tactics was one that certainly wasn't new to television. But while at CBS and ABC, Silverman rocket-fueled this strategy to new dimensions—the spinoff. *Mary Tyler Moore* begat *Rhoda*, *Phyllis* and *Lou Grant*. *Happy Days* begat *Laverne and Shirley*, *Mork and Mindy*, and *Joanie Loves Chachi*. *All in the Family* produced so many spinoffs, it was more like Six Degrees of Archie Bunker.

SILVERMAN: Another kind of program development are spinoffs, and I am guilty of taking advantage of them. It's using the strength of our regular schedule to spin off other shows. Going back before my time, *Gomer Pyle* was a part of Mayberry [*The Andy Griffith Show*]. So this was something that historically, went back to the earlier days of television. It can work. That's a very effective way of program development.[9]

So here we are. *Columbo* is toe-tagged (for now at least, by NBC), the network is in tatters, Fred Silverman needs new shows quickly, and Fred Silverman loves spinoffs. Is it really any surprise that NBC's new boss latched onto the idea of a new *Columbo* series?

COLUMBO (in *Double Exposure*): My wife's got no head for crime. We go to those whodunit movies, she always picks the wrong murderer.

FISCHER: Of all the idiotic ideas Silverman ever sired, this was by far the dumbest, but maybe he figured he could parlay the Columbo name into a successful franchise at a tenth the cost. He was adamant and came to the three of us [Fischer and *Columbo* co-creators Richard Levinson and William Link] to create and produce it. None of us wanted anything to do with it.[10]

RICHARD LEVINSON (Columbo co-creator): We thought it was a mistake, because it looked like a rip-off, the exploitation of a successful idea. I just don't see how it can work. I think audiences will turn off to it.[11]

FISCHER: Dick decided that maybe the project was better done by us than some nonentity who would sully the Columbo image. We immediately decided that the woman should be approximately Peter's age, probably ethnic Italian, warm and outgoing, sharply intelligent without flaunting it. She would be childless, giving her room to maneuver. She would have the large extended family Peter was always referring to.[12]

WILLIAM LINK (*Columbo* co-creator): We wanted an actress like Brenda Vaccaro, who isn't an ugly woman in any sense, but she was more like Peter in the looks department, and the way she acted. I could believe that she was an Italian cop's Italian wife. The pretty wife... that was the cliché in all the other television series. Dick and I wanted to break cliches when we could, in a good way.[13] [Vaccaro would be offered the role but turned it down to star in a CBS show called *Dear Detective*, which lasted four episodes, nine fewer than *Mrs. Columbo*.]

FISCHER: We had mature actresses in mind for the part, people like Maureen Stapleton, Jean Stapleton, Zohra Lampert, maybe Anne Jackson. One morning we woke up, and we were faced with Kate Mulgrew. Nobody knew quite who she was. All we knew was that Silverman liked her and decided to cast her. Pretty, young, talented, a good actress—and completely wrong for the role of Mrs. Columbo. I wanted to call her "Mrs. Schwartz."[14]

SILVERMAN: You look at that girl Kate Mulgrew, and say, "She belongs in television." She has a face that lights up the screen.[15]

JOHN MCMAHAN (Sr. VP of NBC Entertainment): We were really impressed with her style, her presence, and the way she could dominate a scene. In the end, we decided a fresh new face was needed to bring Mrs. Columbo to life. Kate Mulgrew also plays older than her years, and that's a real indication of an enormous range of talent.[16]

KATE MULGREW (March 1979): Freddie Silverman was at ABC when I left the soap [daytime serial *Ryan's Hope*], and he personally asked me to stay. When I told him I had to move on, he said he'd have something else for me. He called and offered me *Mrs. Columbo*. When Fred Silverman wants something, he gets it. I am in awe of this man. I trust Freddie. If he says it's right for me, it's right for me.[17]

FISCHER: There was nothing warm or ethnic about Kate. If Peter Falk had ever run into her on one of his own shows, he would have arrested her immediately for murder.[18]

To promote the suddenly-seen wife of the network's most iconic character, Mulgrew put in the standard NBC appearance on *The Tonight Show with Johnny Carson*. She had her own try at spinning the match made in, not heaven, but Fred Silverman's office.

MULGREW: It makes a great deal of sense. Columbo was eccentric, right, when we met. And I imagine, I think we met probably in college and I fell desperately in love with that genius…. I don't know what they [show producers] saw originally. I mean my information is still sort of starved. But I think that ultimately they realized what I realized when I took the role which is that it makes a delightful match. I mean it makes great sense I think, when you really think about it, because the love affair is the first thing. I mean, two bright people together, that kind of chemistry works in a sort of extraordinary fashion.[19]

"Extraordinary" is not the word most people would attach to a Falk-Mulgrew union, and the network knew it. As Richard Levinson explained, "NBC's idea is that after one or two segments, you will forget your objections to her, which I think is wrong."

MULGREW: I did see one *Columbo* once, quite a while ago. She's the antithesis of Columbo, efficient, rather clean, vivacious and practical. Even though he's much older, she's the sort of woman he'd fall in love with. I suppose people were led to think she was matronly and dowdy. I hope they are genuinely pleased when they see me as Mrs. Columbo. To those who say I'm too pretty, too young, or too sexy, I say fiddlesticks. I'm selling something every woman in America can understand—authenticity. Kate Columbo is every bit a human being. The only unreal element of the show is that she keeps solving major crimes. But again, that's TV license. I think it's going to be fun.[20]

KATE MULGREW as the much-maligned Mrs. Columbo. Did she pave the way for Jessica Fletcher?

Fun, it wasn't.

Mulgrew had no interest in a series after *Ryan's Hope*, but Silverman was determined, and convinced her to come aboard by including a set of contract amenities such as guaranteed money, future projects, time off, and—shades of Peter Falk—script changes.[21] After confirming its star, *Mrs. Columbo* was rushed into production quickly. So quickly, that nobody had quite figured out an actual name for the Lieutenant's wife. For lack of anything better, the crew called Kate by her own name—and that was that. With the need for speed, staying on NBC's accelerated production schedule proved to be punishing for everyone.

MULGREW (June 1979): It's 16, 17, 18 hours nonstop with no time for reflection, no time for yourself. I mean, it's fine for a while. I'm very strong. I can take a lot of it, but this is almost six weeks of it. I get out about 9:30. I go home, I take a bath, I study. I try to get the lights out by midnight, and I'm up at 4:30. How long can you go like that? The scripts are very good, very well written, but I'm just afraid that the scripts will be dealt an injustice because of the pressure under which we have to work. Somebody's going to get very sick, and then they're really going to be behind schedule. I just do not understand their thinking.[22]

RICHARD ALAN SIMMONS (Executive Producer, *Mrs. Columbo*): I haven't had a day off since mid-December, and when you work twenty hours a day, have two days to write a script and one day to prepare it, you get tired. If I go to Fred Silverman and tell him it's impossible for me to do my job... you write the next line of dialogue.[23]

MULGREW (1980, after the series was canceled): I tried to rise above the mediocre stories. If they ask me to do mediocre material, they are saying in effect that I am mediocre and I am not. I gave it absolutely everything I had. But the writing was not good, the producers didn't have it together, and they expected so much so fast. I demanded a say in it. I would end up fighting with all the producers and the writers. But what am I supposed to do, sacrifice my character? Keep my mouth shut forever so I can work for NBC? I have my integrity as an actor, believe it or not, and I want to be able to say what is fact. And the fact is that I'm embittered because they are all tough, manipulative people. All scared to death and walking on eggshells, as afraid of losing their jobs as I am. It was never my intention to shut down. I wanted to shoot, but I wasn't going to shoot crap. But I wasn't responsible for the cancellation. If anything, I was responsible for its brief success.[24]

MULGREW [on rewriting scripts]: There wasn't a definite character. Every week I was playing somebody else and desperately trying to get back to the original character. *Kate Loves a Mystery* was anybody's guess each week. I wasn't going to look like an idiot on national TV. I wanted to sack the writers.

The writing was terrible; a 3-year-old could figure out the plots. I would call Fred Silverman and raise hell about the material, and I'd just get a lot of odd looks, you know, "Here she goes again." And then, inevitably, invariably, I'd get roses, a nice little gold watch, anything to keep my mouth shut.[25]

GRANT TINKER (Chairman and CEO, NBC 1981-1986): For Fred, as things got bad at NBC, he became desperate, and there was a flop sweat aspect to it all. Maybe he lost his edge. He just went into a batting slump. Nothing he touched turned to anything but… something awful.[26]

An interesting side note to the "something awful" *Mrs. Columbo* tale is the story of one of Mulgrew's co-stars. Lili Haydn (misspelled "Lilli Haydn" for the credits of *Kate Loves a Mystery*) played 8-year-old Jenny Columbo, yet another surprise popping up in the Lieutenant's household. Haydn was the daughter of feminist comedienne Lotus Weinstock and underground filmmaker David Jove, and her unconventional childhood, including living in a commune, eventually led to her starring in Jack In the Box commercials and *Mrs. Columbo*. Earning $1,500 per episode (over $6,000 in 2023 dollars), Lili was footing half the family rent at age 8.

Haydn's career took a turn when she discovered a love for the violin. *Mrs. Columbo* helped pay for lessons, and she was playing with the Los Angeles Philharmonic at age 15. Today she is a renowned rock violinist, having played with and opened for Robert Plant, Tom Petty, Sting, Herbie Hancock, Roger Waters, and others. So we do have something to thank Fred Silverman for.[27]

Of course, Silverman is the convenient villain in all this. But perhaps, if he had had the instinct to get out of his own way, the story might have been different. David Levinson (no relation to Richard Levinson) presents an interesting thought experiment.

DAVID LEVINSON (*Mrs. Columbo* Producer, first season): Kate Mulgrew was a nice actress, but there was no way to overcome the premise. Peter [Falk] went berserk. He didn't like the idea of *Mrs. Columbo* anyhow, but now it looks like he's Woody Allen; you know, he's married to this girl who's young enough to be his daughter. The Mrs. Columbo character made no sense at all. She's a housewife. To have her as a neighborhood reporter at least gave her some kind of excuse for poking her nose around. But it was such a stretch. It would have worked if we could have cast Maureen Stapleton. That's who everyone saw as Mrs. Columbo. Not Freddy Silverman![28]

Hold that notion for a moment. Now, fast forward to 1983. CBS approached Richard Levinson, William Link, and Peter Fischer about creating a new mystery series with a strong female lead, "one not bailed out by a man," as described by Link.[29] In his autobiography, Fischer writes that he borrowed an idea from a recent CBS TV-movie starring Helen Hayes as writer Agatha Christie's Miss Marple character. "I thought, why don't we meld Miss Marple and Miss Christie into one character, a mystery writer who actually solves murder mysteries using logic, good sense, observation, and a twinkly sense of humor."[30] Voila, Jessica Fletcher and *Murder, She Wrote* were born.

Perhaps it simply slipped Fischer's mind that the concept was actually given a go-round in 1973 as part of NBC's Wednesday Mystery Movie wheel, where Hayes played an elderly whodunit novelist in *The Snoop Sisters*. The series lasted only four episodes, but is notable in its unique portrayal of an amateur lady sleuth. In television history, this was a rarity. Female detectives such as *Honey West* and *Police Woman* were not totally uncommon, but beyond *Nancy Drew* and *The Snoop Sisters,* at the time there was only one other female-headlining amateur investigator in American TV history. Her name was Mrs. Columbo.

As the Levinson/Link/Fischer team was trying to solve the 1978 puzzle of what to do with the Mrs. Columbo character, Dick Levinson asked, "What is her franchise [the formula, or series premise], and where is her husband? And how is she, as a housewife, going to stumble across a murder each week?"[31]

Certainly, these were very valid and obvious questions that needed answering. But they paled next to determining the actress who would be playing the lead character. And if it had indeed been Maureen Stapleton, or Jean Stapleton, or Brenda Vaccaro, as Link, Levinson and Fischer suggested, it's reasonable to think that those three *Columbo* vets would have stuck it out to shepherd the project through. After all, it was Mulgrew's casting that drove them off the show in disgust. It's not fanciful to think that if they had the right actress, they could have made whatever adjustments were needed to make the Mrs. Columbo character become a (somewhat) credible amateur detective.

Fischer's description of Jessica Fletcher: "She's a voracious reader. Make her an English teacher who writes murder mysteries... a stand-alone character free to move about unencumbered by children or a husband. Her hometown would be the scene of some of these mysteries, but we would put her on the road... as a successful author, travels would be natural."[32]

With this blueprint, Fischer created Fletcher in 1983. Could he have made similar adjustments to Maureen Stapleton-as-Kate Columbo in 1978? In the

TV history timeline, female amateur sleuth mystery *Mrs. Columbo* pre-dates female amateur sleuth mystery *Murder, She Wrote*. It's intriguing to consider if perhaps, just maybe, *Mrs. Columbo* could have *become Murder, She Wrote*, with a long TV life and enough respectability to persuade Peter Falk himself to turn up occasionally to utter, "Honey, just one more thing…." But Fred Silverman and his fixation on Kate Mulgrew makes that a mystery that neither Mrs. nor Lt. Columbo will ever be solving.

Perhaps it was a case of right Kate, wrong time. Silverman's hand-picked choice for *Mrs. Columbo* received a 1980 Golden Globes nomination for Best Actress in the role, losing out to Natalie Wood in a TV take of *From Here to Eternity*. And Mulgrew's television career has certainly not lacked for activity, most notably *Star Trek: Voyager* and *Orange Is the New Black*.

But Mulgrew credits one person in particular for keeping her acting career on track—Angela Lansbury. The ex-*Columbo* guested on *Murder, She Wrote*'s third season episode "The Corpse Flew First Class" at a time when roles were not coming her way. "I have only one person to thank for this, and that is the great, great Angela Lansbury… I got an offer—and to play the murderer, too—and I flew to it because I was always being cast as the good girl. The murderer, what heaven!"

Mulgrew came back for two more episodes, and recounts the advice Lansbury gave her: "The acting comes and goes, it's ups and downs… You must hang in until you hit it, and you will hit it."[33]

By the time *Kate Loves a Mystery* dragged itself across the finish line on March 19, 1980, it had become literally and figuratively divorced from its *Columbo* origins. No lieutenant hubby, no Dog, no Peugeot, no cigars littering the house. All those *Columbo* callbacks simply reminded disappointed viewers of who came first. As David Koenig's *Shooting Columbo* notes about the NBC brain trust, "Privately, they realized that the Columbo connection created false expectations for the audience."[34]

Expectations, not just about the character of Mrs. Columbo, but about the quality of *Mrs. Columbo*. As ridiculous as the show appears today, it was more-or-less comparable to much of 1979's television fare. But it was not comparable at all to its predecessor and serves as a reminder that the quality of *Columbo*, even as its best years were in the rearview, vastly outdistanced anything else on television at the time.

Fast forward to 2023. *Poker Face* starring Natasha Lyonne was introduced to instant popularity and acclaim, much of it based on its shared DNA with *Columbo*. This included the inverted mystery format, Charlie Cale's keen observational skills and logical reasoning, her relatability to ordinary folk and underestimation by the killer, her sense of justice, and other mutual traits. But the irony is that she is also shadowing the TV footsteps of one of the pioneers of the amateur female sleuth template—Mrs. Columbo.

Accordingly, it's Mrs. Columbo herself who'll get the last word on the snakebit spinoff that, perhaps despite itself, helped break new ground for television detecting.

KATE MULGREW: When they gave me my own show, I thought it would survive the stigma of *Columbo*. But it didn't.[35]

15.
Explaining Patrick McGoohan

Columbo's guest villains are often fertile ground for intertextual observations. For Janet Leigh's appearance as actress-dancer Grace Wheeler in *Forgotten Lady*, producers used actual footage from Leigh's appearance in the real 1953 movie *Walking My Baby Back Home* for when Grace watches film of herself in the fictional movie starring Grace Wheeler, *Walking My Baby Back Home*. Just three episodes later, Ricardo Montalban plays renowned matador Luis Montoya. In the first two minutes, Montoya is seen watching film of "himself" in the bullfighting ring, which is actually Montalban playing a bullfighter in the 1943 film *Santa*.

One of *Columbo's* most prominent contributors was Patrick McGoohan, with four appearances as a killer and five as a director across the program's 69 episodes. McGoohan rose to fame as a spy in the British TV series *Danger Man*, retitled *Secret Agent* for American viewing. He followed with his iconic performance as the numbered but no-named agent in 1967's *The Prisoner*. It is this role and series that *Columbo* calls back to when McGoohan plays a spy in *Identity Crisis*. More than once, McGoohan's character Nelson Brenner uses the same "Be seeing you" catchphrase uttered by Number 6 in *The Prisoner*.

McGoohan had a heavy conceptual influence on *The Prisoner*, and helmed and penned a handful of its scripts. Most notably, McGoohan wrote and directed the final two series installments, "Once Upon a Time" and "Fall Out." In these episodes, his Number 6 character is finally able to escape The Village where he has been confined, and you'll be hard-pressed to find two more totally bonkers episodes of any television series ever aired in the U.S.

Although not as wild as those affairs, McGoohan's unconventional directing

WAS PETER FALK a prisoner of Patrick McGoohan's *Columbo* vision? *(Photo from 1998's Ashes to Ashes)*

style was on display in what most *Columbo* fans agree is the worst chapter of the classic run, *Last Salute to the Commodore*. As David Koenig's *Shooting Columbo* details, McGoohan had free reign to improvise, rewrite and stretch the Columbo character to ill effect. But Peter Falk felt that McGoohan was a boon to the show, affirming, "We have been fortunate to work with many exceptional people over the years, but Patrick McGoohan's contributions to the show stand out as something very special."[1]

Outside of the official *Columbo* team, one could plausibly argue that it was McGoohan who had the most outside influence on the entire series. On balance, his acting was generally top-notch, his directing was hit-or-miss, and his rewriting efforts were often panned (though certainly not by Falk). Such was the case with McGoohan's last work on *Columbo*, 2001's penultimate episode, *Murder with Too Many Notes*.

For this intertextual look at McGoohan's impact, we'll take a detour outside of the Classic Era. In 2023, I impulsively decided that I was going to have a go at tracking down the original script for this episode with the simple goal of learning exactly what changes McGoohan had made to the initial work of the aspiring writer who submitted the original screenplay, Jeffrey Cava.

By all accounts, the celebrated, egocentric, often-brilliant McGoohan had taken a perfectly decent *Columbo* plot and made a cascading series of terrible choices that resulted in what has been generally regarded as one of the lowlights of the 69-episode *Columbo* library. Along the way, beyond merely altering some words on pages of a Courier 12-pt. font screenplay, it became a story of Hollywood hope and heartache.

Koenig's book devotes several pages to the disaster. Jeffrey Cava was a youthful assistant editor at Universal Studios where *Columbo* was produced, and on spec—that is, without any guarantee that it would be bought—he created a script that centered around his interest in film music.

In Cava's original vision, celebrated musical conductor and composer Francis Paradiso has been getting uncredited assistance on his latest movie scores from a youthful assistant and aspiring conductor, Daniel Mason. For the award-winning music to his latest film, *The Murderers*, Paradiso pirated most of the soundtrack from Mason, who has received no public acknowledgement of his efforts. Of course, if the world did know that someone else was providing the bulk of Paradiso's work, the egotistical maestro's reputation would be sunk. When Mason threatens to spill the musical beans, the evil conductor's solution is, naturally, homicide.

Writer Cava concocts a unique murder method. Young would-be conductor Mason always practices his craft on the roof of the building where Paradiso creates his scores. The high-rise has an unused freight elevator shaft—unused but not inoperative. Paradiso drugs Mason, then places the body atop the shaft. Paradiso returns to his ground-floor studio, then sends the elevator slowly upwards just before he begins a live performance for a studio audience. When the lift reaches the building's top, the shaft's trapdoor opens upward and Mason's comatose body is rolled off, plummeting to the alley below. Meanwhile, Paradiso seems to have an airtight alibi of hundreds.

As merely an aspiring screenwriter rather than an established one, Cava's work lay unread for many months, eventually getting a look from Peter Falk, who was quoted before episode production as claiming, "In my judgment, it is one of the most ingenious murders in the history of *Columbo*."[2] Impressed, Falk gave it the go-ahead, and the script was being readied for production when Patrick McGoohan came aboard as the episode's director.

Cava had already worked with *Columbo* co-producer Jack Horger to trim the too-lengthy script before Falk had a look at it. But now, it was McGoohan's turn to apply the knife and make room for his own embellishments. His unrestrained additions and subtractions to the script resulted in trivial circumstantial clues that had no connection to the conductor villain, and unfunny and unflattering scenes with Peter Falk that sapped the patience of even the most forgiving *Columbo* fan.

What happened? Exactly how, and why, was Cava's work so changed by McGoohan? If found, the original script could provide answers.

David Koenig described Jeff Cava as a film music "superfan," so I fired up my Google machine for a search. It led me to the website Film Score

Monthly, describing itself as "one of the leading voices in film music [with] appreciation of the original dramatic underscoring composed for motion pictures, television, new media—and of the talented composers who create it." FSM is a robust community of film music devotees. If you're looking for an interview with the composer of *Evil Dead Rise*, release date of the CD score for *What's Eating Gilbert Grape?*, or serious discussions of the music of *Matlock*, *Fantasy Island*, and more (including *Columbo*), FSM is definitely your online hang. And for Jeff, it was.

But it's where I also found the sad report that Jeff had passed away in September 2020. FSM founder Lukas Kendall posted the news and noted Jeff's professional history at Universal and Paramount, where he had been working on home video restorations and documentaries of classic movies. Said Kendall, "He was, quite simply, a mensch… who went above and beyond to assist with any project he could."

Kendall followed this news in May 2021 with word that "the family of our late friend Jeff Cava is looking to find good homes for Jeff's significant collection of soundtrack CDs." The email contact for the project was Jeff's sister Elizabeth. Unsure if this would prove to be helpful, I reached out to her, explaining my hope that she could help me discover Jeff's original *Murder with Too Many Notes* script. Her reply was unexpected: "He was my little brother, and his death has still left me reeling. What he wrote and what was ultimately shot, was an extremely painful process for him." She added, "If there's any way to get justice after the fact, I'd be happy to help with this. I was always his protector when we were kids, but I couldn't protect him from stuff like this."

While Elizabeth began her own search for the screenplay, in the interim she put me in touch with Bill Paxton, a friend of Jeff's at Universal who was now Head Librarian of the Universal Film Library. In the early Nineties, Jeff and Bill were friends trying their hand at screenwriting in Los Angeles. They shared their scripts with each other, looking for feedback and collaborative advice. Jeff was angling to sell a movie script, but when that was unsuccessful, Bill convinced him to try his hand at something for television.

Weeks later, *Murder, with Too Many Notes* was born. Bill liked it. One of *Columbo's* producers at the time was Jack Horger, whom Paxton had known when Horger was an editor at *Murder, She Wrote*. Paxton assisted getting stock footage for *Columbo* episodes, so he looked to Horger as a way to advance Cava's script. It worked.

"Jack called me up and said, 'Bill, this is a really good script.' He said, 'Peter really loves these stories that take place in show business. I'd like to

JEFFREY CAVA, the better of the *Murder with Too Many Notes* screenwriters.

show it to him.' I put Jack in touch with Jeff, and next thing you know, Jeff says that they want to buy the script, and he was all excited."

It is here where the inexperienced Cava likely made a critical miscalculation. "I said, 'Jeff, the very first thing you have to do is to get an agent. Whatever you do, get an agent.' He did not get an agent."

What happened next is a vivid memory for Paxton. "In those days, Jeff was an emotional guy, very integrity-based. He would call me sometimes and we would talk through things. This time, he was really upset. He told me, 'Patrick McGoohan is trying to steal my script!' I said, 'He can't do that. It's registered.' [Scripts registered with the Writers' Guild of America (WGA) create a public claim to authorship.] But according to Jeff, he said that McGoohan took his script, and changed the names of every character in it, and re-registered it with the Writers' Guild."

This was the first twist in my script quest. With McGoohan and Cava each deceased, reconstructing events would be difficult. Alleged actions are one thing, but confirmation is another. Here is where the original script would be able to provide at least some small validation or contradiction. Fortunately, the efforts of Elizabeth Cava paid off. Among Jeff's belongings was his original script, which she graciously passed along to me.

On the front cover page, the work is titled *Murder, with Too Many Notes*. (Yes, the comma is in the original title.) In addition: "First Draft 1-24-92 Copyright 1992; Original WGA Registration #485193 1-27-92; Renewal

Registration 5-27-97 Renewal #666335."

Following this is the Character List page. Some of these roles would be eliminated from the final episode version and others added, as might naturally happen in script rewrites and revisions. But there are several characters who are holdovers from Cava's initial effort, and none of them retain the names he gave them, save Lt. Columbo. Conductor Paradiso becomes Findlay Crawford, to be played by Scottish actor/comedian Billy Connolly. Victim Daniel Mason's name is switched to Gabe McEnery. The closest any major or minor moniker comes to the original Cava choice is Director Nicholas Ritter, who is renamed Sidney Ritter in the episode.

Additionally, there are other small and seemingly subjective alterations. Cava's score composed by the victim is called *The Murderers*, now changed to *The Killer*. Stellar Studios becomes Monolith Studios. Of course, there could be logical and perfectly legitimate reasons those tweaks were made, and in isolation, they don't have significance. But on the point that Cava was said to be initially upset about, name changes did indeed happen.

Paxton continues, "Jeff was crying; he was so upset. I was aware of the Writers' Guild arbitration, and said, you have to go to the Guild and tell them what this man did. So he filed a grievance against him. I remember that there was a back-and-forth about how he [Cava] was only going to get the story credit, and McGoohan would get the teleplay credit, and that really upset him."

To document his complaints, Cava needed to provide an arbitration statement to the Writer's Guild of America, detailing his contributions to the script, and how they did, or did not, differ from the finished product. Once again, Elizabeth was able to retrieve this piece to the puzzle. Amidst music notes from episode composer Dick DeBenedictis, a thank you card from Peter Falk, production shooting call sheets, and dusty VHS tapes, Cava's account was lurking in a set of three boxes of materials collected from his Universal and *Columbo* experiences.

The statement is dated January 16, 1999. The words are decades old, but they read as fresh as a contemporary oral history, the story of one fledgling writer's personal mission to create a quality episode of *Columbo*.

"I first had the idea to write the teleplay *Columbo: Murder with Too Many Notes* in December of 1991. I recognized that conceiving a story and script for a pre-existing format that already had its own well-defined central character would be an important lesson to me in the development and possible success in my writing. The Lieutenant would be a challenge for me to fill a blank script page with story, which is exactly what the task that I'd set for myself was meant to be.

"I have long since loved film music and its impact on movies. This setting would not only let me offer my point of view on the importance of film music, but would also dramatize… the emotional value of music both in film and in the fictitious world of my character's everyday life." Unlike a typical generic murder-for-money plot device, Cava was offering up a unique environment that motivated, inspired and excited him. And he also clearly wanted it to educate, interest and excite us, the viewer. It was a textbook passion project.

Cava's five-page statement walks through the elements of the script that he originated: the murder's premise, the protégé's eccentricities, the weaponized vertical lift elevator, the conductor's arrogance, the killing's execution. He notes clues that were kept and ones that were dropped. He recounts how he moved forward an important clue—the lack of a scream by the falling victim—from Act 6 to Act 3 because "placing it earlier made Columbo's suspicions much more warranted." Cava shows a clear understanding of "the emotional and mental 'chess game,' pitting Columbo against his villain in a way that lets both the pursuer and the pursued believe, 'I've got you, but you still think I don't.'"

But Cava's document produced another mystery. On the title page, he calls himself "Writer A." This obviously makes sense. But he also describes other script drafts as having been written by "Writers B and C." Wait, two other writers? Wasn't Patrick McGoohan supposed to be the sole villain responsible for all the script rewrites?

Cava ascribes many of the character name changes to Writer C, so one can assume that this was McGoohan. What was Writer B's role? According to Cava's statement, "Wherein my drafts used the lack of a baton as a clue, Writer B initiated the presence of a baton, engraved with a love note from Gabriel's girlfriend, as the primary clue…. The use of Writer B's device of the baton eliminated other clues in my original draft." [Although in the final filmed version, the baton isn't really used as a clue at all, never mind as a 'primary clue.']

Another search through Jeff's *Columbo* boxes was needed, and sister Elizabeth's discovery of the final arbitration settlement papers produced the identity of Writer B. The notice was cc'ed to Jeffrey Cava, Patrick McGoohan, and Jeffrey Hatcher. Hatcher was the credited teleplay writer for the previous *Columbo* episode, 1998's *Ashes to Ashes* starring McGoohan. Hatcher has an extensive list of plays, films and books to his credit, yet it appears that the baton was his only significant addition to the *Murder with Too Many Notes* script.

As Cava had told Bill Paxton, the arbitration committee indeed "tentatively determined" that Cava would only get a story credit, and the entire teleplay would belong to McGoohan. But Cava's multi-page inventory of script similarities and crucial differences apparently swayed the arbitration board. The WGA recognized how much of Cava's original teleplay survived McGoohan's tampering. "After carefully considering the material submitted to the Guild for the determination of credits, the Arbitration Committee has determined that the writing credits shall read as follows: Teleplay by Jeffrey Cava and Patrick McGoohan; Story by Jeffrey Cava." And this is what we see in the episode's opening credits.

The arbitration notice then takes just 16 words to unintentionally but accurately summarize the entire relationship between Cava and McGoohan: "Please note that an 'and' designates writers working separately, and an ampersand ('&') denotes a writing team." As if Cava didn't already realize it, he and McGoohan were not going to be hammering out the script's final draft together downing pints at an L.A. tavern.

Cava, looking to get a foothold in the Hollywood screenplay game, was distressed by the whole process. How did McGoohan react? According to Paxton, Jeff clearly remembered McGoohan's blithe response to the conflict: "'Well, sorry, old boy.'" Elizabeth Cava has a bitter reaction to McGoohan's alleged brush-off: "Ouch. Did McGoohan even try to help Jeff with the script? Why did McGoohan decide to do it that way?" The rules of the Writer's Guild may point to a possible answer.

Writer's Guild arbitration conflicts are not uncommon, particularly in the often-cutthroat Hollywood community. After an initial script sale, precisely worded credits determine residual payments. This would be the compensation paid for the reuse of a credited writer's work, such as an episode rerun. In other words, looking at credit disputes often have a simple dictum—Follow the Money.

As the current WGA Credits Manual points out, "The first writer on an original screenplay shall be entitled to screenplay credit if such writer's work represents a contribution of more than 33 percent to the final shooting script. Any subsequent writer must contribute 50 percent to the final shooting script."[3] Comparing the original script to the finished broadcast product, one wonders exactly what McGoohan contributed to get to his 50 percent contribution threshold.

We know that he added a lengthy and excruciating slow-car crawl, with Columbo steering his Peugeot through L.A. acting as a police escort while a hammered Crawford trailed along behind. The continual stop-and-starts to the procession and Columbo's banter with Crawford serve no useful purpose. If the point was to have Columbo annoy the suspected killer, the Lieutenant certainly annoyed the viewing audience. Another dreadful scene had Columbo and Crawford in the conductor's rehearsal studio, where a full orchestra played the instantly recognizable themes to *Jaws* and *Psycho*, which a painfully ignorant Columbo couldn't identify. Once again in New *Columbo*, Peter Falk ignores his own advice, given long ago to Johnny Carson: "People wouldn't like a character that doesn't have dignity."

For the curious, Cava's original screenplay has been posted through the Columbophile Blog to allow Columbo deep-divers to give it their own look.[4] As with all creative works, opinions of the screenplay will no doubt draw a range of responses. My own take is that the script is perfectly serviceable as a first draft. If Cava was indeed open to change, if McGoohan hadn't crowbarred his own terrible scenes into it, and if Peter Falk didn't exaggerate his old man-nerisms, it had potential to be a solid Nineties episode.

The script is indeed overlong. At 131 pages, it would have run close to two and a quarter hours minus commercials. In particular, the extended opening is ripe for shortening. And the finale's final proof that Daniel Mason scored *The Murderers* comes in the form of a too-convenient pre-mailed package with a postmarked date prior to Paradiso's claiming that he alone wrote the score, a package not even discovered by Columbo.

But Cava provides several good clues that McGoohan either ignored or botched. Columbo suspects something's amiss when it appears that victim Mason did his rooftop "conducting" facing in an unlikely direction. Most significantly, Paradiso has to cover his tracks for the unlocked freight elevator that opens and rolls Mason off the roof, so he attaches a rusty lock that comes from his Peugeot, which is the same model as Columbo's, only in pristine shape. Completing the subterfuge means that Paradiso has to go the roof immediately after the fall instead of rushing to see the body on the pavement, the best of the clues that focus Columbo's sights on Paradiso.

It must be noted that nowhere in his official arbitration statement does Cava make a direct accusation that McGoohan was trying to steal his work. The presence of a third writer would likely make that claim more difficult to stick. But the practice that Cava was objecting to is unfortunately not unusual. It would not be the first time in movie history that a rewrite job made unnecessary and arbitrary changes to an original scribe's work in order to get a writing credit.

In Hollywood, script rewriting is as natural and essential as drawing oxygen. Paxton says that Cava was under no delusion that his work would remain untouched. "Jeff was open to advice. And he would admit that he was an

PETER FALK appreciated Cava's efforts.

overwriter. He wrote long, and he knew that. He wanted the feedback. There was no objection to rewrites. The objection was to McGoohan's trying to cut Jeff out completely. To my knowledge, there was no collaboration whatsoever.

"You know, he would have loved it if he had been brought in to be even a little part of what they did; 'Listen kid, this is how we do this in the big time, you have to cut this and this,' I think Jeff would have welcomed that feedback. He was so passionate.... It wasn't about the money, it was about the credit for something you wrote. That really meant something to him. The fact that he thought McGoohan tried to steal that, that's what offended him

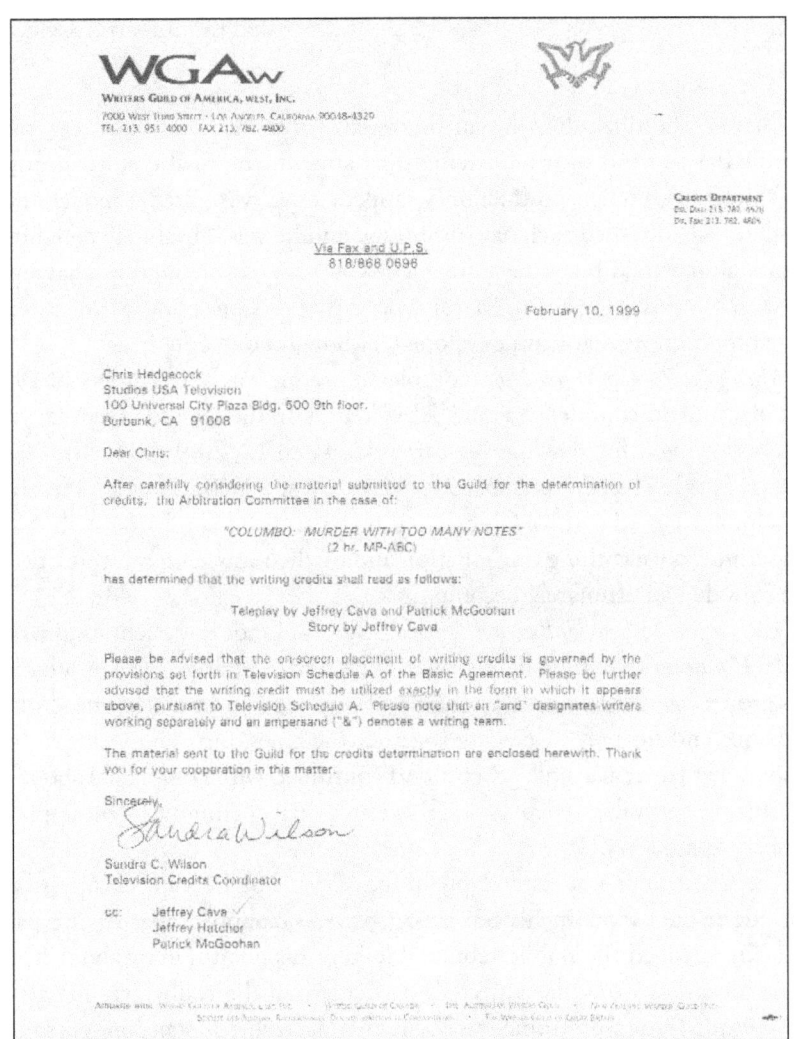

THE ARBITRATION LETTER with the final verdict for the writing credits of *Murder with Too Many Notes*.

so much. It was so vile and reprehensible that I could not believe that a man of McGoohan's stature would do that."

Cava closed his 1999 arbitration statement to the WGA recognizing the irony in what he was seeking. Over a quarter-century removed from writing it, and almost five years after his passing, this realization has special resonance uncovering it today: "It is my hope that this arbitration will afford me a shared credit, the credit I believe I have worked to deserve. This is probably out of line, but as I finish this statement, I can't help but realize that I wrote a script about an upstart artist who is murdered by the mentor who takes his credit. Where's Rod Serling?"

Despite the difficulties he encountered, Cava was, as Paxton describes, "thrilled at the end of it all. Seeing his name on the final credits meant so much to him." When production wrapped, Cava was gifted a model of the set that he had visited each day of filming, and he was "absolutely delighted." Although it would be understandable if Cava soured on anything having to do with screenwriting again, Paxton asserts that this was not the case, as there were other scripts that Cava developed, although none bore fruit.

Murder with Too Many Notes completed production in December of 1998, but in a sure no-confidence signal, ABC kept it on the shelf for over two years before slotting it for viewing. Air date was March 12, 2001, and Jeffrey Cava was ready. He rented event space for the episode's premiere at a Vine Street L.A. lounge bar, The Three Clubs, inviting friends and family to the showing. He scripted a welcoming introduction and by then was acutely aware of what the episode had ultimately become.

The review in *The Hollywood Reporter* was not kind. Ray Richmond wrote, "The *Columbo* execution has grown tired and repetitive. The production has grown bloated and lazy. Columbo always used to be a step ahead of his audience and his prey in piecing together the clues, but time seems to have eroded that particular skill." Richmond continued with complaints about the "agonizing formulaic teleplay.... The traditional 'hedunnit' style is played almost for mockery."

The assessment understandably stung Cava, but he kept a copy of the critique tucked away in his boxes of *Columbo* paraphernalia. At the party, he acknowledged the public rebuke. He kept his good humor about it, but some bitterness would be expected, particularly if the really terrible parts of the episode came from someone else and you're the one standing up to take the arrows.

"Many of you know that tonight has been a long time in the works.... *Columbo* was a show that I always admired, mainly because of his adversaries. A really good murder is difficult to plan, and *Columbo* allowed the time to plan and execute a good murder, and in doing so managed to emerge, most of the time, as quality television. I hoped that my script would be all of that.

"Of course, last Friday's *Hollywood Reporter* review will tell you that I achieved nothing close to this lofty goal. We all know that a tremendous lot can be said in reaction to any critic, but I'm not the one to do so. No writer ever is.... So screw *The Hollywood Reporter!*"

His sister was at The Three Clubs viewing. "The episode was airing, people were drinking, and I just remember that Jeff kept pacing back and forth throughout the night. And things would come up and he would suddenly yell at the screen. This was almost non-stop. It was funny… but of course, ultimately not totally funny for him."

Bill Paxton did not attend, not because he didn't care, but because he cared too much. "For me, it felt like I was going to celebrate somebody who was crippled in a car accident and got a $10 million settlement. It just didn't feel right."

Perhaps the party served as a final catharsis for Cava. After all, the screenplay was his personal pet project. Regardless of how we judge his original script, it was a work that he poured his film-score passion into, and Peter Falk and others at Universal had felt that it was worth buying. That alone meant something. But then, rightly or wrongly, he believed that his passion had been flayed into something else altogether by others. Well, by one person in particular.

The whole experience was, according to Elizabeth Cava, "a mixed bag. It gave Jeff hope that he could be a writer, and he never gave up on that, even as messy as everything was. So he continued to write, but it also took a toll on him. Once you have the writing bug, it never really leaves you—if it's in your blood, it's in your blood."

Friend Paxton speculates on the might-have-been. "If Jeff had just had an agent, I think he would have had a writing career in the business. He was talented. With an agent, he would have had someone behind him who could have protected him, someone who could have sold more of his scripts. But Jeff was a quirky guy, and he had his own way of doing things. He was naively trusting of people."

"Jeff really wished that he had taken Bill's advice to get an agent," adds Elizabeth. "I don't think he didn't want to, but finding time for his job, to write, to find a good agent… I don't think he was made out for that."

There is one final unknown regarding Jeff Cava and Patrick McGoohan, and of all the questions this script search raised, this mystery may be the most curious. After McGoohan's death in 2009, a posthumous appreciation was penned, appearing on the Ultimate Columbo Site. The writer of this appreciation? Jeffrey Cava.[5]

Dated March 14, 2009, Cava's 800-word homage has no direct mention of his difficulties with McGoohan. He describes him at various points as "gracious," with "dry humor," "irreverent," "irreplaceable," and both having a "connection that was mutually realized."

But there was one passage that takes on more significance when understanding the scripting backstory of *Murder with Too Many Notes*. See if you can spot it here: "In my early experiences with him, Patrick, though welcoming, was a seemingly hard man externally who many might feel was perhaps too thick-skinned to get to know or even approach. And while that distinctive character trait may have been counter to the manner in which I felt our joint *Columbo* venture should be realized on screen, it was never thick enough to prevent me from wanting to spend as much time as I could around him, no doubt much to his irritation."

The appreciation stunned Bill and Elizabeth, who were unaware that it existed until after Jeff's death. "I don't believe the Jeff Cava that I knew had those kind of feelings about Patrick McGoohan," says Paxton flatly. "Did they change over the years? Did he find it in himself to say 'why be bitter' and forgive him? Maybe."

Elizabeth provides another, sisterly perspective. "Jeff never wanted conflict; he was a gentle soul and never looked for a fight. He wanted to have a mentor, and I think he probably looked up to McGoohan and wanted him to be what he wrote about in that appreciation. He would make his memory and remember him in a positive way, rather than saying, 'What an S.O.B.'"

While pursuing his screenwriting ambitions, Cava's passion for film and his photographic memory were put to good use as he immersed himself in movie restoration projects, most notably the 2007 restorations of *The Godfather* and *The Godfather II*. In his later years, there were health issues and harder times.

Murder with Too Many Notes was Cava's first and only screenplay credit. It was McGoohan's last. After this final *Columbo* contribution, his career was essentially complete, save for a handful of voice acting roles, such as "Number 6" in a 2000 *Simpsons*.

McGoohan was never a collaborator. After the worldwide Sixties success of his *Secret Agent* and *The Prisoner*, both of which he totally controlled, no producer would let him steer the ship of any project, which was "totally frustrating.... Clout. I had clout in England. And you have to have it. *Columbo* was okay because Peter had the same sort of situation that I had. He had say-so. Peter had a very successful series and they'd do anything he wanted."[6]

It is well-documented that Falk was enamored of McGoohan's talent and, for better or worse, indulged him with unparalleled freedoms in his *Columbos*. A notorious rewriter even outside his work with Falk, in retrospect it is highly unlikely that McGoohan would have ever consented to seriously work with a writer on his first screen effort.

Jeffrey Cava may have wanted a mentor. But a mentor must want a mentee. Of all the roles in Patrick McGoohan's long career, it may be the one that interested him the least.

V.
Watching and Rewatching *Columbo*

There are many reasons we love Classic *Columbo*.

The character is iconic—a respectful, working-class everyman with human foibles, imbued with warmth, intelligence, and determination. Peter Falk's brilliant portrayal of the character adds depth, steely resolve, and mischievous charm. Clever plotting draws the viewer into the unique inverted mystery format of stylishly-filmed murders, laying out a trail of subtle clues inviting us to join Columbo as he doggedly looks for a stress point in the powerful, privileged and/or pampered villain's story that will expose guilt.

This much, we get on first viewing. It's why the NBC Sunday Mystery Movie wheel was so successful for seven years after its original Wednesday night launch in 1971. There was no VCR replaying (unless you were burning money like Ward Fowler), no streaming, no DVDs, no time-shifting DVRs. You watched it once, then waited for the network summer repeats. For those one-time broadcasts, you could enjoy a lot of what made the series great, but it was perhaps difficult to fully appreciate in a single sitting. For what was beneath the surface, for what you might have missed that first time, you had to rewatch.

And now, technology allows us to do just that, repeatedly.

Everyone's repeatability mileage will vary, but one key I've noted is the *Columbo* connective tissue that binds the episodes together. The plotting, the dastardly villains, the soundtrack, the Seventies elegance and polish, the direction, the sets, the casting, the understated humor, all encourage us to stream the Seventies episodes again and again, even if an installment comes up short of the quality of the masterpieces. It's why you might find some heretofore hidden value in relative duds like *Old Fashioned Murder* or *Short Fuse*.

In writing this book, my goal has been to provide even more reasons to watch and rewatch *Columbo*. Hopefully, you are encouraged to keep a close eye and ear on those proverbial little things that made this character a product of his times. Of course, the pleasure of *Columbo* is in the escapism; the show was not designed to be studied in a sociology class. But the 45 episodes of Classic *Columbo* were a pop culture sensation, and it would have resisted such popularity if it hadn't reflected, at least in some small way, American values. As our pop culture archeologists of the future will tell you, this reflection included the intersection of our humble Lieutenant with the social issues of the decade.

ELLIOT MARKHAM: Let's look at your itinerary. You showed up at my office, at my lecture, and now at my construction site.
COLUMBO: Well, actually, I just happened to have some have spare time.
MARKHAM: Perhaps you should spend your time a little more productively.
– *Blueprint for Murder* (1972)

Murderers like Elliot Markham may not think so, but spending your spare time watching and rewatching *Columbo* is always productive. We're not just reliving the investigations of TV's top cop—we're reliving a critical and turbulent decade of American life.

Footnotes & Sources

Preface
1. "Peter Falk on Johnny Carson Talks *Any Old Port in a Storm*" (youtube.com, Oct. 5, 1973)
2. "What Is Culture" (bu.edu)
3. Hua, Hsu, "Stuart Hall and the Rise of Cultural Studies" (*New Yorker*, July 17, 2017)

Introduction
1. Richard Levinson and William Link, "How We Created *Columbo*" (*American Film*, March 1981)
2. David Martin-Jones, *Columbo: Paying Attention 24/7* (Edinburgh University Press, 2021), p. 50. Martin-Jones maintains that "there is no singular, coherent "Columboverse," only a multi-verse of infinite variations on *Columbo*. [It] only really has coherence within each stand-alone episode."
3. Columbophile, "The Most Chilling *Columbos* of Them All" (columbophile.com)
4. Dana Schwartz, "I Want to Watch the *Columbo* Episode about Trump" (bustle.com, Nov. 6, 2020)
5. David Koenig, *Shooting Columbo* (Bonaventure Press, 2021), p. 208

Columbo's Cultural Footprint
1. mediaessentials2e_ch4 ("TV Guide Inc." entry on encyclopedia.com)
2. "A Cop (And a Raincoat) for All Seasons" (*Time*, Nov. 26, 1973)
3. Philip H. Dougherty, "Advertising: Time of Affluence" (*NY Times*, Jan. 19, 1973)
4. *Green Acres* ("A Star Named Arnold Is Born," S3 E29)
5. "History's Moment in Media: Johnny Carson Became NBC's Late Night Star" (mediavillage.com)
6. *Dean Martin Celebrity Roasts* ("Ronald Reagan Roasts Frank Sinatra," 1978)
7. Rich Little interview (*Delaware County News*, cited wellesnet.com message board)
8. Lee Hale, *Backstage at the Dean Martin Show* (Taylor Trade Publishing, 2000), p. 229
9. Koenig, *Shooting Columbo*, p. 166-168
10. Fred L. Worth interview, (Trivia Hall of Fame, triviahalloffame.com)
11. "Issues Pursued in Copyright Lawsuit Are Not Trivial", NY Times, Nov. 13, 1984
12. Ken Jennings, *Brainiac* (Villard, 2007), p. 167.
13. Worth interview (Trivia Hall of Fame). Long-forgotten is the other bogus "fact" that Worth inserted on page 107 of his book—that Mrs. Columbo's name was "Mildred"!
14. Nester's Map & Guide Corp v. Hagstrom Map Co. (law.justia.com)
15. Columbophile, "Was Lieutenant Columbo's First Name Really Frank?" (columbophile.com, March 18, 2018)

16. William Link interview (interviews.televisionacademy.com)
17. J. Kingston Pierce, "Bringing *Columbo* to the Printed Page" (The Rap Sheet, Oct. 13, 2010)
18. "Innovations Spur Boom in VCR Sales" (*NY Times*, Nov. 12, 1984)
19. Jake Rossen, "Paw Enforcement: A History of McGruff the Crime Dog" (mentalfloss.com, July 27, 2017)
20. sherrynemmers.com
21. Wendy Melillo, *How McGruff and the Crying Indian Changed America* (Smithsonian Books, 2013), p. 157
22. *Stop a Crime* (youtube.com)
23. Zach Schonbrun, "McGruff the Crime Dog, Outliving His Creator, Fights On" (*NY Times*, Oct. 9, 2017)
24. Mark Dawidziak, *The Columbo Phile: A Casebook* (Mysterious Press, 1989), p. 309
25. Peter Falk interview (reddit.com, March 1, 1995)
26. "*Columbo*, Romania and the Communist Party" (youtube.com)
27. Willa Paskin's *Decoder Ring* podcast provides invaluable information through diligent research that demonstrates the exaggerated nature of Falk's story.
28. *Colombo: Spot Coop* (youtube.com)
29. Anna Wynn, "Wait, Why Is There a Columbo Statue in Budapest?" (*Daily News Hungary*, July 14, 2018)
30. Sean Aitchison, "Why Does Japan Love *Columbo*? An Investigation" (Anime News Network, Dec. 4, 2023)

Columbo and Social Culture: The Me Decade
1. Tom Wolfe, "The 'Me' Decade and the Third Great Awakening" (New York, Aug. 23, 1976)
2. The TV Professor, "Columbo and the History of Gym Franchises" (thetvprofessor.com, June 11, 2021)
3. Koenig, *Shooting Columbo*, p. 162

Class Conflicts and Power Plays
1. Josh Spiegel, "Columbo: A Class of His Own" (brightwalldarkroom.com)
2. Elisabeth Vincentelli, "Comfort Viewing: Three Reasons I Love *Columbo*" (*NY Times*, July 24, 2020)
3. Jeff Greenfield, "Columbo Knows the Butler Didn't Do It" (*NY Times*, April 1, 1973)
4. Dawidziak, *The Columbo Phile*, p. 6
5. Lilian Mathieu, "Columbo: Class Struggle on TV Tonight" (2013), p. 2
6. Levinson and Link, "How We Created *Columbo*"
7. "Anti-War Protests of the 1960s-70s" (whitehousehistory.org)
8. Mathieu, p. 4-5
9. Mathieu, p. 5, 26
10. Mathieu, p. 11
11. Alex Crowley, "The Psychology Behind Willful Disrespect" (thealexcrowley.medium.com, June 26, 2023)
12. Mathieu, p. 5

Liberation and Lady Killers
1. Susan J. Douglas, *Where the Girls Are* (Crown, 1995), p. 194-195
2. The book here, with its subtitle *The Secret Rooms of the National Museum*, is a clear knock-off of Michael Grant's 1975 volume Eros in *Pompeii: The Secret Rooms of the National Museum of Naples*. Grant's book examines the large collection of erotica and sexual symbols and imagery produced by ancient Romans before their civilization was buried under the Vesuvius eruption of A.D. 79. Columbo's faux edition cover shows us an almost-but-not-quite dead ringer of an actual 1st century fresco titled Satyr and Nymph.
3. Columbophile, "*Columbo* Inspires New Nashville Art Exhibition" (columbophile.com, Aug. 21, 2022)
4. Christyne Berzsenyi, *Columbo: A Rhetoric of Inquiry With Resistant Responders* (University of Chicago Press, 2021), p. 105

5. Berzsenyi, p. 112
6. Berzsenyi, p. 111
7. Berzsenyi, p. 117
8. Kathy Caprino, "What Is Feminism, and Why Do So Many Women and Men Hate It?" (forbes.com, March 8, 2017)
9. Janey Davies, "The Psychology of Female Killers: Why Do Women Kill?" (learning-mind.com, Oct. 10, 2019)
10. Berzsenyi, p. 104
11. Douglas, *Where the Girls Are*, p. 213, 216

Coping with Future Shock
Alvin Toffler, *Future Shock* (Random House, 1970)
1. *Future Shock* documentary (youtube.com, 1972)
2. Martin-Jones, *Columbo: Paying Attention 24/7*, p. 121-125
3. Martin-Jones, p. 127
4. Martin-Jones, p. 124-125

Race and Representation
1. Law Offices of Christopher J. Cherella, "The 'CSI Effect' on Jurors" (wicriminaldefense.com, Jan. 15, 2021)
2. *Chevy Mystery Show: Enough Rope* (Vimeo 28:09, July 31, 1960)
3. The Lt. Columbo Forum (pub10.bravenet.com)
4. Amelie Hastie, *Columbo: Make Me A Perfect Murder* (Duke University Press, 2024), p. 56-61
5. Hastie, p. 56
6. Los Angeles Police Department (Wikipedia)
7. Although *Murder Under Glass* does feature plot-specific scenes set in Chinatown, and Asian representation at a dinner with Paul Girard.
8. Survey L.A. Citywide Historic Context Statement (planning.lacity.gov), p. 38
9. Camille Zubrinsky and Lawrence Bobo, "Prismatic Metropolis: Race and Residential Segregation in the City of the Angels"(harvard. edu), p. 339
10. Zubrinksy and Bobo, p. 336
11. LAPD (Wikipedia)
12. Hastie, p. 207
13. "The Library of Congress Celebrates the Songs of America" (loc.gov)
14. "When the Saints Go Marching In" (Wikipedia)
15. Johnny Cash performs "I Saw the Light" and "When the Saints Go Marching In" (youtube.com)
16. Caitlin Byrd, "It's Offensive: SC Senator Urges the Citadel to Remove Confederate Flag from Chapel" (*The State*, March 2, 2021)
17. *Ransom for a Dead Man* script (Dec. 22, 1970)
18. *A Friend in Deed* script (Jan. 3, 1974)
19. Martin-Jones, *Columbo: Paying Attention 24/7*, p. 159

Murder for the Whole Family
1. In *Harry O* (1974-1976), David Janssen's private investigator Harry Orwell also operated without a gun.
2. John J. O'Connor, "TV: *The Gun*, a Journey to Tragedy" (*NY Times*, Nov. 13, 1974)
3. Peter Kihss, "No Harm in Horror, Comics Issuer Says" (*NY Times*, April 22, 1954)
4. Hearings for the Investigation of Juvenile Delinquency in the United States Before the Subcomm. to Investigate Juvenile Delinquency of the Sen Judiciary Comm., 87th Cong., 1st & 2d Sess. (1961-62)
5. Mass Media Hearings: A Report to the National Commission on the Causes and Prevention of Violence, Dec. 1969 (www.ojp.gov), p. 297
6. Mass Media Hearings 1969, p. 305-306
7. Mass Media Hearings 1969, p. 337
8. Mass Media Hearings 1969, p. 312
9. Mass Media Hearings 1969, p. 339
10. MediaSmarts, "What do We Know About Media Violence?" (mediasmarts.ca)
11. "The Wild Wild West – Violence,

Cancellation, and Syndication" (www.liquisearch.com)
12. "Television and Growing Up – The Impact of Televised Violence," Report to the Surgeon General's Scientific Advisory Committee on Television and Social Behavior, 1972 (ojp.gov)
13. Sex and Violence on TV, Hearings before the Subcommittee on Communications of the Committee on Interstate and Foreign Commerce, House of Representatives, 94th Congress, Second Session, (July 9; August 17-18, 1976), p. 261
14. Sex and Violence on TV, p. 262
15. Sex and Violence on TV, p. 375
16. Sex and Violence on TV, p. 377
17. *Make Me a Perfect Murder* script (Aug. 1, 1977)
18. Marshall Myer, "Police Shootings at Minorities, The Case of Los Angeles," incl. in Readings on Police Use of Deadly Force, p. 158
19. Jeremiah, "The Top Five Reasons Why Columbo Is an American Paradox" (The Fandomentals, June 15, 2018)

Deconstructing Murder and Media
1. Hastie, *Columbo: Make Me a Perfect Murder*, p. 146-147, 161
2. Renee Hobbs and Amy Jensen, "The Past, Present and Future of Media Literacy Education" (uri.edu, 2009)
3. BBC News, "Does Subliminal Advertising Actually Work?" (bbc.com, Jan. 20, 2015)
4. Charles Bensinger, "A Grand Tour of Video Technology" (*The Video Guide*, 1981, cool.culturalheritage.org)
5. 1974 Sony U-Matic Videocassette System VCR Machine ad (www.ebay.ca/itm/362612382427)
6. *Make Me a Perfect Murder* script

Just One More Think
1. Berzsenyi, *Columbo: A Rhetoric of Inquiry With Resistant Responders*, p. 3
2. Susan Krauss Whitbourne, "A New Look at Why People Invade Your Personal Space" (*Psychology Today*, Nov. 16, 2019)
3. Simon Worrall, "You Need Your Personal Space – Here's the Science Why" (*National Geographic*, Jan. 19, 2018)
4. Susan Krauss Whitbourne, "Five Things You Need to Know About Personal Space" (*Psychology Today*, April 6, 2019)
5. Nirmala Ferrao, "Protect Your Personal Space – Win At Psychological Warfare" (www.onmanorama.com, Jan. 11, 2017)
6. Australian Institute for Professional Counselors, "Principles and Techniques of Motivational Interviewing" (aipc.net.au, Jan. 12, 2015)
7. Steven Gaffney, "How to Confront Liars Using 'The Columbo Method'" (smallbusinessadvocate.com, July 6, 2011)
8. Changing Minds, "Closure Principle" (changingminds.org)
9. Mark Griffiths, "The Psychology of Columbo" (*Psychology Today*, Feb. 20, 2018)
10. Changing Minds, "Closure Principle"
11. Joshua Uebergang, "How to Brainwash People: Techniques to Put an Idea in People's Minds" (towerofpower.com.au)

The Politics of Murder
1. Dawidziak, *The Columbo Phile*, p. 240
2. Hastie, *Columbo: Make Me a Perfect Murder*, p. 46
3. Ron Elving, "The NRA Wasn't Always Against Gun Restrictions" (npr.org, Oct. 10, 2017)
4. Hastie, p. 55
5. AllSides, "Authority" (allsides.com/translator/authority)

Nineties Columbo: A Man Out of Time
1. Spiegel, "Columbo: A Class of His Own"
2. Vincentelli, "Comfort Viewing: Three Reasons I Love *Columbo*"

3. CrimeFictionLover, "Subversiveness and Curiosity: What Makes Columbo the Greatest TV Detective" (crimefictionlover.com, Oct. 10, 2018)
4. Greenfield, "Columbo Knows the Butler Didn't Do It"
5. Spiegel, "Columbo: A Class of His Own"
6. Siobhan Lyons, "*Wall Street* at 30: Is Greed Still Good?" (theconversation.com, Dec. 7, 2017)
7. Kevin Polowy, "'Greed Is Good:' Oliver Stone Explains Origin and Relevance of Classic *Wall Street* Line 30 Years Later" (yahoo.com, Sept. 22, 2017)
8. Political Calculations, "The Ebb and Flow of the Baby Boom Generation" (politicalcalculations.com, Oct. 5, 2011)
9. Spero Financial, "How Do Different Generations View Money?" (spero.financial)
10. "Understanding the Values of Baby Boomers" (medigap.com, Aug. 18, 2023)
11. Richard Worzel, "The Greediest Generation" (futuresearch.com, July 7, 2014)
12. Koenig, *Shooting Columbo*, p. 177, 185
13. Mathieu, "Columbo: Class Struggle on TV Tonight," p. 2
14. Berzsenyi, *Columbo: A Rhetoric of Inquiry with Resistant Responders*, p. 12
15. *Crime Trends: 1990-2016* (Brennan Center for Justice)
16. Crime statistics (Gallup, news.gallup.com/poll/1603/crime.aspx)
17. Henry Molofsky, "*Cops*: The Violent Legacy of a TV Show that Sculpted America's View of Police" (*The Guardian*, June 11, 2020)
18. Crime statistics (Gallup)
19. Crime statistics (Gallup)
20. Molofsky
21. Sarah Whitten, "How *Cops* Shaped Public Opinion about Police & People of Color" (cnbc.com, June 13, 2020)
22. Molofsky
23. Nicole Sperling, "*Cops*, Long-running Reality Show that Glorified Police, Is Canceled" (*NY Times*, June 9, 2020)
24. Aaron Doyle, *Entertaining Crime: Television Reality Programs* (Routledge, 1998), p. 2 of Chapter 2: "Cops: Television Policing as Policing Reality"
25. Falk, Peter, "Columbo Returns! What You Can Expect from Him Now" (*TV Guide*, Feb. 1989)
26. Spiegel
27. Vincentelli
28. Talen Lee, "Are Columbos Bastards?" (Press.Exe, Jan. 31, 2022)
29. Joe Dator, "Rediscovering *Columbo* in 2020" (*New Yorker*, Oct. 27, 2020)
30. Schwartz, "I Want to Watch the *Columbo* Episode about Trump"
31. Ashley Spurgeon, "And Another Thing: The Beauty of *Columbo*? The Lack of Mystery" (nashvillescene.com, Dec. 1, 2020)

The Legacy of the Thinking Detective
1. David Fantile and Tom Johnson, *Reel to Real: 25 Years of Celebrity Interviews* (Badger Books, 2009), p. 216-217.
2. Jennifer Keishin Armstrong, "How Sherlock Holmes Changed the World" (bbc.com, Jan. 6, 2016)
3. Randall Stock, *Sidney Paget Original Sherlock Holmes Drawings & Artwork: A Census & Checklist* (bestofsherlock.com, Jan. 26, 2020)
4. Dawidziak, *The Columbo Phile*, p. 37
5. Joseph Bell, *The Arthur Conan Doyle Encyclopedia* (arthur-conan-doyle.com)
6. "A Point of View: The Enduring Appeal of Sherlock Holmes" (bbc.com, Aug. 17, 2012)
7. John K. Kruschke, "Posterior Predictive Check" (*Doing Bayesian Data Analysis*, 2015, sciencedirect.com/topics/mathematics/posterior-predictive-check)
8. Kyle Freeman, Introduction to *The Complete Sherlock Holmes, Volume II*, p. xxvi

9. Adrienne Tyler, "Sherlock Holmes Rights Explained: Why Nobody Owns the Great Detective" (screenrant.com, Aug. 21, 2019)
10. Columbophile, "A Hypothetical *Columbo* Reboot: How Might It Work?" (columbophile.com, April 19, 2020)

A Hitch in Crime
1. P.J. Grisar, "Why We Have *Columbo* to Thank for Steven Spielberg" (Forward, Dec. 13, 2021); Dawidziak, *The Columbo Phile*, p. 15-19
2. Rip Rense, "Richard Levinson and William Link: Hall of Fame Tribute" (emmys.com, Nov. 21, 2017)
3. "All rights reserved under international and Pan American copyright conventions" definition (avvo.com)
4. Martha Green, "Hitchcock Hideaway" (*Palm Beach Post*, June 7, 1964)
5. William Link interview on *Alfred Hitchock Presents* (televisionacademy.com)
6. The Hitchcock Zone, *Family Plot* (the.hitchcock.zone/wiki/Family_Plot_(1976))
7. R.L. Terry, "Alfred Hitchcock: The First Director to Brand Himself: Part 2" (rlterryreelview.com, Sept. 20, 2018)
8. Paige A. Driscoll, "The Hitchcock Touch: Visual Techniques in the Work of Alfred Hitchcock" (bgsu.edu, 2013); Jason Hellerman, "How Alfred Hitchcock Used Visionary Cinematic Language to Tell His Stories" (nofilmschool.com, Aug. 20, 2024)
9. Columbophile, "The Most Chilling *Columbo* Murders of Them All" (columbophile.com, March 21, 2021)
10. Link interview on structure of *Columbo* (televisionacademy.com)
11. Ian Farrington, "Dial M for Murder" (ianfarrington.wordpress.com, July 10, 2018)
12. Adam Philips, "Alfred Hitchcock Dials Up *Dial M for Murder*" (the hitchcockreport.wordpress.com, Nov. 14, 2010)
13. Sheldon Hall, "Dial M for Murder" (*Film History*, Vol. 16. No. 3, 2004)
14. "Carly Higley, About the Playwright: *Dial M For Murder*" (Utah Shakespeare Festival, www.bard.org)
15. Joel Gunz, "*Columbo*: A Follow-up to *Alfred Hitchcock Presents*?" (alfredhitchcockgeek.com, Nov. 4, 2013)

Columbo Gets His Wings
1. Lou Thomas, "'Every Person Is a Universe:' Wim Wenders on *Wings of Desire*" (BFI, July 4, 2022)
2. Jim Hemphill, "'Imagine How Angels Would Look at Us:' Wim Wenders on Restoring *Wings of Desire*" (*Filmmaker Magazine*, Oct. 19, 2018)
3. Richard Luck, "Angels of Old Berlin: An Oral History of *Wings of Desire*" (*The New European*, Oct. 27, 2022)
4. Cynthia Wang, "Peter Falk, Wim Wenders's *Wings of Desire* Partnership" (*People*, July 4, 2011)
5. Luck, "Angels of Old Berlin"
6. Casey Jarrin, "*Wings of Desire* Is My Secular Religion: Berlin's Rebel Angels, Peter Falk, and Nick Cave in the Postmodern Muck" (Perisphere, Aug. 31, 2021)
7. Richard Raskin, "What is Peter Falk Doing in *Wings of Desire*? (au.dk)
8. Thomas, "'Every Person Is a Universe"
9. Luck, "Angels of Old Berlin"
10. Luck, "Angels of Old Berlin"
11. Dominic Patten, "NBCUniversal Scores New Trial Over $70M in *Columbo* Profits" (Deadline, Dec. 2, 2019)

The Curious Case of *Columbo Takes the Rap*
1. Michael Riedel, "Lt. Columbo Solves B'way" (*NY Post*, July 11, 2007)
2. Kentucky Muse, "Murder, They Wrote" (ket.org)

The Debacle of *Mrs. Columbo*
1. Michael Shonk, "TV Series Review: *Mrs. Columbo/Kate Loves a Mystery*" (mysteryfile.com, April 27, 2015)
2. Rex McGee, "The Short Harried Life of *Mrs. Columbo*" (*American Film*, June 1979)
3. McGee, "The Short Harried Life of *Mrs. Columbo*"
4. Peter Fischer, *Me and Murder, She Wrote* (CreateSpace, 2016), p. 91-92; McGee
5. Dawidziak, *The Columbo Phile*
6. Erik Pedersen, "Fred Silverman Dead: Legendary TV Executive & Producer Was 82" (Deadline, Jan. 30, 2020)
7. Dean Hargrove interview on Fred Silverman (televisionacademy.com)
8. Fred Silverman interview (Part 9 of 13, televisionacademy.com)
9. Silverman interview (Part 9)
10. Fischer, p. 91-92
11. McGee
12. Fischer, p. 92
13. Wes Britton, *Remember When* podcast (July 31, 2022)
14. McGee
15. Sally Bedell, "Up The Tube", p. 266
16. McGee
17. Rowland Barber, "Here Comes Columbo's Wife" (*TV Guide*-Canadian, Feb. 24-March 2, 1979)
18. Fischer, p. 93
19. *Tonight Show* (Feb. 23, 1979, transcript by totallykate.com)
20. Barber; Lewis Grossberger, "Comes On Like a Mack Truck" (*TV Guide*, March 10, 1979); Vernon Scott, "Surprise! Surprise! It's The Mrs." (*St. Louis Post Dispatch - TV Guide*, Feb. 25-March 3, 1979)
21. Grossberger
22. McGee; Al Coombes, "Kate Hates This Mystery" (*StarWeek Magazine*, March 15-20, 1980)
23. McGee
24. Coombes
25. McGee
26. Grant Tinker interview on Fred Silverman (emmylegendstv.org)
27. "Lili Haydn, Recognizing Humanity" (Innerviews, innerviews.org, 2015)
28. Classic TV History Blog, "An Interview with David Levinson" (classictvhistory.wordpress.com, May 12, 2016,)
29. William Link interview (interviews.televisionacademy.com)
30. Fischer, p. 7
31. McGee
32. Fischer, p. 8
33. Rob London, "How Angela Lansbury Changed Kate Mulgrew's Life on *Murder, She Wrote*" (collider.com, June 19, 2024)
34. Koenig, *Shooting Columbo*, p. 171
35. Al Coombes, "Kate Hates This Mystery" (*StarWeek Magazine*, March 15-20, 1980)

Explaining Patrick McGoohan
1. "Barbara Pruett, "Patrick McGoohan & *Columbo*" (web.archive.org/web/19981206185852/http://www.clark.net/pub/bjpruett/pmweb/columbo.htm)
2. "Murder with Too Many Notes" (columbo-site.freeuk.com/notes.htm)
3. Screen Credits Manual (wga.org)
4. *Columbo: Murder, With Too Many Notes* script (Jan. 24, 1992), columbophile.com/wp-content/uploads/2023/06/MURDER-NOTES-1st-Draft.pdf
5. Jeffrey Cava, "Patrick McGoohan: An Appreciation" (The Ultimate Columbo Site, home.freeuk.net, March 14, 2009)
6. Bill King, "Patrick McGoohan: An Interview with the Man Behind *The Prisoner*" (The Tally Ho, 1988)

Index

– Italicized page number denotes photo

Aaron, Hank, 28
ABC Evening News, 61
Adventures of Superman, The, 101
Aerosmith, 24
Agenda for Murder, 21
Aitchison, Sean, 41
Albert, Eddie, 25, 53, 100
Albertini, Giampiero, 41
All in the Family, 26-27, 106, 146, 203-204
Andy Griffith Show, The, 204
Any Old Port in a Storm, 13, 26, 52, 133
Archerd, Army, 29
Arkin, Alan, 36
Armstrong, Neil, 28
Arthur, Bea, 72
Asner, Ed, 28
Avengers, The, 103-104
Ball, Lucille, 23, 28, 77
Balsam, Martin, 49
Banana Splits, The, 79
Barnaby Jones, 9
Barry, Gene, 55, 126-*127*, 180
Batman, 27
Bauchau, Patrick, 21
Baxter, Anne, 65
Berle, Milton, 29
Bernstein, Carl, 56
Berzsenyi, Christyne, 64-65, 71, 128, 152
Big Chill, The, 32
Bishop, Joey, 25, 28
Blackman, Honor, 52, 70
Blair, Linda, 105-*106*
Blees, Robert, 108-109, 122
Bochco, Steven, 92
Boggs, Hale, 103-104, 109
Borgnine, Ernest, 29
Born Innocent, 105-*106*
Bower, Antoinette, 19
Brady Bunch, The, 17
Broderick, Matthew, 79
Bronk, 10
Butterfly in Shades of Grey, 18
Buzzi, Ruth, 29

By Dawn's Early Light, 15, 34, 51, 54, 94, 128, 132, 141
Bye-Bye Sky High IQ Murder Case, The, 42, 63, 114, 172
Candidate for Crime, 15, 20, 51, 109, 143
Cannon, 10, 17, 114, 142, 152
Capote, Truman, 28
Carlos, John, 89
Carne, Judy, 60
Carson, Johnny, 8, 20, 25-26, 30, 125, 140, 206, 221
Carter, Jimmy, 43
Carter, June, 93
Cash, Johnny,
Cassavetes, John, 52, 116, 129
Cassidy, Jack, 14, 52-53, 58, 128
Caution: Murder Can Be Hazardous to Your Health, 20, 123
Ceausescu, Nicolae, 38-39
Chamberlain, Wilt, 28
Charlie's Angels, 17, 27, 72, 203
Charo, 29
Cheap Detective, The, 19, 191
CHiPs, 27
Christine Cromwell, 21
Clark, Susan, 54, *67*
Close, Glenn, 32
Columbo: A Rhetoric of Inquiry with Resistant Responders, 64, 128, 152
Columbo Cries Wolf, 20-21
Columbo Goes to the Guillotine, 148
Columbo Likes the Nightlife, 97, 148, 158
Columbo: Make Me a Perfect Murder (book), 19, 88, 92, 143, 162
Columbo of Shinano, 41
Columbo: Paying Attention 24/7, 12, 78, 97, 112
Columbo Phile, The (book), 39, 48, 142, 175, 178
Columphile Blog, The, 5-6, 14, 34, 63, 68-70, 158, 182, 221
Complete Unabridged Super Trivia Encyclopedia, The, 31, 33
Conrad, Robert, 43, 53

"INDEX" 237

Conrad, William, 29
Conspirators, The, 30-31, 52, 58, 62, 193
Conversation, The, 112-*113*
Cooking with Columbo, 33
Cooper, Jackie, 51
Coppola, Francis Ford, 111-112
Cops, 152-157, 159
Cosby, Bill, 64, 107
Cosell, Howard, 29
Court, Margaret, 66
Coward, Noel, 49
Crime and Punishment, 126
Crouse, Lindsay, 21
CSI, 87
Culp, Robert, 16, 24-25, 51, 53, 83, 118, 184
Curtis, Tony, 105
Dagger of the Mind, 22, 41, 52, 170, 175
Danger Man (see *Secret Agent*)
Davies, Janey, 70-71
Davis, Bette, 28
Davis Jr., Sammy, 28
Dawidziak, Mark, 6, 39, 48, 142-143, 166, 175, 178
Dead Weight, 12, 34, 44, 53, 64, 100, 128
Deadly State of Mind, A, 82, 133, 139
Dean Martin Celebrity Roast, The, 28-31
Death Hits the Jackpot, 35
Death Lends a Hand, 25, 51, 53, 77-79, 83, 98-99, 112, 116, 184
Dehner, John, 43
DeLuise, Dom, 29
Dickinson, Angie, 72
Diller, Phyllis, 28
Dillman, Bradford, 67
Dinah!, 93
Dishy, Bob, 14
Dostoevsky, Fyodor, 126
Double Exposure, 53, 83, 86, 100, 118-119, 121, 128, 204
Double Shock, 12, 47, 132, 185
Douglas, Kirk, 28
Douglas, Michael, 149-*151*
Douglas, Susan J., 72
Driskill, Bill, 105
Dr. Who, 12
Draper, Fred, 109
Dunaway, Faye, 18
Ellsberg, Daniel, 50
Erhard, Werner, 44
Etude in Black, 16, 22, 25, 34, 52, 63, 72, 92, 116-117, 121-122, 129-130, 133, 167, 170
Exercise in Fatality, An, 7, 26, 43, 51, 53, 80 84, 117, 128

Fade In to Murder, 15, 84, 109, 121
Falk, Miksa, 41
Falk, Peter, 5, 8, 13, *15,* 17-20, *23*-27, 29-31, 33-41, 47-49, 61, 63, *81,* 88, *127*-128, 131, 140, 145, 147-148, 157-158, 163-164, 166, 173, 175-176, 180, 188-*191*-195, 199, 201, 203, 206-207, 209, 211, *214*-215, 218, 221-*222,* 225-227
Ferrer, Jose, 51, 79
Fischer, Bobby, 162
Fischer, Peter S., 96, 202-206, 210
Fleming, Art, 31
Fonda, Henry, 29
Forbidden Planet, 79
Ford, Gerald, 43, 56
Forgotten Lady, 13, 16-17, 52, 70, 100-101, 105, 117, 140, 168, 170, 213
Foxx, Redd, 25, 28
Friedan, Betty, 60
Friend in Deed, A, 22, 55, 59, 74, 87, 91, 98, 109
Fringe, 12
Furuhata Ninzaburo, 41
Future Shock, 74-*75*-86, 112
Gabor, Eva, 25
Gabor, Zsa Zsa, 28
Garagiola, Joe, 28
Geer, Will, 90
Gelbart, Larry, 106-107
Get Christie Love!, 73
Get Smart, 27
Gideon Oliver, 21
Gleason, Jackie, 28
Godfather, The, 111, 226
Godfather II, The, 111-112, 226
Gold, Joe, 43
Goldblum, Jeff, 32
Goldenson, Leonard, 103
Goldwater, Barry, 28
Gomer Pyle, 204
Gordon, Ruth, 68, 70, 128
Graves, Teresa, 73
Grant, Lee, 53, 68, 128, 184
Green Acres, 25
Greenfield, Jeff, 47, 49, 51, 149-150, 152
Greenhouse Jungle, The, 14, 52, 66, 86, 135, 168
Griff, 10
Griffin, Merv, 25
Griffith, Andy, 17
Gun, The, 99, 143
Gunsmoke, 103
Hackman, Gene, 112-*113*
Haggerty, Dan, 28

Hall, Monty, 28
Hamilton, George, 20, 82, 139
Hammett, Dashiell, 56
Happy Days, 26
Hargrove, Dean, 95, 203
Harper, Valerie, 61
Hartley, Mariette, 62
Hastie, Amelie, 6, 19, 88-89, 92, 112, 143-144, 162
Hefner, Hugh, 28
Helms, Richard, 50
Henderson, Florence, 28
Hirschfeld, Al, 24
Hirschfeld, Nina, 24
Hoover, J. Edgar, 36
Hope, Bob, 28
Humphrey, Hubert, 28
Hurt, William, 32
Identity Crisis, 56, 62, 83, 90-92, 101, 106, 112, 115, 117,213
In-Laws, The, 36
Ironside, 10, 17, 152
It's All in the Game, 18
Jackson, Anne, 205
Jackson, Mahalia, 94
Jeopardy!, 31, 33
Jeffersons, The, 107
Johnny Cash Show, The, 94
Jordan, Michael, 21
Jourdan, Louis, 51, 58, 129
Just One More Thing, 39
Kaplan, Gabe, 28
Kasdan, Lawrence, 32
Kazan, Lainie, 108
Keil, Jack, 36-37
Kelly, Gene, 29
Kelly, Grace, 186
Kennedy, Robert, 89, 102
Kiley, Richard, 55
King, Billie Jean, 66
King Jr., Martin Luther, 89, 102
Kissinger, Henry, 28, 39
Kline, Kevin, 32
Klugman, Jack, 49, 58
Knievel, Evel, 28
Koenig, David, 6, 19, 94, 150, 211, 214-215
Kojak, 8-9, 17, 27, 40, 114, 152, 159, 203
Krivascy, Ray, 36
Landis, Jessie Royce, 54
Last Salute to the Commodore, 5, 43, 66, 131, 214
Laugh-In, 60
Laverne and Shirley, 26, 204

Law and Order, 16, 153
Lear, Norman, 106-107
Leigh, Janet, 52, 70, 101, 213
Letterman, David, 39-40
Levinson, David, 209
Levinson, Richard, 11, 17, 21, 34, 49, 58, 76-77, 88-89, 95, 98-100, 112, 116, 126, 135, 143, 145, 149, 152, 175, 178-182, 185-187, 196, 198-199, 204-206, 209-210
Link, William, 11, 17, 21, 34-35, 49, 58, 76-77, 88-89, 95, 98-100, 112, 116, 126, 135, 143, 145, 148-149, 152, 175, 178-182, 185-187, 194-200, 204-205, 209-210
Little, Rich, 28, 30
Little House on the Prairie, 26
Lost in Space, 79
Lou Grant, 204
Love Boat, The, 26, 203
Lovely But Lethal, 51, 65, 68, 185
Luckinbill, Laurence, 71, 107
Make Me a Perfect Murder, 63, 65, 68, 86, 98, 107, 111, 121-122
Maltese Falcon, The, 56
Man from UNCLE, The, 27
Mannix, 39, 76-77, 112, 152, 196, 199
Many Loves of Dobie Gillis, The, 79
Marshall, Peter, 28
Martin, Dean, 28-31
Martin-Jones, David, 6, 12, 78, 80, 83, 97, 112
*M*A*S*H*, 26-27, 106, 203
Mathieu, Lilian, 6, 48-51, 56, 151
Matter of Honor, A, 13, 34, 41, 56, 173
McBain, Ed, 181, 197
McCloud, 5, 17, 30, 105
McCoy, 105
McDowall, Roddy, 92, 133
McEachin, James, 88, 92-*93*, 107, 198
McGoohan, Patrick, 6, 19, 34, 51, 54, 56, 115, 128, 142, 213-*214*-215, 217-223, 225-226
McMillan & Wife, 5, 30, 105
McNee, Patrick, 103
Melillo, Wendy, 36, 38
Melle, Gil, 78, 185
Miles, Vera, 65
Milland, Ray, 51-52, 186
Mind Over Mayhem, 78, 80-*81*, 140
Mod Squad, The, 152
Modern Utopia, 12
Montalban, Ricardo, 56, 213
Montgomery, Lee H., 80-*81*
Moon, Sun Myoung, 43
Morita, Pat, 34
Mork and Mindy, 26, 204

"Index" 239

Most Crucial Game, The, 16, 20, 51, 53, 61, 83, 118, 120, 130
Mr. T, 28
Mrs. Columbo, 201-*207*-212
Mulgrew, Kate, 31, 202-*207*-212
Murder, a Self Portrait, 21
Murder by Death, 19
Murder by the Book, 13, 28, 52, 76, 92, 128, 148, 160, 177, 184
Murder in Malibu, 153
Murder, She Wrote, 210-211, 216
Murder Under Glass, 51-52, 129
Murder with Too Many Notes, 214-226
Nader, Ralph, 28
Namath, Joe, 28
Negative Reaction, 19, 91, 117, 133-134
Nemmers, Sherry, 35-*37*-38
Newman, Paul 24
Nielsen, Leslie, 68, 90
Nixon, Richard, 24, 39, 43, 50, 56, 143
Now You See Him, 13, 171
Odd Couple, The, 25
Old Fashioned Murder, 15, 65, 71, 84, 228
O'Connor, Tim, 71
Oglivie, Morgan, 64
O'Neal, Patrick 51
Orlando, Tony, 28-29
Paige, Janis, 62
Pal Joey, 29
Partridge Family, The, 26
Paskin, Willa, 40
Perry Mason, 26
Peter Gunn, 26-27
Playback, 16, 18, 83-86, 99-101, 109, 112, 119, 121-122, 140
Pleasence, Donald, 52, 58, 70
Pleshette, Suzanne, 44
Police Woman, 72, 210
Prescription: Murder, 8, 12, 25, 46, 48, 55, 76, 89, 97, 102, 124, 126-127, 132, 152, 172, 180-181, 183, 194, 200
Price, Vincent, 29
Prinze, Freddie, 28
Prisoner, The, 115, 213, 226
Publish or Perish, 14, 28, 141
Ransom for a Dead Man, 12, 15, 22, 41, 53, 63, 65, 68, 76, 94, 100, 116, 128, 130, 166, 184
Reagan, Ronald, 29, 32, 95, 143
Reasoner, Harry, 61
Reddy, Helen, 60
Reed, Rex, 29
Requiem for a Falling Star, 51, 65
Rickles, Don, 28, 30

Riggs, Bobby, 28
Ripa, Kelly, 196
Robin and the Seven Hoods, 30
Roddenberry, Gene, 107
Route 66, 102
Russell, Nipsey, 28
Saint, The, 39
Sanford and Son, 25
Savalas, Telly, 29, 40, 147
Schlafly, Phyllis, 60
Schwartz, Dana, 160
Scooby Doo, Where Are You?, 27
Scott, Pippa, 70
Scotti, Vito, 19-20
Secret Agent, 213, 226
Sex and the Married Detective, 21
Shaft, 89
Shooting Columbo, 6, 19, 94, 150, 211, 214
Shore, Dinah, 93
Short Fuse, 90, 92, 133, 228
Silverman, Fred, 31, 202-209, 211
Simmons, Richard Alan, 129, 150, 208
Sinatra, Frank, 28-31, 203
Smith, Howard K., 61
Smith, Jaclyn, 147
Smith, Sandra, 66
Smith, Tommie, 89
Space: 1999, 26
Spielberg, Steven, 53, 148, 177, 184
Spitz, Mark, 29
Stanton, Frank, 104, 203
Star Trek, 12, 76, 89, 107, 162
Star Trek: Voyager, 211
Starsky & Hutch, 9
Steinem, Gloria, 60-61
Stepford Wives, The, 197
Stewart, Jimmy, 29
Sting, The, 105
Stitch in Crime, A, 90, 162
Strange Bedfellows, 18,
Strangers on a Train, 184
Suitable for Framing, 55, 61, 66, 85, 109, 129, 132-133
Swan Song, 92-93, 117, 133, 194
Tanny, Vic, 44
Tenafly, 88-89, 92-*93*, 198
Tillis, Mel, 29
Tinker, Grant, 209
Toffler, Alvin, 74-79, 82-86
Toma, 10
Tonight Show, The, 8, 25, 125, 206
Torres, Angelo, 25

Trace of Murder, A, 35
Trebek, Alex, 33
Trivia Encyclopedia, The, 31
Troubled Waters, 15, 86, 99-101, 105-106, 136, 165
Try and Catch Me, 62, 68, 127-128
Twilight Zone, The, 12, 79
Ultimate Columbo Site, 88, 225
Undercover, 92, 168, 194
Untouchables, The, 102, 159
Vale, Jerry, 29
Van Devere, Trish, 68, 107
Van Dyke, Dick, 19, 133
Van Patten, Joyce, 15, 19-20, 71
Wall Street, 149-*151*
Waltons, The, 26, 203
War Games, 79
Warren, Lesley Ann, 82
Warwick, Dionne, 28
Washington, George, 28
Watson, Deshaun, 64
Weinstein, Harvey, 64
Welles, Orson, 29, 78
Werner, Oskar, 84
Where the Girls Are, 72
White, Bette, 28
Wild Wild West, The, 103-104
Wilde, Cornel, 107
Wiley, Richard, 105
Williams, Hank, 92
Williams, John, 186
Williamson, Nicol, 44, 82
Windom, William, 55
Winters, Jonathan, 29
Winters, Shelly, 28
Wolfe, Tom, 42, 44
Woman Under the Influence, A, 24 , 191
Woodward, Bob, 56
Worth, Fred L., 31-33
Yesterday, 12

www.ingramcontent.com/pod-product-compliance
Lightning Source LLC
Chambersburg PA
CBHW070054080526
44586CB00013B/1047